D1283856

TWO ROADS DIVERGED

A SECOND CHANCE FOR THE REPUBLICAN PARTY, THE CONSERVATIVE MOVEMENT, THE NATION—AND OURSELVES

Mark Sanford

Former Governor, South Carolina
Former Member, U.S. House of Representatives

TWO ROADS DIVERGED

For information, contact Vertel Publishing at
2837 Rivers Avenue
Charleston, South Carolina 29405

First edition

Manufactured in the United States of America
1 3 5 7 9 10 8 6 4 3 2

Hardcover ISBN: 978-1-64112-027-2
eBook ISBN: 978-1-64112-028-9

Library of Congress Cataloging-in-Publication Data has been applied for.

To my sons, Marshall, Landon, Bolton, and Blake

Two roads diverged in a wood, and I—
I took the one less traveled by.
And that has made all the difference.

—Robert Frost

CONTENTS

★ ★ ★

Preface: Two Roads Diverged · **xi**

Introduction: Recalibrating the Conservative Conscience · · · **xix**

PART ONE: SECOND CHANCES · **1**

   1. My Second Chance Gained and Lost · · · · · · · · · · · · · ·3

   2. A Second Chance for the Republican Party · · · · · · · · · ·43

   3. A Second Chance for the Conservative Movement · · · · ·68

   4. A Second Chance for America · · · · · · · · · · · · · · · · · ·95

PART TWO: WHAT WE CAN DO · · · · · · · · · · · · · · · · · **107**

   5. Nine Things We Can Do for the Party and

      the Movement · 109

   6. Eight Things We Can Do for the Nation · · · · · · · · · · 137

   7. Thirteen Things We Can Do for Ourselves · · · · · · · · 171

Parting Thoughts · **209**

Epilogue: Epistles · **215**

   To Democrats · 216

   To the Trump Voters · 221

   To the MAGA Folks · 225

   To Evangelical Christians · 230

   To the Commenters on My Facebook Page · · · · · · · · · · 234

   To Congressman Jim Jordan · · · · · · · · · · · · · · · · · · 240

To Senator Ted Cruz · 244
To Senator Josh Hawley · 248
To Matt Gaetz and Marjorie Taylor Greene · · · · · · · · · · · 252
To Nancy Pelosi · 254
To Former President Donald Trump · · · · · · · · · · · · · · · 259
To President Joe Biden · 264
To My Sons · 269

Acknowledgments · **271**

TWO ROADS DIVERGED

Robert Frost wrote these words about someone faced with a crossroads: "Two roads diverged in a wood, and I—I took the one less traveled by. And that has made all the difference."

For reasons Frost does not explain, the speaker takes the "road less traveled," and Frost leaves us with the words "And that has made all the difference." But Frost doesn't say whether the difference that less-traveled road made was for the better or for the worse, just that it made not only a difference, but *all* the difference.

We each face crossroads at different points in our lives. Many of us take the road *more* traveled rather than the less-traveled road, and those who do invariably arrive at the next destination more safely than do those of us who chose the other path. But sometimes, for reasons we can never satisfactorily explain, we take that less-traveled road, and we find, as Frost says, that the choice to take that course brings very different consequences.

For better or worse, our country took a road less traveled in 2016, and we spent the next four years making our way through hazardous terrain that has led us into uncharted political territory. Now, in different but still powerful ways, we are continuing down the same path toward ruin with the Biden administration. His administration has committed to more new spending in its first hundred days than any other on record. Four trillion in new spending is anything but moderate, though he promised to govern from the center. He was portrayed as a moderate and embraced this image. It made sense, given his many years in the Senate. After all, it's an institution by its very design biased to protecting the views of the minority, and so people understandably surmised that someone who had spent over thirty-five years there would be sympathetic to its traditions.

His governance has not fit this.

Over the administration's first few months, some of the largest expansions in government since Franklin D. Roosevelt (FDR) in the era of the New Deal have been advanced on a single-party basis. The filibuster, with its inherent advantages to the minority's perspective, and something that not so many years ago Biden defended, is now seen as a relic that should be jettisoned because it slows single-party governance. Yet the design that so bothers all of us when we think about "getting things done in Washington"—and that so frustrated Trump's efforts to go in politically opposite ways from Biden—is the very design of our political system. It should be celebrated. The day we get to true single-party governance will be the day we get to a post-constitutional America. Our virtual speed bumps in the form of checks and balances and divided government have given some measure of stability in preventing us over the years from lurching from one side to the other. Accordingly, it needs to be recognized that Biden is working against this when he pushes for legislative victory by way of single-party votes. The same is true when he agrees with Senator Schumer on the idea of discarding the filibuster. And the same criticisms would fit the Trump administration regarding judicial appointments and more.

In short, we are spinning out of control. It's as if centrifugal force is pulling us further and further apart. At some point, if we pull hard enough in opposite directions, things break. Divided we cannot stand, and yet increasingly we live in a land that is not only divided but bitter in its division. Given the vitriol pervading Washington, many days it seems there is no path to redemption.

But one thing Frost neglected to mention is that every fork in the road inevitably leads to yet another. Like ripples on a pond, the ever-expanding effect of choices made grows with the passage of time. And just as that first choice makes all the difference, so, too, do successive choices that follow. Time has a way of expanding the effect of each of our significant decisions in life, but the fatalism of Frost's phrase "And that made all the difference" belies the fact that sometimes God gives us second chances—and with them the chance to learn from one's previous decision and begin anew and fresh.

As I write this in the late spring of 2021, our nation stands at another crossroads. The road we take going forward will determine the future we leave to those who will follow us. The implications of these decisions will be borne by our children—and their children's children. Our choices today are significant because they will stand as monuments in reflecting who we really are and what we stand for and believe.

I took a road less traveled at a different crossroads in 2009, and it was not along the Appalachian Trail. That year I fell deeply in love with a woman who lived five thousand miles away and was not my wife. I completely mishandled that chapter of my life, and its consequences were disastrous. It was a journey that cost me dearly, and I don't know that I will ever fully comprehend its total cost. Just as those ever-expanding ripples on placid waters define the reverberations that Frost alluded to in his description of paths taken in the journey of life, so, too, will the consequences of my choices reverberate until the day I die. I wish I could go back and do many days differently in my life, but those days stand out above all others.

But going back is not real life.

We get our one shot at each day, and on some days we do far better than we could ever have imagined while on other days we fall far shorter than we could ever have dreamed. And though we can choose our sins, we can never choose their consequences, and under their weight we move forward as best we can in this all-too-short journey called life.

In the wake of all that came after 2009—divorce, trust lost, and condemnation abounding—I was cut off and alone. Isolation forces deliberation and soul-searching, and I tried both to make amends where I could to the people who would accept them and, with some measure of humility, to absorb the condemnation of those who would not forgive me.

The story of that road I took is part of this book not because I want to justify my actions but as a way of registering the fact that my life's path has given me an acute appreciation of Frost's notion of crossroads and the consequences of differing paths—as well as the power of grace, the chance to learn from one's past, and the opportunity for refocusing that comes with that learning.

Even those most wounded among us have something to offer. We can learn and see more if we take the time to look at things through another's eyes. Whether we have the humility to do so is one of the great mysteries of life, but it's through the normal course of speaking, listening, and learning that we have the chance to gain each other's perspectives and become the wiser for it.

This book is my attempt to do just that, because while some of the people I let down forgave me and others never will, it's still incumbent upon all of us to point to truth as we see it, regardless of our wounds. Accordingly, this book is more critical of Republicans and conservatives than it is of Democrats and liberals. I do this not because I agree with the left—my conservative credentials would put me in the near-Neanderthal category of the political spectrum. Nor do I believe they hold a greater grasp on truth. I do it because for conservative ideals to advance, I believe we first must clean our own house. Though I never cared for his style, I voted overwhelmingly with Trump and the Republican Party on matters of policy where policy was allowed to be the issue. Too often it was not, and accordingly there is a real need for a review of not what Republicans got right but what we got wrong over the last few years. This book attempts to do this for the same reason our military focuses on what went wrong in an after-action review. We can learn from our mistakes.

Doing so is vital because people don't knowingly take the advice of hypocrites, and the Republican Party of late has been filled with hypocrisy. Because of that, my aim, prompting, and goading toward Republicans and conservatives are included with purpose. There are many pages that follow wherein a Republican might rightfully point out where a Democrat or a liberal philosophy was worse. Though this may be true, it's irrelevant when one wants to better one's own ideas. What we get right as Republicans and conservatives is also good for Democrats and Independents. Whether we like it or not, we are all in this together. A hard-core liberal should write a book on how to better the Democratic Party and the liberal movement, and I look forward to reading it. Our country is made better when the best version of both political philosophies is robustly offered in the halls of Congress. But I can't add value and perspective to what I don't know, so my aim in this book is to give thoughts from a conservative on what might come next for conservatives. I also continue to believe in the Bible's admonition of first taking the log from your own eye before you worry about the splinter in the eye of another.

I believe categorically in human freedom. The institutions, traditions, and political debate that have kept American independence alive for nearly 250 years are unquestionably sustained and made stronger by including both liberal and conservative perspectives. When these viewpoints are advanced by the two parties rather than one party simply contorting itself to hold power, it's better for each one of us regardless of our political views.

As Oscar Hammerstein once said, "Liberals need conservatives to hold them back, and conservatives need liberals to pull them forward." One side should thwart the other when it oversteps and prompt it when it fails to act. That the American way is made stronger with a robust competition of ideas is core to my thinking and again is the basis upon which all that follows is written.

In offering my perspective, the fact is none of us is perfect. To a greater or lesser degree, we are all wounded messengers. Some hang on to the fiction that this truth doesn't apply to them; yet if we accept it, I believe good things begin to happen—not only in absorbing another's perspective but in really hearing it, because our points of connection lie not in our strengths but in our weaknesses.

This doesn't make wrongs right or absolve us from consequences, but it opens our eyes to the fact that you can't really hear or empathize with another perspective until you get off your high horse.

What I'm suggesting is that our political moment today is critical, and it's therefore vital we listen to each other as Republicans, Democrats, and Independents. None of our imperfections absolves us of the need each day to get back up and try as best we can to make the world a little better place—whether that lies in helping the neighbor empty his garbage or pointing to what we see wrong in today's political environment. We need to reengage as Americans. We can't solve the complex problems that confront our society if some of those who have the most to give remain silent and indifferent, cloistered behind gates in the Hamptons or Palm Beach. My father's admonition from the Bible holds true: "To whom much has been given, much will be required."

My journey is unique. After I took the mightiest of falls, the people who knew me best put me back in Congress two years after my term as governor ended and then reelected me to Congress twice more. That taught me about the importance of second chances and how, collectively and individually, we can learn from them.

But those very lessons also sealed my own electoral defeat.

By the midterm election of 2018, many of the people in the First Congressional District of South Carolina had joined with the Republican Party at large in taking a different, less-traveled road in politics with their support of President Trump. In that political moment in time, adherence to conservative philosophy paled in importance relative to support for one man, and as I chose to defy the president, the voters stood with him, not me.

How my seemingly unforgivable sin was politically pardonable but not bowing to Trump was not will always baffle me, but I hope in time to come to understand it. As Frost said, making that choice led me onto a road less traveled. And, once again, it made all the difference.

This book is about those roads—the political and the personal, the traveled and the less traveled—and the choices we Americans face going forward today.

As a nation we have a second chance…if we are wise enough to recognize it and brave enough to take it.

INTRODUCTION

RECALIBRATING THE CONSERVATIVE CONSCIENCE

Written in 1960, Senator Barry Goldwater's book *The Conscience of a Conservative* is viewed as one of the seminal writings making a case for conservatism in American politics. A modest book of 123 pages, it was ghostwritten by Goldwater's speechwriter, Brent Bozell, and Bozell's brother-in-law, William F. Buckley Jr., both of whom were lifelong conservatives who believed thoroughly in the principles Goldwater advanced. With chapters on states' rights, civil rights, agriculture, labor, taxes and spending, welfare, education, and a final chapter on "The Soviet Menace," the book quickly sold through its ten-thousand-copy first printing and ultimately sold more than three million copies. Though Goldwater lost his 1964 bid for the presidency, many argue that the thinking and philosophy in his book paved the way for Ronald

Reagan's attempted presidential runs in 1968 and 1976 and his wins in 1980 and 1984.

Part of the book's significance lies in its clarity. It concisely and practically applies conservative philosophy to what Goldwater believed were the challenges of political life in 1960. I once heard it said that if you can't boil your business idea down to fit on the back of a business card, you don't yet have a clear idea. By this measure, Goldwater had real clarity, but in other ways the book now reads like the Old Testament as weighed against the New Testament. Parts of the Old Testament were written as long lists of thou-shalt-nots, and many people boil down the New Testament to two thou-shalts: "Thou shalt love God with all thy heart," and "Thou shalt love thy neighbor as thyself."[1] On his list of policy highlights in his 1960 book, Goldwater talks a lot about what should *not* be taking place, and although he is dead on in most of his assessments, over the years conservatives have often found themselves relegated to the role of doing nothing more than blocking areas of government's growth. Too often conservatives have allowed themselves to be cast in a negative light.

Are we just the party of obstruction, the people who block things? There's got to be more to conservatism than being against new ideas and different people.

What if we flipped it around, New Testament–style, and talked about the advantages to saying yes? What if we started finding positive ways to apply true conservative philosophy to today's challenges? Might that not be more relevant to young voters? What if

---

1 Matthew 22:37; Matthew 22:39

we created a small list of conservative thou-shalts instead of our too-long list of conservative thou-shalt-nots?

We have been here before. As of 2021 we stand at an ideological crossroads like the one Barry Goldwater stood at in 1960. Goldwater believed that 1950s Republicans had capitulated on core conservative principles in the same way Trump-era Republicans believed over six decades later. Goldwater felt that Eisenhower's notion of being conservative on economic matters but liberal on other issues made for a policy mix that at day's end was not conservative. He strongly believed that continuing and expanding New Deal programs that had outlived their original purpose represented a selling out of conservative values and ideals. As with anyone who is firm in their ideology, he didn't see his ideas as negotiables. He believed principles were timeless and sacrosanct. Though his political rise was limited to the Senate, his lonely stand against lukewarm political principles paved the way for the likes of Ronald Reagan and Margaret Thatcher and their advancement of conservatism.

Given how far the party has fallen, today's crossroads represents an even greater opportunity for renewal and correction—one that could lead to good things for all Americans. And I say all Americans, not just conservatives, intentionally. Over my twenty-five years in politics, I came to respect and believe in a divided government. Neither side has all the answers. And even if it did, one-party rule is by its very nature corrupting.

The British politician Lord Acton famously said, "Power tends to corrupt, and absolute power corrupts absolutely." My personal experience in politics has cemented this axiom, and history codifies it. If one cares at all about perpetuating our country's center-right orientation and the political system that has encouraged it, we need spirited debate from both the left and right so we can forge solutions that have some of both. In an open political system, no one should win all, or all of the time. The vigorous debate between differing perspectives and interests holds at bay the tyranny our Founding Fathers so feared, and makes for solutions that can be digested by a widely diverse population of 330 million.

Before Donald Trump's arrival in Washington, the conservative movement as represented by the Republican Party had devolved into a lukewarm mess. Reality was the Republican Party didn't really represent conservatism any longer. Trump's inauguration on January 20, 2017, made this painfully apparent. I was there on that day and was afforded my own look at determining the crowd's size because members of the House, the Senate, and the Supreme Court are seated behind the president for the swearing-in ceremony. As one takes in the view down the Mall, the political cast assembled, and the pomp and ceremony that accompany it, the day always comes as a sobering reminder of the genius of the Founders in the traditions they created to surround the peaceful transition of power.

You also soak in little things. I remember being struck by the way Trump did not include his wife as he walked up to the edge of the dais and took in the moment and the adulation of the crowd that stretched before him. I watched Melania intently, wondering what she was thinking. All I knew was there was no way my former wife, Jenny, nor the wife of any friend would have put up with this.

What I didn't appreciate in that moment was how Melania's nonreaction of placid indifference to Trump's behavior would be mirrored by millions.

As the band took up "Hail to the Chief," there was not a whisper from any of the party leaders that Trump was hijacking the Republican brand. Why would there be? You can't change what you no longer have, and people generally don't get agitated about losing something that is not theirs. There was no strong objection within Republican circles to what Trump began to change in the Grand Old Party because to many of them, the GOP had come to stand for surprisingly little. The people who truly believed in conservative ideals were disillusioned and tired of the Republican Party's abysmal efforts to advance their ideas. The party had come to mean even less for most Americans. Only some of us noticed or cared about this at the inauguration in 2017, but the GOP was taking a hairpin turn onto a road less traveled—and it was one that had disappointingly little to do with basic conservative principles.

If you ask most people what the Democratic Party stands for, they'd probably say something like, "It stands for the people." Except for wanting to make health coverage more widely available, most people wouldn't be able to give you a lot of substance beyond that, but in the world of politics, "for the people" is not a bad place to start.

If you asked me the same question on what it means to be a Republican these days, well, you would think I ought to be able to do that, given my many years in Republican political waters. But in the era of Trump, giving that answer proved tough. Once I would have said, "lower taxes" or "less regulation" or "smaller government," but these are features, not a simple business card–size essence of a meaningful brand. One might also take the tack of saying, "It stands for freedom," but Trump's style was far too autocratic to allow that answer to stick, and his flirtations with leaders like Vladimir Putin undercut the GOP's moral high ground on freedom.

So let's sit down at the proverbial kitchen table and make a more forward-looking list of what it should mean to be a Republican and a conservative today. Call it Barry Goldwater 2.0 or a modern-day *Conscience of a Conservative*, or even plain common sense, but we desperately need a conservative conscience, and more so, we need its timeless principles to be applied to the challenges of the day.

It's important we do first things first in life, so it's critical that conservatives go back to embracing a governing philosophy. A conservative one. Maximizing human freedom within the confines of a sustainable political system is the main aim of conservatism. Both have seen serious erosion over the last ten years, and here is where we need to go back to the basics.

The different political blocks used in the construction of freedom really do matter. Things like justice, rule of law, private property rights, reason, sustainable spending, and the institutions and mores that protected them were carefully decided upon and codified by our Founding Fathers so that we might flourish collectively and individually as Americans.

As is the case in anything designed by man, what they assembled was not perfect—and for two hundred years we have fought as

Americans toward a more perfect union. We certainly have never made it to the Promised Land that Dr. Martin Luther King Jr. articulated and dreamed of, but we have come too far to allow the backsliding each of us is witnessing in American politics today. Staying on our current path will diminish the odds of any of us achieving the American Dream.

We all know it. We may not admit it or articulate it, but our present course on many fronts is in no way sustainable. It's for this reason it is so important to go back to the basics of what made our country great...and it wasn't government largesse. For the first 150 years of our country's existence, right up until World War II, federal government spending represented less than 10 percent of our economy, and for most of that time, it was less than 3 percent. Today our federal government is responsible for 31 percent of American spending, and I don't believe we are three or ten times better off than we were back then.

Over that century and a half of remarkable growth, as we moved from a series of colonies to being the world's greatest power, it was not the government's size but rather the principles we got right and stood for that catapulted us forward. And they were by and large conservative in nature.

In rethinking and updating Goldwater's *Conscience of a Conservative,* let's review what conservatives once believed and why it might be worth returning to these ageless ideas that unleash human freedoms and the prosperity that comes with them. What follows going forward must be lived and not read. Ultimately, that's the point of this book. It's incumbent upon all of us to reawaken the

American public to the dangers of our present course, the threats to our republic, and the hazard of what's increasingly being unleashed from Washington.

Ludwig von Mises said in 1922, "Everyone carries a part of society on his shoulders; no one is relieved of his share of responsibility by others. And no one can find a safe way for himself if society is sweeping towards destruction. Therefore everyone, in his own interests, must thrust himself vigorously into the intellectual battle. No one can stand aside with unconcern: the interests of everyone hang on the result. Whether he chooses or not, every man is drawn into the great historical struggle, the decisive battle into which our epoch has plunged us."[2]

Look around, and at the events of January 6, 2021, at the US Capitol, if you have any doubts that an intellectual battle stands before us. And as with so many real struggles, they begin with people's perception of justice. Some see it one way, others another, and these differences amount to the lighter fluid that starts the fires of struggle and conflict. Adam Smith would argue government's purpose begins there, that arbitrating those differences and defining their scope are the main points of why we have government. Human freedom and liberty spring from the ability to see things your own way, but the foundation of acting on those beliefs lies in having your freedom to do so safeguarded and protected. As conservatives we want government, but we want it limited only to what government can or must do.

---

2 Ludwig Von Mises, *Socialism: An Economic and Sociological Analysis. Translated by J. Kahane.* (London: J. Cape, 1953), 515.

Here are ten classic conservative principles that can be applied today:

- Justice
- The rule of law
- Private property rights
- Markets and trade
- Limited government
- Civil society
- Freedom of religion
- A reason-based republic
- Limited spending, debts, and deficits
- Civil Liberty

JUSTICE

As a citizen, my rights extend only to the point they begin to infringe on yours. It's the government's role to enforce and protect this division, and it is the rule of law that determines where the line between them lies. Millions of people doing whatever they want, however they want, to whomever they want is a recipe for chaos and the injustice that comes with it. It's for this reason the Founders began with justice in forming their more perfect union in the preamble to our Constitution.

Conservative-leaning governance and laws would favor maximizing the zone of individual autonomy, whereas leanings to the left would limit them. But real justice goes far beyond the ordering of public and private roles and even the relative *positions* of private roles. It goes to the larger question of whether there is justice in the public role itself. In other words, should government even be doing what it's doing?

Think about a host of current issues that tie straight to the Founders' idea of justice. The themes of Black Lives Matter, pandemic mask mandates, and debt all tie to this fundamental idea and should illuminate why conservatives should affirmatively stand for justice at all times.

Take the focus of late on Black Lives Matter and of George Floyd's death in Minneapolis. What's at play here is much larger than race or single cases of excessive police force; it's about whether our Constitution means what it says in its promise of equal protection—justice—under the law. Equal protection, and the justice it embodies, begins to get real in these cases because no matter the aggravating circumstances wherein people do things that solicit reaction and force, we are all promised equal protection under the law. Justice can't exist without every citizen having an equal chance of being heard. The power of government as served by law enforcement must be limited to just getting the job done. A police force must not become judge, jury, and executioner. Its role is limited to delivering suspected law breakers to our criminal justice system, where they will then be granted due process in being presumed innocent until found guilty. People often focus on all the things a person may have done wrong to invite force, such as an off-putting victimhood mentality or strident language and behavior, but none of it matters when one focuses on the simple principle at play—justice.

Consider the questions surrounding mask mandates. Justice means calibrating the awesome powers of the state, which makes conservative thought that much more relevant in the here and now. In times of crisis, people rightly expect leaders to lead. Thus, there is an incredible bias among people in government to "just do something" in a crisis, lest they be seen as not leading. This is exacerbated by the fact that doing too much can be explained away in the wake of a crisis, but not doing enough has more risk than upside for the officeholder. Over the years we have all seen silly cover-your-butt actions by bureaucrats and politicians alike. Doing something, and doing more rather than less, is the government's orientation because being frozen in indecision is hardly a formula for reelection. It's this mentality rather than justice that drives the decision of all too many in power. And so you get all kinds of goofy suggestions and mandates on masks—and more—that creep up against the idea of justice and limited government.

Our youngest son's senior year was effectively taken from him at Georgetown University based on a litany of rules from Washington, DC. Many were not based on science, common sense, or justice, but instead on the political currency that mattered most to those who held power—the need to appear in control. While other schools continued with class and graduation ceremonies, many northeastern schools were relegated to graduation pictures beside a cardboard cutout of their dean, even after scores of these same young people had gathered only months before on the beaches of Fort Lauderdale. In this odd patchwork of red and blue state reactions, it was fascinating to see the statistics in a state like California or New York compared to Florida with its much older population but relatively libertine approach to masks and social distancing.

When I was governor of South Carolina, hurricane-evacuation planning and preparation took an inordinate amount of time every fall. I had become governor in part because of a botched hurricane evacuation by my predecessor, and as the first governor in a long time hailing from the coast, I had an appreciation for how very real this issue was for coastal residents.

What's of interest is the way in which this issue, like so many that come with the weight of government's power, once again ties back to the idea of justice. With each approaching storm, all the political biases were toward early action. Action was in my political interest, never mind the costs to the taxpayer or private business. But statistically, nine out of ten approaching hurricanes don't ever come ashore. During my tenure, many ran farther up the coast and made landfall in North Carolina. But nobody can know what the storm is going to do three days out, so justice was necessarily part of our decision-making process. I thought it meant being deliberate and offering as limited a response as possible, because premature evacuation orders meant added cost not only for the taxpayer but also—and equally significantly—for the hospitality businesses along the coast. Bookings and visitors and the jobs and earnings for working people that came with them were lost not just during the week of an evacuation order but in the week that followed due to lost reservations. Though it made for long nights, we would therefore recalibrate every few hours based on the Hurricane Center's updated forecast.

In these kinds of matters there is no perfect answer, but it does mean weighing competing interests and really thinking through what real justice would look like. Policy makers should seriously consider limiting government's reach and maximizing that of the citizen. Sadly, too often there is but one consideration, and that is how it will look politically and play in the press.

Finally, I'd ask you to think about the injustice of spending money we don't have. Think about what it means for our young people and, if they really comprehended its long-reaching effects, what this would mean for their collective political voice. This may be a pipe dream, given the old saying "If you are not a liberal at twenty-five, you have no heart. If you are not a conservative at thirty-five, you have no brain," but considering the magnitude of our current national debt, what's at play is frightening.

We are borrowing from our children's future to pay for government services today. It's wrong, and conservative philosophy should highlight this in ways that are real to young people. We should be screaming from the rooftops, but people seem to have forgotten about the importance of political philosophy. Though spending matters, Americans are ridiculously quiet on what I believe to be the biggest threat to liberty and our way of life.

Forty-three percent of all US government spending last year was borrowed money. That is a ghastly number. Essentially one in every two dollars is borrowed, and young people will be the ones stuck with the consequences. Similarly, a whopping 35 percent of all new dollars created by the US Treasury over this country's entire two and a half centuries of existence were created in one single year—2020. Equity and justice would require containing the government's appetite for more.

My point in all this is that there are hundreds of real-world and practical applications on which to apply a conservative's take on justice, which is as sorely lacking as it is desperately needed in today's political environment.

THE RULE OF LAW

Justice's first cousin is the rule of law. You can't have justice if people are treated differently, and therefore the rule of law has always been premised on equal justice under the law.

Take the issue of immigration. For conservatives, the current debate on immigration is ultimately about the rule of law. None of us can have individual rights and the freedom they represent without laws that limit another person's ability to infringe upon those rights. Can you imagine watching a football or basketball game that has no rules? No helmet, no problem; fifty players on one side against eleven on the other, no problem. In basketball, forget the dribbling; it's too hard. Even the act of war has rules attached to it—torture and chemical weapons are out of bounds. The game of life needs rules too. In Russia they have rules—whatever Putin says, goes. But while this rule works for those with power or proximity to power, it eliminates freedom and fair play for all others. Our system has always been based on no man being above the law. In the American system, the rule of law is supreme, and blindfolded in the justice it dispenses. In all open political states, freedom has been enshrined with a rule of law that gives people a playbook from which to organize their activity. Using the football game analogy, they know that when they watch a game on ESPN, there will be eleven players on both sides every time. For human endeavors to work, the rule of law is vital.

Which brings us back to immigration. We allow about two million people a year to come to America legally. Given the waiting line that exists, in some cases people wait for years for the privilege of coming to America. Many countries are much less welcoming. It's widely accepted that no sovereign nation can really call itself sovereign without secure borders. It's why we must go through passport control when leaving one country and going into another. But some people find an easier way. They skip the wait line and just walk across the border.

But wait, if they can do that, why can't I do the same in some other area of life that matters to me? Why pay taxes? That doesn't work for me. Why drive the speed limit? It doesn't work for me. Everyone could come up with their own chafing point with the rules, and if we all did that, our system of government would no longer work function. And yet when it comes to immigration, with straight faces, well-meaning advocates and political figures alike simply change the subject. They point to human plight or human potential, and while the situation in places like Guatemala or Honduras might be bad, if that's the standard we adopt, why not also open the borders to everyone living in Chad or Nigeria?

When one takes issues like this back to the principal at play, things get simple. For this reason, when I was governor, I worked to enforce a thing called e-verify. Many businesspeople were upset with me, saying that undocumented workers were a part of what made their business work, but my counterargument was that my job was to enforce the law. Plain and simple. If they wanted to employ this labor, they should work to change the law. My job was not to turn a blind eye to the breaking of what should be sacrosanct in our political system—the rule of law.

PRIVATE PROPERTY RIGHTS

Have you ever washed a rental car? If you have, you're most unusual, because there is typically a big difference in our behavior toward things when owning versus renting. People rent things so they don't have to worry about the pesky details that come with ownership. Think about the garbage cans on your street that must be wheeled out each week for the trash collector. Ever wheeled out the cans for everyone on the street? Not just once for an elderly neighbor but week after week for the whole street? Though I own a farm with siblings who love to pretend we live in a utopian state wherein everyone will take care of the property we share, that's not how the movie plays. Not surprisingly, they cut grass in front of their homes but not the rest of the property. The reality is that everyone's business is no one's business.

If that were not the case, downtown Havana would not look like downtown Havana. Sadly, our family farm is beginning to look more and more like the ruins now blighting that once-great city. Both Havana and our farm are monuments to the way collectivism does not work. As it stands now, why would I take a Saturday to scrape and repaint a window, as in our case was needed a few years ago? There are twelve of us who own the farm, and though fixing the window would require 100 percent of the work, I would get one-twelfth of the benefit…so human nature being human nature, the window goes unpainted. This is the so-called tragedy of the commons.

Private property rights are not about stuff but our attitude toward it. If you want to get something done, put one person in charge and hold him responsible for the results. Private property rights unleash human initiative and work ethic, and people have an amazing proclivity to focus on their own stuff. There are a host of other values to private property, ranging from its worth as a store of value to the value it ascribes to work itself. People from Dr. Martin Luther King Jr. to Pope John Paul II have talked about how our work is a direct expression of our human dignity, and in my view, any system that devalues the fruits of one's efforts also devalues human dignity.

I'm hardly original in my thinking. In *Federalist Paper No. 10*, James Madison argued how the first object of any government is the protection of property rights.

In his book *Democracy in America*, Alexis de Tocqueville explained that the genius of America was its protection of private property and the fact that there was no landed aristocracy. He argued that the protection of private property translated into the protection of all other rights, even for the lowliest of farmers.

In *The Mystery of Capitalism*, Hernando de Soto made the case that the protection of capital and private property rights has led to economic prosperity in the West while the lack of this same protection has led to economic disparity and plight in poor countries.[3]

The list goes on, but the concept is simple—no one watches out for your things as well as you do. And in a government where all things are shared, no one really watches anyone's things. Government money is easy to spend, and therefore it's important it be offset with strong private sector and private property rights. A government big and powerful enough to give you things is powerful

---

3 Hernando de Soto, *The Mystery of Capital: Why Capitalism Triumphs in the West and Fails Everywhere Else* (New York: Basic Books, 2000).

enough to take them away. Our safeguard here comes in private property rights that are upheld by the rule of law.

MARKETS AND TRADE

Free markets and free trade aren't perfect, but they are far superior to the alternatives. In the early twentieth century, Joseph Schumpeter talked about "creative destruction" and the financial hardships that come with capitalism as some businesses fail while others succeed and take their place. We don't have many horse-buggy manufacturers anymore, but we do have auto manufacturers, and even the ones we know may fall to the next generation of electric vehicle manufacturers. Businesses are always changing, because Adam Smith's so-called invisible hand guides consumers in the marketplace toward where they think they can get the best deal. David Ricardo's theory of comparative advantage similarly drives trade. Both these guys lived a long time ago, but their theories are still practical and real as we think about government edict versus consumer choice today. Adam Smith believed there was unintended public good brought about by individuals acting in their own self-interest. For example, as a vendor might strive entirely in their own interest to create the best hamburger shop, other spots would have to lower their prices or better their quality to pull consumers their way. This, when multiplied across billions of wants, products, and services, creates not only markets but also the forces of Adam Smith's invisible hand. Ricardo's comparative advantage means that while they grow great wheat in Kansas, oranges don't grow there. So rather than setting up a greenhouse and attempting to do so, why not trade your wheat grown in Kansas for oranges grown in Florida? Most people would say these concepts are reasonable, yet today they are under assault as never before.

If we go the way of government control, consumers are left with a variety of poor substitutes that come with an expanded government role. Leaving aside the graft and nepotism I have seen accompany it, a larger governmental role—buy it here because the government says this is best—is hardly a formula for lowest price, best service, or quality.

Doubt me?

Take a trip to your nearest DMV office. When I was governor, one of our most popular reforms entailed employing a few market-based ideas in our offices, and consequently, DMV wait times tumbled from sixty-six minutes to fifteen. But this is not the way of government, and although there are many to choose from, a good example of the way government insulates itself from market forces occurred during my second year in office as governor. In this instance some businesses in the name of "protecting the consumer" used government regulation to protect themselves. We wound up in a particularly ridiculous fight over legislation for hair braiding, of all things. Local cosmetologists had become upset with the fact that unlicensed women were freelancing in their trade, particularly in braiding hair for students during their spring break along the coast in places like Myrtle Beach. There is an amazingly long list of state-sanctioned professional boards in everything from geology to real estate to daycare, and yes, South Carolina even has one to oversee cutting hair. These professional boards bring with them the power of government and the ability to fine businesses and even put people in jail. We were bewildered when the Board of Cosmetology promulgated rules that would require fifteen hundred hours of training before one could be licensed to braid hair in South Carolina. There was much back and forth, and after getting it down to three hundred hours, the legislative body finally settled on a compromise of sixty hours...in a bill that I ultimately vetoed. This is the text of that letter.

December 6, 2004
The Honorable David H. Wilkins
Speaker of the House of Representatives
Post Office Box 11867
Columbia, South Carolina 29211

Mr. Speaker and Members of the House:

I am hereby returning without my approval H. 4821, R-430, a bill containing various sections relating to licensure requirements for optometrists, licensure requirements for hair braiders, and registration requirements for cardiovascular invasive specialists. Identical versions of Section 2, which sets licensure requirements for hair braiders, and Section 4, which provides registration requirements for cardiovascular invasive specialists, were also passed by the General Assembly in H. 4455, R-147, which I have also vetoed today. I am restating the reasons for my objection to the similar sections in H. 4455 below.

I am vetoing this bill because I believe it is unduly burdensome and imposes unnecessary restrictions on hair braiders. Section 2 of this bill requires persons who braid hair to receive sixty hours of cosmetology education as a prerequisite to receiving state certification. Even though the intent of this section is to lessen the extreme, newly-applied requirement of 1,500 hours of education on hair braiders, I do not believe a person who braids hair should be burdened with any government-sanctioned educational requirements when there is no great public safety concern.

I believe this bill unfairly requires mandatory educational training for hair braiders when professions with a greater potential impact on public safety such as water treatment operators, chemical operators, residential builders, and general contractors are free from similar requirements. By comparison, a concealed weapons permit only requires eight hours of education and the educational requirement for selling real estate, which often involves complex financial transactions, is sixty hours of education—the same amount that this legislation would require for the braiding of hair.

My veto of H. 4821 stems from my fundamental belief in the need to limit the scope of government. I firmly agree with President Ronald Reagan who said in his first inaugural address that "Government can and must provide opportunity, not smother it; foster productivity, not stifle it." I believe that mandating education courses as a prerequisite for individuals to perform hair braiding would serve to unnecessarily smother opportunity for many South Carolinians. Therefore, I would urge the General Assembly to remove all licensure and educational requirements for hair braiders early in the next legislative session so that they may be free to work without restrictions as soon as possible.

Sincerely,
Mark Sanford

Think about it. What is the public policy consequence of a bad hair braid? By my reckoning, it is a bad hair braid and nothing more. You can get your license to fly an airplane in forty hours. Helicopters are even more complex, and yet you can get your license to fly one in forty hours as well. The lunacy of the fight my administration found itself in led to John Stewart of *The Daily Show* to report on it. It's a hilarious clip and worth viewing. In it reporter Samantha Bee interviews Pat Adams of the South Carolina Board of Cosmetology on the "growing national epidemic of illegal hair braiders." Ms. Adams talks of the dangers of somebody just working from an umbrella stand "anyplace they please" and likened illegal braiding to drunk driving as she noted, "Just like a drunk driver, nothing's wrong until you hit and kill someone."

Leaving her hyperbole aside, Adam Smith anticipated words like hers long ago when he said, "As it is the interest of the freemen of a corporation to hinder the rest of the inhabitants from employing any workmen but themselves, so it is the interest of the merchants and manufacturers of every country to secure to themselves the monopoly of the home market."[4]

LIMITED GOVERNMENT

Thomas Jefferson said at his first inaugural address in 1801, "Still one thing more, fellow citizens—a wise and frugal Government, which shall restrain men from injuring one another, shall leave them otherwise free to regulate their own pursuits of industry and improvement, and shall not take from the mouth of labor the bread it has earned. This is the sum of good government."

Have we come a long way or what?

Our federal government is no longer limited. These days New York City Democrats use government to impose their beliefs about whether people should be allowed to drink a Big Gulp and consume sugar. Republicans ask government to impose their beliefs about whether people should be allowed to consume medical marijuana. Democrats ask the government to impose their beliefs about who should be allowed in the military. Republicans do the same in using government to determine who should marry whom. It's not that either party wants to limit government, they just want it to do their stuff.

And this is a problem, given the endless list of things the federal government might be used to remedy based on the many challenges

4 Adam Smith, *An Inquiry into the Nature and Causes of the Wealth of Nations* (Oxford: Oxford University Press, 1976), 494.

found in any society. The latest attempt to take a crisis and grow the federal government's role relative to state and local government can be found in federal police reform originating in Washington. But while real problems exist, federal government policy as the cure-all is hardly synonymous with limited government.

Part of limited government means that it's not part of your life every day. Over the last four years, many people in far less "free" parts of the world have enjoyed far more freedom than we did as Americans. The former president's Twitter rants were omnipresent, and a never-ending voice from Washington is not consistent with limited government. Trump wanted and needed to be center stage. If there was a funeral, he wanted to be the corpse; if a wedding, the bride and groom. Unending noise alone from government can amount to an obnoxious assault on both freedom and limited government.

CIVIL SOCIETY

I find it easiest to think of the importance of civil society by thinking of the world as three intersecting circles—government, business, and civil society. Only the government has the power of coercion. If you don't pay your taxes, they send you to jail. Business can be defined by people acting in rational self-interest—if I can find a cheaper supplier or dealer, I'm going to the other vendor. And with civil society you have everything outside the circles of business and government, such as all the civil associations that do good, ranging from Habitat for Humanity to the Girl Scouts to the Heart Association. In them, people come together as a community of citizens who are linked by common interests and collective activity. Here there is no force; people find each other, and if it doesn't work for them, they simply move on. If we want to keep freedom, it's vital to keep as much of society as possible in business and civil society, but especially in civil society. This gets hard when government grows unchecked, which again is why conservative philosophy is so needed today. It's not that government can't do everything business or civil society does, it's just that there is a real cost to them doing it, and that cost is an ever-growing government. Thomas Jefferson observed in 1788, "The natural progress of things is for liberty to yield and government to gain ground."[5]

Jefferson's peers were more dire in their warnings. Thomas Paine said at the very founding of our country, "Society in every state is a blessing, but government, even in its best state, is but a necessary evil; in its worst state an intolerable one."[6] The mission of protecting civil society and restraining political society was at the very foundation of our republic, but the concerns of our Founders are too often lost as people fall prey to the promises of "more" from people like Alexandria Ocasio-Cortez and Andrew Yang.

FREEDOM OF RELIGION

One of the kindest guys I know is a friend by the name of Jay Winthrop, and I suspect that a good part of his warm disposition is

5 Thomas Jefferson, The Papers of Thomas Jefferson Vol 1. (Princeton: Princeton University Press, 1950).
6 Thomas Paine Common sense Thomas Paine, Common Sense and Other Writings. (New York: Modern Library Classics, 2003).

simply in his DNA. In 1630, one of his ancestors, John Winthrop, left England in search of a place that would allow religious freedom. Those Puritans formed the Massachusetts Bay Colony on land that is now called Boston, and we celebrate Thanksgiving as a day that memorializes many of their traditions on that first Thanksgiving. In coming to America for religious freedom, the same could be said of a host of faiths over the years, including the French Huguenots, who were instrumental in forming my hometown of Charleston. A heritage of faith is in not just in my friend Jay's DNA but in that of all of us.

The Founders believed in a higher power, and I have always found it telling that they placed freedom of religion first in our Bill of Rights. It reads, "Congress shall make no law respecting an establishment of religion, or prohibiting the free exercise thereof; or abridging the freedom of speech, or of the press; or the right of the people peaceably to assemble, and to petition the Government for a redress of grievances."[7] I think it's relevant that on the back of every US coin or dollar bill are the words "In God we trust" or that the House and Senate begin each day with a prayer. Some would argue these acknowledgments of faith are outdated, but I would argue they are deliberately placed, as they are based on the Founders' belief in the importance of faith to preserving liberty. If power and authority come from government or a king, it's one thing; if from God, another entirely.

With due respect to my more liberal friends, I think we have gone too far in our attempts to take God from the public realm.

---

7 U.S Constitution. amend. I.

A conservative voice is needed here—not a strident and moralistic tone but a reasoned one that speaks to the importance of this building block of liberty. I think the Founding Fathers really knew what they were doing here. It wasn't freedom *from* religion, but *of* religion. Inasmuch as they wanted a pluralistic society, religion was vital. Faith was important not only in broadening one's worldview beyond the simple horizon as to what each one of us might see as truth but also in creating a culture of tolerance. After all, if one could coexist with the neighbor whose faith said you were going to burn in hell while he ascended into heaven, you could probably find ways to tolerate their political views. The intolerance of competing faiths that came in things like the Crusades was a story they knew all too well, but this doesn't make excising faith from the public sphere the answer either. The fact that communist regimes have been as forceful and thorough as they have at excising religion and faith under their rule should tell us something. Big government has always attempted to crowd out faith, as big government has never wanted competition in allegiance, but if you want to keep liberty, government needs all the checks and balances the Founders prescribed.

Our history is very important here. Before the Revolution, places like Virginia had an official church, the Church of England. This left Presbyterians or Baptists in the colony out in the cold, and sometimes persecuted. This troubled Jefferson, who referred to his early battles in this as "the severest contests in which I have ever been engaged."[8] This political controversy ultimately resulted in the Virginia Statute for Religious Freedom, and Jefferson considered its

---

8 Thomas Jefferson, The Papers of Thomas Jefferson Vol 1. (Princeton: Princeton University Press, 1950).

passage one of his biggest accomplishments. He not only applied its thinking in our Constitution's mandate for religious freedom, but at Monticello, it is one of the three things he dictated were to be inscribed on his tombstone. It reads, "Here was buried Thomas Jefferson. Author of the Declaration of American Independence, of the Statute of Virginia for Religious Feedom, and Father of the University of Virginia." That Jefferson considered the codification of religious freedom one of his life's greatest works should underscore its importance for the rest of us.

A REASON-BASED REPUBLIC

It's commonly believed that Benjamin Franklin, upon leaving America's first Constitutional Convention, was asked whether we had been given a republic or a monarchy, to which he replied, "A republic, if you can keep it."

To do so would require reason; accordingly, another of the Founding Fathers' building blocks in preserving freedom was reason. They feared the tyranny of the masses and the irrational behavior that could come with it. As conservatives, it is vital we embrace reason. There are many current issues I could use to illustrate its importance in both policy and political terms, but let me zero in on the environment.

Goldwater doesn't mention it in his book, and the Republican Party of late has not given environmental issues their due, but a conservatism that leaves out the planet we call home strikes me as neither conservative nor reasonable. To many, the GOP has become synonymous with the distrust of science and denial of climate change. And yet, President Teddy Roosevelt was a Republican and an ardent conservationist. Republicans should reembrace the issue of conservation and remember that as conservatives, nothing could be more conservative or rational than our survival as a species.

What if conservatives and the Republican Party were to state emphatically that we *believe* in facts and science, wherever that might take us? Sounds reasonable to me. Basing policy on science rather than political whim or myth is wholly consistent with what the Founders envisioned in creating a reason-based republic. Inexplicably, the party has given up its great legacy of stewardship and conservation. It's time to go back to our roots. Teddy Roosevelt once stated, "The nation behaves well if it treats the natural resources as assets which it must turn over to the next generation increased and not impaired in value."[9]

Teddy put his thoughts into action and was father to our enviable National Parks System. During his presidency he established 150 national forests, five national parks, and eighteen national monuments on more than 230 million acres. It's a remarkable conservation legacy, and one with staunch Republican roots.

Why shouldn't conservatives today build on this and offer not bigger government but science and limited-government-based solutions to Mother Nature's ailments and the systemic natural threats to our way of life and even to civilization itself? What Roosevelt understood was that we should be conservative not only with our financial

---

9 Theodore Roosevelt, "The nation behaves well." August 31, 1910, in *Theodore Roosevelt on Bravery: Lessons from the Most Courageous Leader of the Twentieth Century* (New York: Skyhorse Publishing, Inc, 2015).

resources but also with our physical resources. That vital philosophy underscores the value of including reason in the world of policy.

The idea dovetails with religious conservatives too. The parable of the talents in the Book of Matthew is a story about being a good steward of what the master placed in the servant's control. The Bible is replete with stories of making the most of what you have been given. Which leaves me baffled as to why religious conservatives and the conservative movement walked away from such a basic tenet of conservatism. "Drill, baby, drill" is not a conservative imperative, and for the people I served along the coast of South Carolina, it was certainly never part of conservative voter sentiment. Even though I had a conservative voting record second to none, I was proud to be endorsed by the Sierra Club in my second race for governor. I know how important the issue of the environment is to me and to my sons—and from my own elections, to those I represented. But more interesting was the fact that I came from a very conservative state and congressional district and still saw this issue's appeal and importance. Why shouldn't conserving our natural resources and the reason fundamental to doing so be important issues in national conservative politics as well?

FREEDOM COMES IN MANY SHAPES AND FORMS, AND CIVIL LIBERTY, THOUGH CURRENTLY FORGOTTEN, IS VITAL TO ALL.

Civil liberty is one of those things that underscores how much we need limited government. Having no government at all does not allow for greater freedom. Anarchy reigns in its place, and foreign powers can use breaches in the wall of freedom to find their way in. But too much government pulls away from freedom as well. Information is power, and there is a reason the late FBI director J. Edgar Hoover wanted to know about the marital infidelities of Dr. Martin Luther King Jr. and John F. Kennedy. Trust me, it wasn't to protect them.

Here along the coast of South Carolina, a live crab can be boiled with amazingly little reaction if the water is turned up very slowly. So it is with politics. Freedom erodes little bits at a time, which makes having philosophical clarity and taking a stand for all freedoms really important. I had to renew my driver's license the other day and noticed I would soon have to have a Real ID driver's license going forward if I wanted to board a plane or enter a federal building. I am not sure whether it was Haley or McMaster who folded on this additional reach of the federal government, but holding the line on civil liberty and the ability to maintain privacy and watch over that which is personal is yet another of those building blocks.

Does Western civilization fall with Real ID? No. But is it yet another chink in the armor of personal liberty? Absolutely. Which was why I fought its implementation both as governor and in Congress. In bipartisan form, we were successful in holding it back while I was governor, and the Tenth Amendment was my main argument. It states that "The powers not delegated to the United States by the Constitution, nor prohibited by it to the States, are reserved to the States respectively, or to the people."[10] I believed the Real ID Act

---

10 U.S Constitution. amend. X.

went against that principle in an attempt to usurp state powers in the issuing of driver's licenses in favor of a federal standard.

The result is a de facto national ID card that should scare every one of us because centralized databases holding personal information have never been synonymous with liberty or even been sympathetic to the liberty the Founders promised each of us. And make no mistake, civil liberty—the ability to have some level of privacy with our personal information and the electronic effects of what we say and how we say it—is a key tenet of the larger notion of liberty.

In short, the personal information that is required with a driver's license has been capably handled by fifty states for a long time, and not so amazingly, we have managed to survive as a republic! This information doesn't need to be centralized and controlled by the federal government, and it's for this reason I pushed as hard as I did for so many years against our country moving in that direction.

LIMITED SPENDING, DEBT, AND DEFICITS

In the movie *Jerry McGuire*, Tom Cruise at one point exclaims, "Show me the money!"

This idea fits with more than the movie, because Nobel Prize–winning economist Milton Friedman was once asked what he considered the ultimate measure of government, to which his reply was, "Government spending." Politicians will talk at great length about limiting government spending, but much more relevant is their actual vote on appropriations bills in Washington. Spending, deficits, and our national debt matter much more than most of the issues discussed in the halls of Congress or in the media that allegedly covers those conversations.

That's especially the case now, given the "culture wars" that currently drive too much of politics. In 2010, our nation's highest-ranking military officer at the time, Admiral Mike Mullen, observed that our biggest national security threat was the national debt. It's really something when someone from a military perspective, rather than from a finance background, notes this in public. Here was the chairman of the Joint Chiefs of Staff saying it was not the Chinese, the Russians, nor the Taliban that we needed to be most focused on, but our national debt.

And guess what's been done about this situation since 2010?

You're right—absolutely nothing.

Erskine Bowles, who co-led the Simpson-Bowles Commission to look at government spending and debt during President Obama's time in office, came away from the experience stating that we were walking into the most predictable financial crisis in the history of man.

Guess what was done with the Simpson-Bowles report?

Right again—absolutely nothing.

President Trump told brazen lies about balancing the budget while not touching the entitlements that drive most of the budget's spending. He ran for office with the promise that he would eliminate the debt over the eight years he might be in office, but instead it proved to be anything but an area of interest, and the debt exploded under his watch. It has now continued to grow exponentially under the Biden administration. What's happening is critical and could spell the demise of our democracy.

The sad part is that no one is even trying to hide their actions. Biden is up front about growing government, and with Trump one could have easily predicted this spending spiral early on in his administration because it was preadvertised in his budget proposal. I was there on Capitol Hill and sitting on the House Budget Committee when then-OMB (Office of Management and Budget) director Mick Mulvaney came to sell the Trump administration's budget.

I dared to say that the budget was a lie, and this made national news, although it was plainly evident to anyone who looked at the way the numbers clearly did not add up.

Guess what was done about this well-evidenced fabrication?

Again, absolutely nothing.

The Republican Party and the conservative cause have both been silenced lately on the most paramount tenet of conservatism—curtailing government spending. If you don't get the budget right, nothing else matters. History and math point to the clear ways this matters more than anything else that is debated in the halls of Congress.

Unsustainable buildup in debt kills civilizations.

Unsustainable debt in time will decimate that nation's currency.

Unsustainable debt sets in motion inflation, which has historically been the great robber of the middle class.

Unsustainable debt fosters political instability, which in turn robs a country of the investment so important to creating opportunity and jobs.

Unsustainable debt prompts stupid government answers. We are constantly told that many of the problems associated with the tidal wave of debt can be remedied with yet more debt.

In short, if you want to ruin a country and the lives of those who live there, go over the edge on debt and deficits. One look at a host of countries across the pages of history highlights this reality. Here Milton Friedman was right on spending, and while it is not the only measure of government, it is what drives government's daily activity, as well as the need for taxes to pay for it. Because taxes and spending have not been balanced for decades, spending drives the growth of deficits and debt. Yet Republican politicians consistently vote for tax cuts while also voting for every program under the sun. They give lip service to eliminating debt and deficits, but they pay real allegiance to spending on local projects they consider vital to their reelection efforts.

This disconnect between what goes out and what comes in is maddening and alarming, but ultimately it comes down to our own blinders. We as voters have let our so-called conservative politicians get away with math that is inevitably destined to harm each and every one of us. If you had a family making $34,000 a year but spending $66,000—even while they already had $250,000 in credit card debt—does that fly? No way. And yet, simply add eight zeros, and you will be about where our federal government sits today. It's unconscionable.

I cannot emphasize enough how important this is. We are sitting on a powder keg of debt, and its ramifications and consequences are unfathomable. In peacetime we have never before seen anything like it. Over the last two hundred years we have never been remotely close to our current level of debt, save during World War II as we fought the Axis powers for our very survival.

If we do not start to balance spending, disaster is coming soon to each of us and those we love.

Given the way spending drives the train on taxes, debt, and deficits, spending is also the clearest reflection of what we really believe about freedom. Let me circle back to this lynchpin issue one more time.

You can spend your time working and sending taxes to the government—or you can spend it earning that same money, saving it, and growing your chance at making your dreams a reality. But make no mistake, it is a zero-sum game. Government's growth is always on one side, and an individual's freedom is always on the other. When one grows, the other contracts, and vice versa.

This has never been an argument for having no government and the anarchy that comes with it, just that government should be limited. That's the key word for conservatism—limited. No one is truly free; we all have a responsibility to pay into the system for it to function in ensuring our rights and the domestic and international freedom that undergirds it. It's just a question of how much is enough because the government's appetite for more never ceases.

My aim in office was certainly for less spending, but even more important, I aimed for sustainable spending, which is what gives us true freedom. Paying more than we can afford, or more than we chose to pay for, is not sustainable, but that is exactly where America finds itself today.

Sustainability is the operative question because whatever level of government we have should be sustainable. From the left it means people who rely on the government won't be left out in the cold, as has been done so many times throughout the ages when government came up short or simply printed more money to extend a financial mirage before then coming up short and decimating people's lives. From the right it means the government we have should be sustainable, and the worthy and important things that the government should do well are thereby also sustained. To do this government must be limited. It can't be all things to all people.

Focusing on the things only government can do also avoids prompting additional rounds of unsustainability, whether coming in the form of borrowing from our children or driving up taxes to the point that economic growth and jobs are hurt, which then triggers the need for yet more government.

In short, if sustainability is a key measure of government, by any measure ours is not. In fact, our county's current financial path has us bound for disaster.

For every program out there, you have diffused cost but concentrated benefit. I remember fighting the sugar program as a freshman in Congress. I joined with Jack Kingston of Georgia and Dan Miller of Florida to push for its elimination. All things being equal, it should have been easy to end. Of the 435 congressional districts that make up the House of Representatives, only about 5 had enough sugar grown in their district to make it an election-winning issue for that district. But that's not how it works. In the early 1990s there were only about sixty domestic sugar producers. The program cost the country about $1 billion in added sugar cost. Divided across the 250 million people living in America at that time, it cost each of us about four dollars more each year in the cost of sugar. Who is going to take a trip to Washington to lobby their representative to save four dollars a year? No one.

But those sixty sugar producers who split the billion dollars, do you think they showed up to lobby? You bet they did.

The largest producer at that time was the Fanjul family. They owned yachts, planes, and even the Casa de Campo resort in the Dominican Republic. They were on the Forbes 400 list, and they played the system like artists. One brother registered as a Republican, the other a Democrat, and their campaign contributions flowed generously to both sides of the aisle. Not surprisingly, when the gavel went down, our measure failed. It was by just three votes, but it should never have been close, given that sugar impacted only about five House districts. I still remember the sight of those grey-suited lobbyists high-fiving each other in the gallery above the House floor as they celebrated their win.

Multiply this phenomenon by one hundred thousand government programs, and you get a sense of why spending is out of control.

But government growth is also out of control because many in the Democratic Party say that public investment in a host of things is more important than an individual's choices on spending. For example, the Biden administration wants to spend $10 billion to create a civilian climate corps. Whether a "new, diverse generation of Americans working to conserve our public lands and waters, bolstering community resilience, and advancing environmental justice" is a good thing or a bad thing is subject to debate. But how it can be called an infrastructure investment doesn't seem as open to debate. Similarly, almost 20 percent of the administration's infrastructure bill's total cost, nearly $400 billion, is proposed for newly defined "infrastructure" like improved in-home care for the elderly and people with disabilities, while only $115 billion is allocated for roads and bridges. To me if it looks, feels, and smells like government consumption, it probably is. I could go on, but my point is that all kinds of things get assigned misleading labels to justify spending. You and I can dearly love elderly people, but classifying them as "infrastructure" does not make it so—and if we are going to go down this road, why not include young people? Given their longer life spans, would they not represent an even better "infrastructure" investment? But that's not what this sort of thing is ever about. Old people vote in much larger numbers than young people, and so with proposals like these, more spending is justified by labeling it under the banner of what will sell—and in this case young will subsidize old, though the elderly already receive the lion's share of entitlement spending. In short, the justifications used to separate you from your money and to allow 535 members of Congress to decide its use are never ending.

Unlike Republicans, Democrats are very up front about spending. I was in Congress with Barney Frank, and though we were polar opposites in our ideas about the role of government, I always admired the fact that he was straightforward about his belief in more and bigger government. He campaigned as a Democrat and voted as a Democrat. I remember many times he would tell me I had voted wrong but that thankfully I was not a hypocrite in my vote as he believed so many of my Republican colleagues were. All too often Republicans campaign as conservatives and vote very differently, and it was that disconnect that helped create the Trump movement and a desperation for something different than Republican politics as they were.

This places a big responsibility on those of us who consider ourselves true limited-spending conservatives. It's time for us to act. It's time for us to make noise. Regrettably, most politicians will never lead on the issue of overspending, which means the rest of us voters have to make it real to them at the ballot box.

Why should we take action? Certainly money and freedom matter, but ultimately this is not an amorphous idea about freedom. It's about looking your children in the eye and knowing you have tried to do right by them. What we have now is generational theft. It isn't cool. It's dead wrong. Because our spending is borrowed, we are stealing both money and opportunity from our children.

This makes it a moral issue. All real principles at the end of the day go to the heart of what we truly believe to be right and wrong. A deficit is nothing more than a deferred tax, and handing my four boys the bill for the government benefits I consume and enjoy today is just that. It's the modern-day equivalent of taxation without representation—an idea our forefathers fought hard against at the time of our country's founding. I have many friends on the left who get very keyed up about the ideas of social justice, equity, and fairness, yet there is no bigger issue of social justice in America than the debt we are handing to the coming generations.

The issues just outlined unfortunately represent only the tip of the iceberg on issues we could explore that are important to conservatives and all Americans. But what's most relevant in thinking about them is that Goldwater's *Conscience of a Conservative* should serve as a guide in framing the application of conservative philosophy on the issues of the day. He got right taking a stand, boiling down into words his philosophy and beliefs, and doing so with simplicity and clarity. It's indeed a worthwhile starting point.

But Goldwater missed his chance to expand many of his explanations to better resonate with audiences less conservative than he was. In trying to figure out today what comes next in politics and our country, we can learn from this mistake.

He had a message about ideals and political philosophy. But to be open to new ideas, people first must trust the messenger, and Goldwater came up short with voters in 1964. He was extremely hawkish about communism and was perceived by many as being too extreme in his beliefs. Johnson hit him hard on those issues in that year's presidential campaign. The opposition eventually crushed Goldwater with just one television ad that featured a small girl counting petals as she picked them from a daisy. It morphed from the daisy to a nuclear countdown and the visual of a nuclear explosion. The inference was that Americans could not trust Goldwater to refrain from using the bomb, given the emphasis he had placed on the need to fight back against communism.

In a similar way, Donald Trump's Twitter tirades and extreme divisiveness eventually caused the American public in 2020 to mistrust the messenger, and Republicans lost control of the presidency and Congress. His tirades about the election cost Republicans the two Georgia seats in the Senate.

I believe Trumpism now must end for the party to go forward. We are not there yet, and I find it amazing that Republican would-be presidential candidates for 2024 condition their candidacy for the highest office in the land on Trump. They go to Mar Largo to kiss the ring. They genuflect. They bow. But a party can't sustain itself orbiting around one man. We need far more humility and a much broader tent of ideas, messengers, candidates, and activists in the Republican Party. But we also need to learn from the Trump movement. Why were people in 2015 so suspicious of the government and the promises of those in government? Why did people feel the government wasn't working for them and those they loved? And how does one drain the swamp of candidates who promise limited government and then advance the opposite when elected?

I think some of the answers can be found by going back to the way as a party we have fallen short on the basics Goldwater outlined in his book. A modern-day *Conscience of a Conservative* should mean recalibration, not dismissal or discarding of timeless ideas. It should mean building on what he got right—his focus on conservative ideals and the ways in which they are the building blocks of human freedom. Those ideals are needed now more than ever.

They should be presented with a positive tone.

They should be offered with humility and empathy.

They should be succinct and to the point.

They should be applied to the real problems of our time.

And what does all this add up to?

Individual freedom. It is the prize. It's the hallmark of American greatness, the lifeblood of a republic, and should represent true north in our political aims.

Justice, the rule of law, private property, an institutional framework for government, trade and markets, civil society, and limited government are all building blocks to preserving freedom. Those are the true conservative themes that have been with us for over two hundred years but are sorely lacking in American politics today.

If we embrace those basics, I believe Republicans can really make something of this second chance we have been granted. Then hopefully we can all come together for a second chance for America.

PART ONE

SECOND CHANCES

1

MY SECOND CHANCE
GAINED AND LOST

I can hear the criticism already; I've heard it before. "So who is this guy, Mark Sanford, who's suggesting what to do?" "He lost his chance to give unsolicited advice." "Isn't he the guy who disappeared?"

I hear you. I am a wounded messenger. Perhaps I did lose the chance to have my words resonate, but I would argue that I am now more grounded than I was at any time prior to June 2009, and I believe my words now have more worth than they did back when I was speaking to millions on several national network shows each week. After my own reflection on these matters, I have come to believe that we are all wounded messengers. Each of us is imperfect or flawed in our own way—sometimes publicly, sometimes not—but even in that imperfection we each have something to say, and when afforded the chance, it's my belief we should take it.

June 2009 reordered my life. It's a year I sorely wish I could take back. Within a year my wife divorced me, and our four boys moved with her a hundred miles away to Sullivan's Island, on the coast of South Carolina. What had been a happy nest in the governor's mansion wherein I could not have imagined solitude instead became a place that personified emptiness, quiet, and loneliness. I went from being a rising star to a hermit and a pariah. I was understandably ostracized, and people wanted to keep their distance. I went from never knowing a stranger and being fearless to feeling shame, guilt, and fear.

It was a self-inflicted gun blast that came with lasting and souring consequences for my friends, those I loved, and those I represented. It was the same in nearly every area of my life. In the months and years that followed, I made amends as best I could for my wrongdoings, some public, some private. Some of them were accepted, some never will be.

But after feeling that life as I knew it, and most certainly my life in politics, were over, the most remarkable thing happened within twenty-four months of leaving the governor's office.

I was granted a second chance.

These circumstances are rare in life, and they are even rarer in Republican Party politics, but people at home along the coast of South Carolina once again elected me to the US House of Representatives, where I wound up being reelected for two more terms.

This second chance was heaven sent, and I'm thankful for it. What follows is a description of events, not a justification. I am in no way seeking to excuse or minimize my actions in 2009, but I learned much from going through them and their consequences.

When God gives us second chances, it is our duty to use them and it is up to us to rise to the occasions we are given. It has been my personal pledge to do so, and through this book I am asking Republicans and conservatives to join me in recognizing that we, too, have been given a second chance thanks to Trump's departure—a second chance for the party and for the conservative movement.

But first let me tell my story so you might better understand how fully I have come to appreciate second chances, and why I believe it's incumbent upon all of us to seize the second chance that Republicans have now been afforded and run with it.

In December 2008, my wife, Jenny, discovered a file of correspondence between me and Maria Belén Chapur, an Argentinian journalist I had met seven years earlier. Jenny's discovery eventually led us to marriage counseling, and amid a busy legislative session, a fierce political battle over stimulus money, and the responsibilities of raising four sons, we did the best we could to sort through what was tough at a private level and what at any given moment might morph into an even more difficult public drama. The months from Christmas through late spring were really hard. By May 2019, Jenny had asked for a trial separation. No one would know because I had commuted each summer on weekends since she and the boys always headed for Sullivan's Island when the boys got out of school.

One month later, I chose a path that caused incalculable pain for all of us.

Late on the afternoon of Thursday, June 18, I drove to the Columbia airport and took a flight that, with a connection through Atlanta that night, would take me to Buenos Aires. I had concocted the strangest of plans in a desperate effort to get my life back.

Jenny wanted a quick and timely resolution to the relationship, and if she didn't get it, she would be taking my news public in early July. She had never been one to bluff. I told her that the counselors we met with had all said that if one took the actions of love, in time good things would follow. I was committed to the actions, but we needed time. We hadn't gotten into this problem overnight, and we wouldn't get out of it overnight. She was, however, fixed on a quick resolution.

In my desperate mind at the time, I figured if I had Belén come up to the farm, she would see rustic cabins in the woods accompanied by big mosquitoes, and it would dawn on her how distant it was from New York, Paris, or Buenos Aires, and she would fall out of love with me. By the same token, given the way I always like to stay busy and be productive, if I went south and saw her country club lifestyle in Buenos Aires—which, while pleasant, was not a place I could get things done—then I, too, would fall out of love and get my life back.

Even with my head swirling, I knew it was too dangerous for Belén to come to South Carolina. But I thought I could go to Argentina over a long weekend and get it all figured out. The open window was narrow. It had to fall between the end of the legislative session and Jenny's deadline of early July.

But my plan proved to be as poorly constructed as it was desperate.

My last action in leaving the office for that fateful weekend was to tell one person that if Jenny called, to say that I was "hiking on the Appalachian Trail." I was certain she would not call since I had been given strict orders that there should be no communication between us during our trial separation. The casually offered Appalachian Trail instructions just crossed a last *t* in my final preparations for that ill-fated journey.

This was just the beginning of a whole catalogue of life lessons that would come my way, but at this point I had no clue about any of that. A white lie that I believed would never be used and was intended for only one person instead became a news item on all the major networks and a punch line for the likes of David Letterman and Jay Leno on late-night comedy shows.

I know now there is no such thing as a white lie, and intent doesn't matter in its construct. I had obviously never planned to mislead the press or the public. I had been an Eagle Scout and had always prized truth and lived by it, and I was mortified to learn my lie had been used as it had in the press.

I learned the hard way that once a lie is launched, you have no idea where it will eventually land. The path to this simple but crucial discovery was littered with pain, and I wish so much I could get a do-over on that day.

But, again, that's not life.

It was just a day like so many others wherein we have a moment that gives us two options. In those split seconds, we don't understand or

comprehend how huge and fateful the ramifications of some decisions are, but as Frost says, those choices make all the difference.

The steps to my political death played out this way.

By the time I had boarded the flight in Columbia, South
Carolina, a political nemesis and state senator by the name of
Jake Knotts was asking for my whereabouts. He concocted a ru-
mor that "no one knows where Sanford is" and contacted State
Law Enforcement Division Chief Reggie Lloyd about tracking me
down. Within hours, by Friday, June 19, state law officials had
attempted to contact me by phone and text. They determined my
last call on Thursday evening had originated from Atlanta at
Hartsfield International Airport. On Saturday, when they had received no return message from me, they contacted my office and
were told there was "no reason for concern." My office provided
no further details at that time.

Sometime later that day, Chief Lloyd stated he had confirmed
that "Sanford's whereabouts are unknown," but Knotts claimed
that Chief Lloyd said that my security detail knew where I was.

The next day, Sunday, June 21, Lieutenant Governor Andre
Bauer said he was informed that "Sanford's whereabouts are unknown," and Monday morning, June 22, news reporters were given
the same information.

From 2:00 p.m. on Monday, June 22, until 10:05 p.m. that night,
a series of questions were asked, and statements were made. This
is where regret becomes poignant. Each of these things, though

unimaginable to me as I boarded my flight, was a result of my little white lie and my actions.

At 2:30 p.m., Knotts issued a statement asking who was in charge of South Carolina during the governor's absence.

At 2:40 p.m., the *State*, the Columbia-based largest newspaper in South Carolina, published an article saying that I had been unreachable "for four days."

At 2:50 p.m., my office issued a statement saying that I was taking some time away from the office that week to recharge after the stimulus battle. They said that while I was away, I would be working on a couple of projects that had fallen by the wayside.

Around 3:00 p.m., the Associated Press located Jenny at our Sullivan's Island beach house. She replied that she didn't know where I was but that she was not worried.

At 3:40 p.m., the lieutenant governor's office told reporters that the governor's office had spoken to me and knew my location.

At 5:00 p.m., Joel Sawyer, in my office, corrected that report and said that no one in the governor's office told anyone in the lieutenant governor's office that they had spoken to me.

The next five hours were marked by political moves from the lieutenant governor's office and reactions from our office. I was completely unaware of the growing storm.

At 10:00 p.m., the lieutenant governor's office issued a statement saying it had been misled into believing that my office had spoken with me. Lieutenant Governor Bauer said he could not take lightly that my staff had not communicated with me "for more than four days." Someone in his office said the conflicting statements arose when Bauer asked to speak with me and my office did not accommodate him.

Then, at 10:05 p.m., Joel Sawyer issued the statement that will haunt me to my grave. "Governor Sanford is hiking the Appalachian Trail."

My office called me in Argentina later that night. I was on a cattle ranch in the middle of nowhere on the Pampas, the wide-open grasslands of Argentina. There the grass appears as if a sea, with its waves stretching as far as the eye can see. With no hills, mountains, or trees to crowd out even a portion of the sky, at night all before and around you are the stars. One's true insignificance is made real on that vast physical landscape, and it was there I felt my first twinges of wrenching desolation. It was as if I were in a tiny boat adrift on the ocean, beyond inconsequential when measured against the unending sea of grass that surrounded me and the heavens above me. It was too late to drive to Buenos Aires to catch the night flight back to the United States, so I tossed and turned restlessly, staring out into the night sky, and the starlit open Pampas, which faded into gray darkness.

I felt as though I had gotten word of my impending execution. I just didn't know its form.

I felt as though life as I had known it was over.

Both were true.

My mind went fuzzy in a combination of dread and fright. I wished so much I could be safely back in my office in Columbia to deal with all of it, a place where we had handled so many crises and challenges so well over the preceding years.

But this was different.

Now *I* was the disaster, and the fires that had been lit could not be stopped. They would run their course. Consequences can't be managed; they are to be accepted and learned from, and my life's most painful tutorial had begun.

At 9:40 the next morning, on Tuesday, June 23, the office issued what they thought would be the end of the story, a statement saying I was taken aback by the reaction to my alleged disappearance and that I would be returning to my office the next day, Wednesday, June 24.

It was far from the end of the story. It was but more gas on the fire.

Around 4:00 p.m., CNN contacted Jenny, and she confirmed that she still had not heard from me, that I had missed Father's Day, and that she was focused on being a mom and taking care of her children. Her dismissal created even more speculation.

At 5:00 p.m., a local news channel reported that a missing state vehicle—the Suburban I had driven—had been tracked down to the Columbia airport. Sources at the airport told the TV reporter that I had been seen boarding a plane. My spokesman stood by the Appalachian Trail story.

Early the next morning, Wednesday, June 24, I arrived at the airport in Atlanta on the overnight flight from Buenos Aires. Met by Gina Smith, a reporter with *The State*, I said that I had been in Argentina for a few days, that I had considered hiking the Appalachian Trail but had decided I wanted to do something more exotic.

"Oh, what tangled webs we weave," wrote Sir Walter Scott, "when first we practice to deceive."[11] I was getting caught in webs I had woven myself.

---

11 Walter Scott, Marmion Vol.4. (Cambridge: University Press, 1885).

At 10:30 a.m., my office announced a 2:00 p.m. press conference, and what followed was a rambling eighteen-minute confession by me, filled with apologies that satisfied no one. I said, "I've been unfaithful to my wife...with a dear, dear friend from Argentina." I said the affair had begun in the last year and that I had gone to Argentina to break it off. I said my wife and I had been working through the issue for about five months. I said I would resign as chair of the Republican Governors Association. And I said much more in my impromptu confessional.

At 4:58 p.m., MSNBC reported that Jenny had asked me for the separation two weeks earlier, and soon after that, she released a lengthy statement in which she said that while she remained proud of my public service, she deeply regretted my recent actions and their potential damage to our children. She said that the trial separation we had agreed to two weeks earlier had stipulated that I should not contact the family, which was why she did not know where I was during my absence. She said she believed I had a chance to resurrect our marriage, and she hoped the media would respect her and the boys' privacy while she sought the "wisdom of Solomon, the strength and patience of Job, and the grace of God" in helping to heal our family.

A few minutes after her statement, *The State* published the series of emails I had exchanged with Belén. The next day her full name was made public in a newspaper in Buenos Aires. A bevy of cameras were deployed outside her apartment in Buenos Aires, at my home on Sullivan's Island, and with me in Columbia. For a guy who had always been private in nature, it was torture. And I wasn't alone in that. After more than a week of being unable to leave her apartment, Belén escaped in the trunk of a car. Jenny and the boys had their own garrison in the form of our Sullivan's Island home, and from there the boys ran lemonade patrols to the journalists encamped in the hot Carolina summer sun at the end of our driveway.

Over the months ahead, there were calls for my resignation. There were five different investigations, among them an ethics committee investigation. Under the category of a person being able to choose their sins but not the consequences, I ultimately settled with the ethics committee and simply paid $74,000 in fines. I had done nothing wrong, and while my lawyers believed we could have fought and won the case, it would have cost me $300,000 in legal fees to prove it. More significant at the time, having another public contest and the media coverage that would have come with it would have further lost the larger battle taking place for even a ray of confidence with the public.

Each day was a new crisis, and I took it one step at a time just trying to survive. Friends regularly came by the governor's mansion at night worried about the specter of suicide.

Eventually the articles of impeachment were dropped. On December 9, a committee of the state legislature voted to censure me.

And on December 11, Jenny filed for divorce.

Writing this is painful. Each paragraph encapsulates a new way in which I blew myself up and let my family and others down.

You get to again live through the downdraft of your life and all that follows in its wake. I suppose I never will completely finish apologizing, but what I tried to do in those first eighteen minutes of my press conference, I repeated often during the remaining eighteen months of my time in office. It was endless—with my staff, in handwritten notes to supporters and friends, before every meeting or speech to a civic club, to random people I met in the streets of the towns and cities of South Carolina.

After a while, people started calling it "the apology tour." After a little more time, people began telling me, "It's time to stop with the apology tour."

But there is something right about owning your past, of saying up front you were wrong and are sorry for what you did.

If you own it, you can learn from it. Without that, you can't.

A combination of this, coupled with shame and guilt, led me to the year and a half of apologies that followed and all the apologies I have made since over the last eleven years.

Saying "I was wrong" changes your internal wiring.

I will always feel more vulnerable than I did prior to June 2009. If someone wants to hurt me, they know exactly how. My bull's-eye of vulnerability is pasted to my chest.

You learn to accept what you can't change.

You learn that no matter the sincerity of your apology, some people will never forgive you. In different forms, that lesson always stays with you. As tough as these things can be, you push through what you could never have imagined as best you can.

By far the hardest of the apologies was with my boys.

How do you explain frailty—life's unexpected turns and inner conflicts—to boys who once saw you as Superman? It became a walk in faith and a tough lesson in my own mortality and weakness.

Where once I preached and lectured to them, now I simply listened; I had lost all authority to say much of anything. As phrases, "I'm your dad" or "Because I said so" proved worthless in yielding any kind of a response once trust was broken. So I did little things designed around rebuilding trust. After so much destruction, it was important to find ways to reconstruct and build.

Toward this end, my sons and I built a cabin and bridge at the farm, and it was my hope that as we nailed and hammered together, we were rebuilding something.

In divorce, or in any of life's breaks and fractures, rebuilding trust takes intention and time. The journey is never complete, but the daily commitment toward its completion is the vital ingredient in rebuilding trust. Mistakes are not corrected cleanly or evenly. Painful feelings last, and regained trust comes slowly, if at all. While the divorce was lightning fast—under the grounds of adultery one can divorce in South Carolina in ninety days—its aftershocks lingered, and most everything I did was called into judgment. Things like a Super Bowl viewing with my youngest son escalated to news headlines, judges, and attorneys.

Belén and I got engaged, only to break off our engagement without marrying two years later.

Time marched forward. Jenny remarried. The boys grew up.

MY SECOND CHANCE GAINED

My second chance story is not unique; from time to time we are all afforded second chances in life. Whether we appreciate them or do something with them is a different story. Some people don't change a bit, and I think this represents a second chance wasted. Others learn from their previous chapter and are the better for it.

I have left public office three times, and in each instance I became spent rocket fuel. Each time, the calls and emails stopped, and those I thought were friends moved on to the next occupant of the office. These times were points of reflection, a chance to look back and review.

When I left Congress the first time, I was leaving a job well done. I left the governorship with shame and regret. In coming back to Congress two years later, I had been forgiven, but then I later left having been found guilty of the crime of speaking out against President Trump. Each time has afforded its own chapter of review and introspection, and with each second chance I grew to be ever more grateful. Time's passage alone has a way of making us appreciate the blessings of life. I love blue sky but appreciate it now far more than I did as a young man, and I suspect at life's end, I'll appreciate it even more. So it goes with the passages and events of life too.

The first time I served as the representative from South Carolina's First Congressional District, in 1994, I won the election by a majority of 66 percent. I ran on the promise of fiscal conservatism, something important to South Carolina Republicans at the time, and I kept that promise, earning a rating of ninety-two out of a hundred from the American Conservative Union. I was also placed at the top of Congress by groups like the National Taxpayers Union for efforts to curb government spending, but because much of politics is zero sum, many of these efforts made me less than popular with state and local politicians where my vow of fiscal conservatism was often at odds with their desires for legislative goodies from Washington. But my constituents appreciated it, and I won my two reelection campaigns by over 90 percent in both 1996 and 1998. I also kept my promise not to serve more than three consecutive terms, and in 2000, I chose not to run again.

In little more than a year I was approached by John Rainey, a regal patrician from upstate who believed in noblesse oblige. Though he could have avoided it, a turning point had come in his life in serving as a lieutenant in Vietnam, and he came to my house talking about the parable of the talents. While many could do the real estate work I had gotten back into, few could be a real contender for the governorship or the US Senate. Jenny and I heard him out, and a little over a year later, I stood for governor, winning with 53 percent, and four years later, I was reelected by 55 percent. I poured a crazy amount of time and energy into trying to be a financially prudent and conservative Republican governor for the six and a half years, until my implosion in 2009.

But spring has a way of coming back around. In 2013, I was still convinced politics was forever over for me. But that year, Senator Jim DeMint surprised the people of South Carolina by announcing his resignation from the Senate to take over the conservative Heritage Foundation. Governor Nikki Haley, who had succeeded me, announced she would appoint Representative Tim Scott to fill DeMint's Senate seat; consequently, there would be a special election to fill Scott's seat in the House of Representatives...which happened to be the First Congressional District, where I had once served.

I had been out of politics for two years and had slowly started to build a career. Real estate, a few boards, and work as a contributor on Fox News kept me busy. When friends began to suggest I should run for Congress, my initial reaction was to say, "Not a chance! The wounds are finally healing."

But at the end of the day, that which had motivated me in the past pushed me over my fears. In some form, we all want our lives to have mattered, and I had long felt called to try to have some impact on the worrisome trajectory of national spending that I had always believed could destroy our country. There was much internal back-and-forth, but in March 2013, I announced my candidacy for my old congressional seat. I was one of sixteen candidates.

I analyzed it with my old pollster and campaign consultant, Jon Lerner, and he believed I had enough name recognition to possibly make it into a runoff but so much baggage that the movie would end there. In his mind, running was an exercise in futility. As he saw it, there was no way mathematically that I could win, so he declined to take the race.

This was where grace and second chances became anything but academic for me. I campaigned hard. I spoke much and listened more. The media was tough, and seemingly every story had to begin with a recap of my implosion. Regular people were much kinder and far more understanding.

I climbed in the polls.

I particularly listened to those who said they wouldn't vote for me. Some said so out of religious convictions, some out of loyalty to

Jenny, some just because they were tired of me. But our team tried to focus the conversation on my strengths. We made really unattractive signs from leftover scraps of plywood spray-painted with the words "Sanford Saves Tax $." They resonated. And I talked about my weaknesses. In one TV ad, speaking straight to the camera I said, "None of us goes through life without mistakes. But in their wake, we can learn a lot about grace and a God of second chances and be the better for it."

I made the runoff, won the primary, and—after a general election that became national news in part because of my story and in part because my Democratic opponent was comedian Stephen Colbert's sister—I won the special election with 54 percent of the vote. A year later, I won the regular election unopposed. Two years after that, in 2016, I won my third term with 58 percent.

I was back in Congress, and I strove to fulfill my vow to serve the people of South Carolina with the same dogged conservatism that had been my guiding principle since day one of my time in office.

But in 2018, my second chance came to a screeching halt. A new wave was sweeping the Republican Party and the nation—with the Republican Party quickly abandoning its long-held belief in low taxes, small government, federalism, and a distrust for autocracy, and transforming into a personality cult centered on President Trump.

Though one might be forgiven and given a second chance for marital unfaithfulness, there was apparently no second chance for political unfaithfulness to this one man. It was the new unforgivable sin in Republican theology, and I would reap its dire consequences.

It all felt particularly unreal to me, given my personal story. In the same way that up was down and down was up as I fell in love with Belén, I watched as down was up and up was down in the Republican Party that year. People had fallen in love with Trump.

He could do no wrong. He was a savior. He was the answer. He was perfect.

They were blinded by their love, and this, too, I knew well.

The list of politicians who have committed sexual indiscretions is regrettably a long one. Some of these men saw their political careers evaporate while others were given a pass. Why the public forgives some and not others remains a mystery to me. The one thing I know is that all of us—not just politicians—who make mistakes and are given a second chance owe it to both God above and those around us to learn from our mistakes and live differently going forward.

That belief guaranteed my political demise.

But how could I have learned the awesome significance of truth and the danger of even the smallest of white lies and *not* speak out against much of what President Trump said and did? Either you learned this difficult lesson and had to speak up, or you didn't. Many sought what they defined as a middle ground—they would stick their head in the sand and pretend they didn't see what they saw and just wait for Trump's time in office to end. But looking the other way is a sin too. One of the fathers of conservative philosophy, Edmund Burke, recognized this long ago, and John F. Kennedy quoted him when he said, "The only thing necessary for the triumph of evil is for good men to do nothing."

More significant for me, to have done nothing would have made a mockery of all my boys and I had spoken about in the years that followed 2009. We all play to different audiences in life, and the one that meant the most to me was and is my four sons. They had been loud and clear on the need for absolute honesty in our relationship and made it plain that they saw this as something of a moral test for me.

Accordingly, my third second chance evaporated as quickly as it came. By June 2018, I had lost the Republican primary. My sin was not my past nor my conservative bona fides; it was my challenge to the untruths told by President Trump.

I had to stand where life had brought me. So I was respectful—but not one who walked in blind deference to the president. I wasn't brave here. I was anything but brave. I just didn't want to be a hypocrite twice in my life.

MY SECOND CHANCE LOST

Making a stand against Donald Trump began for me on February 19, 2016, the night before the South Carolina presidential primary, when I endorsed Senator Ted Cruz for president. My endorsement, I admitted at the time, was not about Ted Cruz but rather that he represented the last train leaving the station that might be able to help in stopping Donald Trump's political advance. As a congressman I had little leverage in affecting the presidential race, but this was the one card I could play, and so in the eleventh hour I did, even though I had long planned to keep clear of the presidential race. Some assumed it was personal, given our wildly different styles, but that was not the case.

I agreed with and supported much of the administration's approach to policy, and the one time I had met Trump had been random and quick but not unpleasant. Just prior to a presidential debate a few months earlier I had been directed backstage via a narrow passageway, and as I came around a corner, we literally ran into each other. In that Trump voice he uses to express alleged conviction, he said, "I've watched you. You're a winner." A few other pleasantries and then he and his entourage were gone. For a second that followed, there was that "What just happened?" moment as I looked questioningly at my aide, Martha, both of us wondering what he'd meant by that.

My last-minute endorsement was too late to have any effect for Ted Cruz, but even as early as 2016 I felt inside that something was happening, and that it was important to take a stand. As I told the press at the time, I was frightened by what a Donald Trump victory would mean for the GOP and the nation.

I wasn't the only South Carolina politician to endorse a non-Trump candidate during that primary season. Both Governor Nikki Haley and Senator Tim Scott had endorsed Senator Marco Rubio. Though perhaps an oxymoron, and time would certainly make it so, there weren't many principled politicians at that time who supported Trump.

As an aside, and an illustration of the way politics really works, our state's lieutenant governor went the other way early and made what turned out to be the best political bet of his life. Henry McAllister had previously been the state's Republican Party chair and attorney general, and had long represented the establishment wing within the state party. Yet he sensed the political winds blowing, changed course, and that January became the highest-ranking state politician to endorse Trump.

When Trump won, McAlister's loyalty to Trump changed the political landscape of South Carolina. McAllister had long wanted to be governor. He had most recently been defeated by Nikki Haley in the 2010 race, so not surprisingly, when Trump asked what he wanted, he said to be governor! There was one small problem, though; South Carolina already had a governor. To make it happen, Trump had to find a position alluring enough to pull Nikki from the seat. She was offered the ambassadorship to the United Nations. It was a political trade made in heaven, with wins for all the politicians. Nikki would gain the foreign policy credentials she needed to enable a run for president, Donald would show the rewards of loyalty, and Henry got to be governor.

But other than inside deals like these, there were few winners. Time with Trump in power would wash away whatever principles most politicians had as they tried to maintain relevance and power during his watch.

I went further than most of my fellow Republicans felt comfortable going. I told the press that I didn't think a lot of what Trump talked about was within the bounds of constitutional authority. I said if you believed in limited government and constitutional authority, you had to stand up to what he was saying. I called him dangerous and destructive. I said his position on immigration was not enough to call him a conservative and that saying he would "get the budget right by curbing waste, fraud, and abuse" was stepping off into financial fantasyland.

And already in February 2016, I had condemned the degrading way he talked. I said you can't call people the disrespectful and ugly things he did without it having a negative effect. I believe the words and tone we use are important in setting the tone for our children, folks at work, worship, and community. But good churchgoing people for some mysterious reason gave him a pass on behavior they would never accept in other places. The same people who had been tough in condemning my infidelity turned a deaf ear to his crass insults and the unrepentant braggadocio with which he had committed his lifetime of infidelities. It was beyond bewildering, and not a little disconcerting.

I said all that in February 2016, but I was ignored. The Republican Party proceeded to step off into its own brave new world with Donald Trump.

By July 2016, I was speaking out against him too regularly for my own good. Republican friends increasingly told me to be quiet. My response was, how do we stay quiet on the trampling of core principles and ideals I thought Republicans held dear? I railed against his pattern of callous disregard for details and his often-incomprehensible stream of consciousness rambles that were long on hyperbole and short on facts. When asked if he would protect Article I of the Constitution—the time-honored limits on the powers of the executive branch—he responded that he would "protect Article I, Article II, Article XII, go down the list."

I said out loud what every member of Congress knew but for reasons of self-preservation stayed silent on: there is no Article XII. Unfortunately, pointing out these obvious facts continued to make the news, which in turn stirred up people at home. They were not

24

upset with Trump for making things up; they were upset that I had called him on it.

In August 2016, in an op-ed in *The New York Times*, I said I was a conservative Republican with no stomach for Trump's personal style and his penchant for regularly demeaning others, and though I was careful not to say I would vote for him, I said that I intended to support and work with our nominee. I attributed this primarily to the importance of filling the existing vacancy on the Supreme Court and others that might open in the next four years. However, I said, "My ability to continue to do so will in part be driven by whether Mr. Trump keeps his word that he will release his tax records."

As most know well, he did not.

But that was enough to make me his enemy, and whatever good-will I might have accrued based on being a reliable conservative vote went out the window.

I said then that the issue was not even about his individual returns but rather the importance of sustaining the fifty-year tradition at the federal level and its maintenance at the state level. It was about the hundreds of down-ballot state and local races and the transparency voters deserved on those who would hold the keys to the executive branch. Each time I ran for governor of South Carolina, I released my tax returns because that was the tradition. I'll admit it felt a bit like a financial colonoscopy. I didn't like it, but it was what had always been done, so I did what was expected to avoid the headlines that would have come in departing from the norm. I repeatedly made the point in those days that if presidential candidates quit releasing their tax returns, why would gubernatorial nominees across the country continue to release theirs?

In February 2017, only a month after the inauguration, I gave an interview to *Politico* in which I said that Trump was fanning the flames of intolerance and that he represents the antithesis, or the undoing, of everything I thought I knew about politics and life.

This interview with Tim Alberta was pointed. Tim's descriptions got people further excited in South Carolina, where excerpts were printed in local papers. Tim wrote of me,

"He lays waste to the president of his own party…Most people in Washington are biting their tongues when it comes to Donald Trump, fearful that any candid criticism of the new president could invite backlash from their constituents or, potentially worse, provoke retribution from the commander in chief himself…Mark Sanford is not like most Republicans in Washington…His policy resume is beyond reproach to those on the right…and this coupled with his past stands and storms…gives Sanford a unique sense of liberation to speak his mind about a president whose substance and style he considers a danger to democracy."[12]

He then went on to quote me. "'I'm a dead man walking,' Sanford tells me, smiling. 'If you've already been dead, you don't fear it as much. I've been dead politically.'"

In the interview Tim went on to ask if I thought Trump was an honest man, and here I picked my words carefully and stopped short of calling him dishonest. Given my history, I told Tim that people in glass houses shouldn't throw stones, but I felt a good part of my chance at coming back to the House of Representatives had been tied to owning up and apologizing for things I had handled wrong.

---

12 Tim Alberta, "I'm a Dead Man Walking: Mark Sanford has nothing left to lose. And he's here to haunt Donald Trump" *Politico*, February 17, 2017.

Not that any of us get it right all the time, but I believe there is eternal relevance in truth. It matters how we approach ideas, and I believe humility is important in our treatment of others. To state the obvious, this was not Trump's style, and he saw an apology as nothing more than a sign of weakness.

His personal style was an affront to all the things I thought God had been trying to teach me about humility, empathy, and more in the aftermath of my own failings. After my experiences in 2009 and what I learned in their wake, I was left with no choice but to call things as I saw them. My sons' concrete beliefs on the issue further locked in my thinking. I got from them more than a few references to what the Bible said, including, "For what will it profit a man if he gains the whole world, but loses his soul?"[13]

And so my course became clear, even knowing its politics might be troubling. I made a stab at justifying my actions. I remember thinking how telling the truth is not criticizing, it's just telling the truth. Right? Others didn't see it that way. The media categorized me as a Trump antagonist and critic. I knew those headlines weren't good, but I said what I had to say and tried to move forward. With Trump, that proved impossible; each day of the period after he won the election and came into office brought a new outrage and a resulting request for, and requirement for me, to comment. As much as I wanted to close my eyes to his outrageous behavior, I believed that when you're vested with the authority that comes with public office, silence in the wake of wrong is affirmation of it. So each day I dug

---

13 Matthew 16:26.

my own political grave a little deeper. But I still didn't fully fathom just how quickly my own words would sentence me to political death.

Others were reading the same tea leaves, and the overwhelming advice from Republicans was that I should get in line and support the president. I just couldn't get there. I would support him and work with him where we agreed, but where we disagreed, I felt I had to be equally forthright.

That was never Trump's way. He never gave full allegiance to anyone, but he demanded 100 percent loyalty. Not to his ideas but to him personally. You were friend or foe; there was no middle ground. Naturally, I was seen as the latter. In March 2017, I signed a Democrat-sponsored letter demanding that Trump release his tax returns, which moved me way up on the enemy list. But I wasn't the only Republican to sign it; the iconic North Carolina representative, the late Walter Jones, did as well.

Walter and I had begun in Congress together in 1994, and he was a great friend. He had a remarkable conscience, which made his stand on the tax return issue no surprise. He had also taken a stand on the Iraq War. I was governor when the war began, so I missed that vote in Washington, but Walter was there. Based on the alleged intelligence about weapons of mass destruction that Cheney and others promoted, he voted yes. When that later proved less than accurate, Walter became one the war's most vocal critics in the US House of Representatives, offering innumerable measures to stop the war or thwart its funding. It took that kind of character to be the only other Republican to stick his head up on this issue.

But the really remarkable act of conscience he made was this: After every soldier's death in Iraq for the rest of his time in Congress,

Walter personally wrote a letter to the family thanking their son or daughter for their service and apologizing for his mistaken vote for the war.

Meanwhile, back in Congress, by April 2017 Trump began sending not-so-veiled threats my way. Before the vote collapsed on a GOP health care bill, word got out that I was considering voting against it, along with several other conservatives. We were all summoned to the Old Executive Office Building beside the White House, where we sat together as if in grade school. There we were told by the president's adviser, Steve Bannon, that it was a shit sandwich, but we were going to eat it. The group did not buy in to his cajoling, so we were all called back to the White House the next day, this time to talk with the president himself.

At the meeting in the Cabinet Room in the West Wing of the White House, the president showed no knowledge of the bill or concern for its threat to conservative ideals and remedy. In his own words, "I just want a win."

At the meeting's conclusion, Office of Management and Budget (OMB) Director—and a former House colleague from South Carolina—Mick Mulvaney pulled me aside. He said, "I hate to do this, but the president told me specifically that he wanted me to look you in the eyes and give you a personal message from him."

Mulvaney's awkward pauses and his inflection intended to intimidate me made it feel as if I were living a scene from *The Godfather*.

"The president hopes you don't vote for this bill," he said, "because he wants to run somebody against you when you don't."

I told him I understood, but the president would have to do what he had to do, because I certainly planned to do what I had to do. It was a surreal moment, listening to a former colleague fulfilling his mission for the commander in chief, soaking in my first actual threat from the newly-seated president.

In response to media questions at the time, I said, "I am committed to working in any way possible with the president, but I ultimately work for the people of the First District. When a bill comes along that does not fit with the people I represent or the promises I made while running, it's my belief that I have to represent that viewpoint regardless of other perspectives in Washington and the consequences of doing so."

Ultimately Speaker Paul Ryan canceled the vote on that bill, but by then the battle lines were fairly concrete. I had known they were forming a few months earlier when the president and his entourage visited the Boeing plant that our team had recruited to Charleston during my time as governor. In a receiving line, I had shaken hands with Ivanka Trump and introduced myself, only to get the iciest of receptions. "There is no need for the introduction; we know exactly who you are," she said. "We watch you on MSNBC and CNN all too often."

The following month, May 2017, I objected publicly to Trump's budget proposal, as delivered to Congress by Mulvaney. I called it what it was—not only a myth but also a lie. I said the budget hinged on what one might call a Goldilocks economy—not too hot, not too cold, and not at all possible. It was total make-believe. Deficits and the debt would explode if its assumptions were wrong, and tragically, elementary math plainly showed the figures were wrong.

At the budget hearing I told Mulvaney, "I'm a deficit hawk, as you well know, and if you're wrong on these numbers, it means all of a sudden we've created a $2-plus trillion hole to dig out of for our kids and grandkids." Mulvaney's transformation had been dramatic. He had gone from only months before suggesting we should shut down the government if necessary to stem the tide of spending and the systemic threat to our country he believed it represented, to selling this delusional stuff. Sadly, he was by no means alone in his philosophic flip-flop during Trump's tenure.

In June 2018 during my heated primary challenge, Trump endorsed my challenger. As a candidate, it's never a good day when the popular president of your party comes out against you. "Mark Sanford has been very unhelpful to me in my campaign to MAGA," he tweeted. "He is MIA and nothing but trouble. He is better off in Argentina. I fully endorse Katie Arrington for Congress in SC, a state I love. She is tough on crime and will continue our fight to lower taxes. VOTE Katie!"

Not surprisingly, I lost the primary, my first electoral loss in twenty-four years.

That night, all four of my sons were with me. After the crowd left, we went down to the local Cook Out and stayed up until three that morning, talking of life and politics. It marked a capstone, the end of our years together in the world of politics. They talked of all they had known, given what they had been born into with a dad in Congress, as governor, and then back in Congress. That warm June night was marked by stories told and the memories that came with them, laughter, and even an occasional tear on my part as we reminisced on the journey we had taken together.

And they all said, "This was the best thing that could ever have happened to you. You have been miserable over the last two years."

Indeed I had been. In my district, I had tried to honestly listen to invigorated left-leaning "Indivisible" and Democratic crowds on one day and Trump-leaning Republicans on the next. It had been a daily tug-of-war.

Fox News, where I had once been a darling and where even after losing the governorship had been a paid contributor, would no longer book me because I had been negative toward the president. When I went on CNN, the office the next day would feel the wrath of Republican voters as hate calls were fielded because I had gone on the "Communist News Network." In light of those difficulties, I wasn't as upset over my loss as I might have been.

And the vote wasn't a blowout either; a few hundred more votes and I would have been in a runoff election, something I had faced twice before and won both times. But Trump's popularity in South Carolina at that time was breathtaking. I saw it not only in my race but in reports on others.

An upstate businessman from Greenville, John Warren, had challenged Henry McMaster for the governorship in the same primary season. He had forced McMaster into an additional two-week runoff, and until the day before the election, his internal polling showed him winning comfortably. It was then, the night before the 2018 election, that Trump came to South Carolina and held a rally for McMaster. Overnight, Warren's numbers fell, and he lost the race.

In the case of the First District, Trump's triumph proved to be short lived. What worked in a Republican primary was not nearly as popular with Independents and Democrats in purple counties like

Charleston. Katie Arrington lost to Democrat Joe Cunningham, and for the first time in thirty-two years, Democrats in South Carolina were able to take a congressional seat from Republicans.

Back on the night of her primary victory, Katie Arrington had exclaimed to the crowd, "We are the party of Donald J. Trump." That was her victory cry, and her loyalty was rewarded. She lost in South Carolina but was given a job at the Pentagon.

A few days after my primary loss, the president took something of a victory lap, dancing on my political grave. In a meeting on an immigration bill, with the entire House Republican Conference—all Republicans elected to the House—in attendance, in HC-5, a subterranean room in the bowels of the Capitol, the president called out and asked, "Is Mark Sanford here?" This in itself was weird. But instead of beginning with details on the bill, he began with, "I want to congratulate him on running a great race."

At this point the room fell silent; people must have been trying to figure where he was going with this. He went on to pronounce me a "nasty guy" and more, and some in the room booed as he crowed about his take on me and my defeat.

Thankfully my flight had been delayed, and I wasn't in the room.

I may have missed his insults, but the following weekend I was on *Meet the Press* and had this to say. "People are running for cover because they don't want to be on the losing side of a presidential tweet... The idea that you can't speak out and say, 'I disagree with you here, but I agree with you on 90 percent of the other stuff'... is a twilight world that I've never seen."

How right I was. But there was a bigger lesson for the GOP in that election, with much more far-reaching consequences than the defeat of one congressman. What the GOP lost in droves in the 2018 election cycle was not only young people and suburban women but what my own race signaled nationally about what the president and party would and would not accept in the way of dissent.

To be an American has always been rooted in the freedom to hold differing points of view. It has always been rewarded and trumpeted as a value and a long-standing hallmark of our political system.

But Trump was changing this. The GOP as I had known it, warts and all, was no longer the Grand Old Party. It was now the POT—the Party of Trump. There was only one litmus test. Are you for or against Trump? "Being on the right" had devolved to simply mean supporting President Trump. Right had become a code word for "something different than more of the same" and "anti-establishment." I had spent my entire time in politics fighting the establishment, and yet, incredibly, in the Trump era I was labeled "establishment."

A year later, in September 2019, I announced what turned out to be a short-lived challenge to the president for the 2020 GOP nomination. My friends had come to me with the proposal, making the point that I had already invested twenty-five years of my life, so what were another couple of months? I might be able to elevate the debt and deficit issue that had long animated my interest in politics. The race for me was never a serious run, but even in this sort of benign challenge of ideas, all debate and dissent were summarily cut off, and at the oddest of times. I had all the conservative credentials one could imagine and a long enough political résumé as a former governor and congressman to be just the kind of person most

Republican voters would at least enjoy hearing from…but in strange times strange things happen, and so there I sat in the Londonderry Republican annual spaghetti fundraising dinner waiting to speak.

And waiting.

And three hours later, still waiting.

Everyone running for even the lowest posts of anything spoke, and though I had been assured I would be recognized, the meeting came and went. When I went up afterward and asked the county chair why I had been skipped over, he explained that there had been some senior people in the state Trump organization in attendance, and it just wasn't worth the hassle he would get if he'd allowed me to speak.

I told him I understood. But at a gut level over those frustrating three hours, I viscerally internalized the real dangers to our political system in avoiding another person's perspective and voice. What followed went well beyond my chance to speak at a local Republican event. Primaries were actually canceled. No contest of ideas was allowed. Trump's hold on the party was strong, with an 87 percent approval rating from Republicans. I sat on the sidelines, along with former Illinois congressman Joe Walsh and former Massachusetts governor Bill Weld.

On November 12, 2019, I suspended my race for the presidency, explaining to reporters that Trump's impending impeachment had made my goal of making the debt, deficit, and spending issue a bigger part of this presidential debate impossible. "From day one," I told them, "I was fully aware of how hard it would be to elevate these issues with a sitting president of my own party ignoring them. Impeachment noise has moved what was hard to herculean as nearly everything in Republican Party politics is currently viewed through the prism of impeachment."

Once again, I made a turn at that crossroads in the woods, and the less-traveled road I took made all the difference.

The GOP also took a less-traveled road, eventually embracing Trump as its candidate, despite everything, and that road would lead to adding the White House to what was about to be lost in the House and Senate.

I was left with no political seat, but what I believed remained firmly intact. The Republican Party under Trump came away from that election cycle with far, far less.

I found myself getting used to being a political dead man walking. It no longer bothered me. As I'd told that reporter, already having died leaves you with little to fear. And I was no longer trying to bridge divides that were clearly irreconcilable.

Back at home in South Carolina, time elapsed, and I tuned out the president's bombast over the lost election. On January 6, 2021, I was sitting at my desk catching up with paperwork, deliberately not tuning in to the inevitable coverage of his "Save America" rally. The Senate was about to certify the electoral results when my friend Bjorn texted and said, "Can you believe what's happening at the place you used to work?" I thought he was referring to some procedural snafu with the Electoral College.

I had seen news feeds that morning and had admired Mitch McConnell's speech on the Senate floor. His words condemning the idea of not ratifying the election results were strong. He said, "I've served thirty-six years in the Senate. This will be the most important vote I have ever cast." Some of what he said was exceptional coming from a man who had, in my view, far too long coddled the president's cavalier approach to our republic and the democratic traditions and institutions that made it strong.

Nonetheless, on that day his words were, "If this election were overturned by mere allegations from the losing side, our democracy would enter a death spiral. We'd never see the whole nation accept the election again... I believe protecting our constitutional order requires respecting the limits of our own power. It would be unfair and wrong to disenfranchise American voters and overrule the courts and states on this extraordinary thin basis... I will vote to respect the people's decision and defend our system of government as we know it."

This had been music to my ears.

But then Bjorn exclaimed, "No! They're storming the Capitol!"

At that astonishing statement, I quickly tuned in to what we all saw that day—a broadcast in insanity.

Protesters storming the Capitol.

The images of the unruly crowd charging into the Statuary Hall of the Capitol were shocking. That was the place where I had done hundreds of satellite feeds over the years and walked countless numbers of constituents thorough on Capitol tours. The TV coverage now showed a sea of people wearing MAGA hats swarming the rotunda of the Capitol. A place midway between the House and Senate Chambers, the rotunda is considered so sacred in the creation of law in our country that only thirty-five Americans have lain in state in that room before being buried with honors. Next on the TV screen was an image of a masked man sprawling in the president of the Senate's chair in the Senate Chamber.

In the end, five were dead in the chaos of that day.

The images and coverage were breathtaking because the whole thing seemed so foreign, not at all the place I knew so well. This was the sort of anarchy one could imagine in a third-world sham of a democracy. I found it unimaginable that it was happening in the Capitol of the United States.

Stirred to action that afternoon, I sent a few tweets calling on the president to speak up and denounce what was happening...though I was not delusional enough to think my tweets would have any effect.

The president just doubled down on his assertion that the election had been stolen, and even as the Capitol was under siege, he was silent. After desperate calls from his allies like Kevin McCarthy, he tweeted nothing more than "I know your pain. I know you're hurt. We had an election that was stolen from us. It was a landslide election and everyone knows it, especially the other side. But you have to go home now. We have to have peace. We have to have law and order...So go home. We love you; you're very special...I know how you feel. But go home and go home in peace."

I was bewildered. But not surprised.

I was glued to the television all evening and then watched late into the night the speeches on the House and Senate floors after order had been restored. In quiet amazement I listened as former colleagues said, "Enough is enough."

All I could think to myself was, "Are you kidding me?"

To give a speech now decrying the horrors of the day while only hours before perpetuating the myth that the election was stolen... to me they sounded hollow and superficial. It seemed like cosmetic repentance.

It was too little, too late. You can't be complicit in crazy for four years but then disavow it when it comes home to roost in your very place of work. Not and be taken seriously.

The thing is, that day's horrors had much deeper roots than inciting words at a morning rally. What occurred had been set in motion over four long years, and all too many people I knew both on and off Capitol Hill had contributed to the turmoil of January 6, 2021.

Those speeches, Trump's words, and the events of that day encapsulate my frustration and my reason for writing this book. The president of the United States should not be given a pass on sedition and treason. *Merriam-Webster* defines *sedition* as "incitement of resistance to or insurrection against lawful authority." The *Cambridge English Dictionary* calls it "language or behavior intended to persuade other people to oppose their government and change it, sometimes by using violence." Wikipedia says, "Sedition is overt conduct, such as speech and organization, that tends toward rebellion against the established order. Sedition often includes subversion of a constitution and incitement of discontent toward, or insurrection against, established authority."

How the president's activity and speeches that day do not fit these clear definitions is unimaginable to me. I'm not a lawyer, and I understand from friends that in cases like this, there is a high legal bar that the government must meet in proving a person conspired to use force. It's a way of protecting First Amendment rights for your average village idiot who runs his mouth about wanting to overthrow the government. But your average village idiot hasn't stood before the country and sworn to protect and defend the Constitution. This is where words absolutely do matter. No president should be allowed to go around for six months saying our constitutionally enshrined system is a fraud and then on the day Congress is set to validate that process fire up and encourage a crowd that then heads to the Capitol to attempt to thwart the legal process.

Common sense tells me if it swims, quacks, and walks like a duck, it's a duck, and therefore what looks, sounds, and feels like sedition to me is sedition. I think the president's acts were sedition, and I think we are terribly mistaken in looking the other way and pretending this does not matter. As surely as past decisions drive future decisions in law, we are setting precedent on what's okay here for a future president. And if you think future presidents behaving in this way as the Capitol is being stormed somehow fulfills the role of commander in chief or honors the pledge to uphold the Constitution, you are delusional or lying to yourself. In this I get it that lawyers will argue most anything, like Johnnie Cochran ably arguing O. J. Simpson didn't kill Nicole. But the difference between what one can prove in the courtroom and what you can see with your own eyes should not be the new standard for the presidency.

After I blew myself up in 2009, I'll bet I heard a thousand times people reprimanding me by saying there should be a higher bar on conduct for those of us in elected office. It didn't matter that I had fallen head-over-heels in love with Belén; there was no excuse. Having been on the journey I subsequently traveled, I agree. My question now is, why wouldn't those same people who rightfully condemned my actions apply the same high standard to President Trump? When Republicans close their eyes to the questionable and even unconstitutional actions of the highest office in the land, we are paving the road to disaster. This is especially the case when

Trump lifted not a finger as a mob assaulted the Capitol. In a room in the personal quarters of the White House, he simply watched. This indeed is not the role of a commander in chief.

That a big portion of the Republican Party would still look to Donald Trump as a leader I find astounding. And by looking the other way, still others are playing with the very foundation of our Founding Fathers' political design. At the core, this is what troubles me most about today's Republican Party.

It is my hope that the events of January 6 represent the beginning of the end of this chapter of political life that has been so spoiled by President Trump's domination of the Republican Party. Unfortunately, Trump's hold is still strong even as I write this. But it is past time for the start of a new chapter. Our representatives need to do more than put their heads in the sand while trying to stay relevant, justifying their inaction with the excuse that they are "representing their district."

Back in the 1700s Edmund Burke said, "Your representative owes you, not his industry only, but his judgement; and he betrays you instead of serving you if he sacrifices it to your opinion."[14]

I hope the road of sacrificed judgment is not the one upon which the Republican Party chooses to move forward. This is a time to look back and assess, and to draw conclusions as to how to face the future in a better way. Crazy has become the new normal, and sadly, as

---

14 Edmund Burke, Edmund Burke's Speech to the Electors of Bristol at the Conclusion of the Poll, November 1774: For Presentation to Members of the House of Commons at the Conclusion of the Poll, May 1997. (Merrion Press for the Edmund Burke Society, 1997).

Republicans we have aided and abetted our own march toward political irrelevance and extinction.

But the beauty of what I learned in being afforded my own second chance is that the story does not have to end here. We can choose a different road. On the one path we can continue with suspended reason, a president encouraging others to hit someone in the crowd, never-ending conspiracy theories, and more. If so, we should also remember that the Bible says that those who sow the wind will reap the whirlwind.

On the other hand, we can try something different. We can take responsibility for our actions and what comes next, recognizing that in a democracy "we the people" are the guardrails. A constitution and political institutions can, for a time, withstand the assault of one man or group, but they can't hold back the collective will of the people. What we tolerate and accept in our government and leaders determines all. The lines in the sand that each of us as citizens draw are vital to our country's well-being. The amalgamation of our individual choices really matters in determining our collective voice and in creating what comes next in the land of the free and the home of the brave.

May we all be bold here, because if not, the corrosive effect of what we have just witnessed and the Republican acceptance of it will prove to be a far greater threat than the misguided efforts of those zealots who stormed our Capitol.

So the stakes are big, and it's consequently important that we are wise enough to embrace this moment and recognize that the conservative movement and the Republican Party have been given a second chance, just as I was. Let's look at what we can do with it.

2

A SECOND CHANCE FOR THE REPUBLICAN PARTY

The Biden inauguration is now history.

Despite many people's fears and in spite of the January 6 efforts to thwart it, power ultimately transferred from one administration to another. Now we can move on to the next chapter of American political history.

In many ways this represents an opportunity for all Americans, but especially for Republicans—given the way midterm elections have historically moved against the party in power.

But as Republicans, *have* we moved on? What, exactly, is our way forward when most in office still play to Trump, and polls show him as the most popular of Republicans in Republican circles? Is casting out or gagging dissenters like Liz Cheney really the best way forward? Many who voted against her or applauded that vote would say we need an even more robust version of the past four years. But in my opinion, a censure of Romney or dismissal of Cheney is not the answer.

If elections are the scores by which politics are measured, the last four years have been an unmitigated disaster for Republicans. We lost the House, the Senate, and the White House. This is reality, not a conspiracy.

Clearly, something's not working.

When the GOP began its drift toward Trumpism, I wasn't alone in distancing myself from it. All four of us who spoke out early against Trump—Bob Corker and Jeff Flake in the Senate and me and Justin Amash in the House—are now gone from Congress. Early adopters may be seen in a positive light in marketing, but in politics it often spells political extinction. When it comes to topics controversial to their own political base, politicians almost always let others go first. The saying in Washington is that it's the pioneers who end up with arrows in their backs.

And so it was. Speaking out cost the four of us, but it should also give us some degree of credibility on these matters and on what should come next in the body politic. After all, it's the decisions that we make against friends, not enemies, that are the hard ones. They are also the calls in life that give us real authority—and what I have lived, learned, and seen screams to me that the Republican Party needs to take a far different road going forward if it's going to be the messenger of conservative ideals and values in Washington.

To that end, let's take a deeper look at what has happened to our Grand Old Party.

Former Speaker of the House John Boehner has suggested that the GOP is somewhere…but sleeping. Others say the antics of the last few years represent what the Republican Party was all along.

I'd argue that what happened was actually simple.

We got here because political leaders in the GOP had over-promised and underdelivered for far too long. Republican voters who really believed in smaller government and less government interference in their everyday lives had been consistently disappointed for decades. True, frustration and disappointment have always been part of the dance of politics. Not so many years ago it was Obama who promised hope and change only to disappoint his followers. But it became more virulent on the Republican side. Not because Democrats were more honest politicians but because there was a friction on the Republican side that didn't exist on the Democratic side. I don't know any Democrats who spend a lot of time talking about shrinking government programs. Certainly they talk about doing things like moving money from defense to social spending, but for the forty years Democrats held the House, neither they nor their constituencies pushed for smaller government and less reach into people's lives. It's just not on their agenda. Quite the opposite.

On the other hand, those things are on ours. Republican politicians always talk about reducing the ways in which government inserts itself into our lives. Even then-candidate Trump talked about and promised much in that regard. But the size and influence of government have just kept growing even as Republicans held different branches of government.

I believe we got here because men who had completed a high school education and used to be able to provide for their families felt increasingly pushed aside and falling behind.

I believe we got here because in some western states where the government owns half or more of all property in that state, ranchers got tired of land-management experts from Washington telling them how to ranch, even though their family had been doing it for four generations. The same could be said of the logger in Oregon or the person who owns a small business in south Georgia.

I believe we got here because Congress punted on making tough legislative decisions and instead let the courts make decisions that should be made by the people. It left people with no voice and greater frustration as they turned to their elected representatives on these matters, and their representatives simply pointed to the courts.

I believe we got here because Wall Street bankers took crazy risks with other people's money, lost that money, and still miraculously earned millions—although no such undeserved windfall came to the working people who didn't stretch financial rules as many on Wall Street had. There is something wrong with a wealthy finance guy or gal in New York being taxed at a much lower rate than a blue-collar working guy or gal because of things like "carried interest"—which neither party has touched. These inequities cemented in many people's minds that the system was rigged and unfair, and that only money talked in Washington.

I believe we got here because those who gave to society got tired of seeing too much taken from society, even as they helped foot the bill for government largesse.

I believe we got here because fair-minded and good people of the heartland of America got tired of being lectured to by people on both coasts, people good with words or numbers but who could never survive without the people they talked down to—the people Hillary Clinton famously described as "deplorables."

I believe we got here because politicians are often arrogant and too often miss or dismiss the real needs, hopes, and wants of the electorate.

I believe we also got here because of gerrymandering and the ways in which Republican districts got more and more red while Democratic seats got more and more blue. The result was a ruling class of guaranteed incumbency. Politicians were awarded never-ending terms and often seemed far more interested in reelection than serving their constituents.

I believe we got here because our culture was being upended. The idea that the public bathroom had become one of the most controversial places in American life didn't fit with the real-world controversies Americans had to deal with daily in paying the bills and getting work. How a man could self-identify as a woman and walk into the bathroom alone with your thirteen-year-old daughter just didn't make common sense.

I believe we got here because politicians too often played to the crowd and the lower instincts that drive mob mentality; the louder the vitriol, the greater the notice.

In short, I believe we got here based on a whole host of fears, a desire to push back against things that cut against what had made America great, and the Republican Party not following the conservative mandate to stem an ever-increasing government reach. And as a result, Republican voters had become frustrated and disenchanted; they had finally had enough. Who could blame them?

Donald Trump saw a real opportunity in 2016, and he took on the role of political strongman. He was an able salesman but with no personal scruples, and he told voters exactly what they wanted to hear in his commitment to make America great again.

It would all be painless. Your station in life would be lifted. Washington would be tamed. Factory jobs would return to the rust belt. Entitlement spending would never be cut, and defense spending would go up, even as we cut taxes and paid off the national debt over the eight years he would be in office. The wall would be built. Cheap imports would be stopped. And the Mexicans and Chinese would pay for it all.

He was ideally suited to the task of telling people what they wanted to hear. It's what he had done his whole life. In fact, there is a story in Washington I've heard several times of him coming into the men's locker room after a round of golf. His companions are complaining of his liberal scoring on the course, to which he allegedly replied, "I cheat on my taxes, I cheat on my wife, I cheat subcontractors—and you expect me not to cheat at golf?"

Whether it's true, I don't know, but what he promised each of us was mathematically impossible. But it's what people wanted to hear. We all want to believe in Santa Claus when it comes to paying for things in Washington, and even if Santa won't pay, we figure someone else will. As the late senator Russell Long from Louisiana used to say, "Don't tax you. Don't tax me. Tax the fellow behind the tree."

But none of this mattered to the voters.

Trump promised he could deliver what they wanted. Voters said to give it a try. In their fervor, they wore red hats and flew Trump flags to signal to the world that they, too, were believers.

While all these things were true, the question remains: Why did this happen now in the Republican Party? After all, Americans had been going along suffering in relative silence for decades. What made Republican voters suddenly decide to make take unexpected turn onto the less-traveled road of Trumpism? What was it about Donald Trump that so appealed to Republicans at this particular time?

AUTOCRACY SELLS.

If you've been denied change long enough, you'll accept most any way of getting there. The longer people are upset, the greater their resolve and will. And after what they perceive to be milquetoast efforts to get them what they want, need, and have been promised, many become receptive to more forceful efforts to do so. This human tendency is recorded throughout the pages of political history. It's been the fuel to many a tyrant's rise, and methods to this technique were recorded in Machiavelli's book *The Prince* back in the 1500s. What occurred here was not new, but it was new in America.

This was one of my initial concerns about Trump. His style was autocratic. He was never a fan of debate or being questioned. The short tenures of those on his team who challenged him cemented that fact. I was appalled, but was out of step because his fans loved this about him. I found his lack of focus on traditional tenets of conservatism like government spending and the debt alarming, but voters were primed for a forceful push. Autocracy had become cool.

Still, I think there was more at play than just the people's desire for a forceful leader. I've found there are always much deeper roots to what we see before us in politics. What's erupting on the airways doesn't "just happen." It's not random. It's always a reaction to something, whether or not we agree with that something. And in most cases, it is something we can grow to understand if we choose to give it time and study.

Sir Isaac Newton in his third law of motion noted that for every action there is an equal and opposite reaction. This formula certainly holds up in politics. The Tea Party was a reaction to spending and bailouts, compassionate conservatism, Obama, and more. At town halls during this time, I heard Republicans rant on the media, George Soros, the left, and what they perceived as Obama's imperial presidency. Perceived injustices had been smoldering for some time, and all it took was a spark to light the fires of appetite for someone who would offer a more robust and forceful defense of their beliefs.

Unfortunately, both in nature and in politics, a little ill wind has a way of growing into a hurricane if the conditions are right. Our storm here will get worse because even with Trump gone, there isn't much out there to calm the Republican Party's frothy political waters. What's happening under Democratic rule and overstep in Washington will only intensify things. Autocracy will continue to have growing appeal because one person with power can argue they can get things done in a way that a system of divided power and checks and balances will not.

DIVISION AND POLARIZATION HAVE INCREASED.

As a country and as a party, we are more divided than I have ever seen in all my years in politics. These divisions are compounding, and I fear they will continue to do so. Urban versus rural.

Heartland versus coast. Wealthy versus middle class. Black versus White. Continue down the list. Some of it comes with a bigger country and with divisions bound to increase with size; some of it comes with the luxury of our prosperous times. When there is not an enemy "out there," many focus on what divides rather than our blessings and how much we have in common.

In the 1950s and 1960s many of these divisions were minimized in the minds of society because increased spending from Washington anesthetized us from the conflict that would have been more apparent without it. The saying is that a rising tide lifts all boats, and this was Washington back then. There was plenty of money to go around. But in the 1970s that began to change with Vietnam, the demands of new social programs, and inflation to boot. And it's gotten worse since then, as the government is now no longer able to paper over our problems. The federal government is still trying, though; we continue to borrow fifty cents on every dollar spent. So for now we will continue to try to paper over things a bit longer, but we are about to run into some hard fiscal limits that will make this impossible going forward. As a consequence, things will get tough politically and economically. We will be left with the country's many sharp divisions but without the financial means to mask or solve them. And that's a problem; a house divided will not stand.

As for political polarization, it's been interesting to watch it manifest. You can see it in the language used by candidates, in media focus and coverage, in the interplay with voters at a town hall, but I saw a small but great barometer in an afternoon basketball game. During my first six years in Congress, there was a standing basketball game every afternoon at three. Depending on votes or committee hearings, sometimes you made it, sometimes you didn't. But it happened, and the Republican and Democratic representatives who may have been arguing against each other only moments before on the House floor were invariably now on the same team giving each other a high five after their team scored. It was congenial, but by the time I returned for my second stint in Congress, it was gone. The spirit of debate was changing. You could feel it. Gone was the debate of an idea as an idea. It had become personal.

In keeping with this change, you have the likes of Congressman Jim Jordan receiving the Medal of Freedom from President Trump within days of Jordan going after Congresswoman Liz Cheney for exercising her constitutionally enshrined freedom to vote as she sees fit on the House floor. Mind you, they were allegedly on the same Republican team! And talk about spiking the ball in the end zone. The Medal of Freedom was created by President Kennedy to recognize those who have made an especially meritorious contribution to national security, world peace, cultural, or other significant public or private endeavors! How a hit on a fellow congresswoman fits this, I don't know, other than that division and conflict within government are oddly rewarded of late.

Seeds of this political polarization were inflamed by the actions of politicians themselves. About the time I first came to Congress in 1994, Newt Gingrich had begun using a new tool in his effort to reach voters and contrast with Democrats, who had held the House for forty years.

Twitter and social media didn't exist then, and as unfathomable as it sounds, neither did Fox News, CNN, or MSNBC. The favorite political vehicle at the time was C-Span, which included a continuous closed-circuit TV feed that broadcast the doings in Congress. Over the several years that led to his rise to the speakership, Gingrich and others would go to the House Chamber and talk for hours about all that ailed people and how the opposition was to blame. Talk radio with its political shock jocks, along with the gradual balkanization of the media, added fuel to the fire of political discord here as well.

The saying in the media is that "if it bleeds, it leads." Conflict sells. Compromise came to represent selling out. And as to be expected, for every action by one side there was an equal and opposite reaction by the other. Republicans like Gingrich demonized Democrats, and Democrats demonized Republicans. Division ramped up even more. The old school of the Republican Party was reticent about this approach, but a newfound, more confrontational and energetic branch saw its power. More division. Current political figures like Congressman Matt Gaetz of Florida were still in elementary school when C-Span was in its heyday, but Gingrich was setting the stage for Gaetz's polarizing style of politics. And ultimately for divisive leaders like Trump.

ANGER ABOUNDS.

Anger is nothing more than an expression of fear. Something has to be done to you, or taken from you, to elicit anger.

The greatest barometer of human sentiment is found in the financial markets around the world as stock, bond, and currency values are measured by the second. There are all sorts of technical-looking charts to justify valuations, but many traders say the real drivers are the simple human emotions of fear and greed. All markets react to those two things.

The political marketplace is no different. Fear and anger or hope and greed. The degree to which fear and anger have been driving the Republican Party lately is again unparalleled in my years in politics. It was certainly a large part of what drove many voters to turn to Donald Trump four years ago. Many of them were understandably afraid and angry over the way America was changing. If your daughter's chance of winning a state competition in athletics was blown away by a young boy self-identifying as a girl, would you not be upset as well? For others it was anger over financial hardship, weariness over having their beliefs ridiculed, and so much more. And here was a flamboyantly outspoken political leader who gave them permission and license to express their fear, frustration, and anger out loud and in ways that had not been previously done. It was no surprise that they flocked to Trump.

And so did Republican politicians. That to me was a surprise, though it should not have been. Statesmen in general went the way of the dinosaurs, and these days if you follow the bread crumbs of voter sentiment, it's easy to see where most in politics will be. The result here has been that seemingly everyone in or around politics is offended these days. The left is offended by the right, the right by the left. It's a never-ending merry-go-round that distracts us all from the very real problems confronting our society. The degree to which even the voters are feeling assaulted by the other side or by some unseen but all-knowing "deep state" has gotten dangerous. January 6, 2021, is witness to this fact, and in a political world long on anger, politicians have played too often not to our better angels but instead to our fears and perceived slights.

DESPERATION BREWS REVOLT.

The Republican electorate had become a bit desperate. Over the years, I have seen voter disorientation and frustration as candidate after candidate changed their tune once they became officeholders. But four years ago it was different. There was a fevered pitch for change among Republican voters that I had never seen before, and desperate people do desperate things. What's telling is that Republicans turned to an autocratic leader who had never stood for their values to fix these things.

How else but desperation do you explain the rise of Donald Trump within the Republican Party? Here was a person with no governing political philosophy, someone who voted for and contributed to Democrats until the eve of his own candidacy. A man without the normal credentials of service to our country in some form, who had a disconnect with the traditional tenets of conservatism, and who had previously been on the opposite side of the guns and abortion issues—previously deal killers to an outsider's advance in the eyes of many evangelical Christian Republicans. Nevertheless, he was enthusiastically embraced even by the religious right. I was stunned as some of those who had been the harshest critics of my moral failings only a few years earlier became the biggest disciples of his candidacy and tenure.

Seems to me, if you start with little in common where you come from and share little in common on where you want to go, you have a formula destined for disaster.

But people bought into Trumpism big time. I remember talking to three retirees at Sun City near Bluffton, South Carolina, in October 2016 before the election. They all planned to vote for Trump, and their reasoning was that we had tried other things and they hadn't worked. They said the definition of insanity was trying the same thing and expecting a different result. They wanted something different.

I remember seeing more than a few emails at the time circulating a short spiel that said, "No one could have been more patriotic than McCain, more genteel than the Bushes, more accomplished than Romney...but none had made it work, and it's time for a change."

So our party tried something new, a new and different form of insanity—electing a flamboyant salesman with a history of many promises and few deliveries.

Where did that leave us? It left us with a GOP that was divided, angry, desperate, and accordingly, open to a different approach. These things paved the way for Republicans to take the unprecedented leap into Trumpism, and this is what's kept many clinging to his leadership even now that he's out of office.

But now what? Where do we go from here?

I think the answer lies in recognizing and embracing four things:

AS AMERICA CHANGES, THE PARTY WILL TOO.

But here is the catch: without the boundaries of conservative philosophy and a few simple virtues like truth, where we go now no one knows. Do we become the party of populist promises? Do we go back to the basics of what made and created the party? We now find ourselves at the very crossroads Robert Frost described could make all the difference, and in some ways we have a blank canvas before us.

Historically the party was unified around conservative themes. Things like the South Carolina Republican creed were odes to this, but I watched philosophical orientation come to mean less and less over my years with the party. What really held it together was a loose coalition of interests. You had national security conservatives, evangelical Christians and the conservative social issues that united them, traditional "Rockefeller" Republicans, and Tea Party and deficit-hawk conservatives.

National security conservatives have grown quieter lately. In part they have been placated. A lot of money has gone to defense. Our forces are robust, well trained, and well equipped compared to many points in our history. The Soviet menace fell to the wayside. At another level, the neocons have been marginalized. Endless war in the Middle East has not proven popular with America.

The same is true of spending conservatives. Although I think this is *the* issue, it doesn't resonate with or animate people today as it should. Fiscal and monetary policy has insulated us from financial reality, and therefore people don't care as they once did when the problem was in fact far smaller. The deficit is not the rallying cry it was in the recent past with the Tea Party.

Rockefeller Republicans? Forget about them. They went the way of the blue dog Democrats. They are extinct. They are gone.

Which now leaves the Republican Party heavily populated by evangelicals and social conservatives… and in search of a philosophy. It explains why Trump has been so beholden to them and why he has played to cultural issues. It also happens that this is the most energized wing of what remains of the GOP. At every turn, culture is being impacted. With globalization, people have felt threatened; accordingly, without a conservative philosophical mooring, we have seen nationalistic and antitrade movements within the party. Mind you, it's a party that once stood opposite on these issues. Culture has been driven to the top of many people's minds with the Kardashians, transgender bathroom wars, and a seeming all-out assault on simple values that have always resonated within the heartland of America. You see culture again highlighted in immigration and the changing face of the American public. At every turn, this is the immediate here and now of politics today.

So in moving the GOP forward, it will be important to recognize this reality, but equally important to try and awaken its membership to the importance of a governing philosophy and issues that, though now quiet, have the ability to do far more harm to those we love than the issues that currently drive the evening news.

THE REPUBLICAN PARTY NEEDS TO BE ON GUARD AGAINST SHALLOW SUBSTITUTES FOR CONSERVATISM.

Here I submit that Trumpism is a cancer. A malignant one.

Like all cancers, it needs to be treated. In time, all cancers will kill or weaken the host if not eliminated—cancers don't get better on their own. It comes from within. Good cells go bad. But something has caused them to go cancerous.

The degree to which Trump lingers like a cancer in the psyche of the Republican base is a testament to how fed up the voters have become with business as usual. This is real and needs to be addressed. It's also disturbingly relevant that Trump can be seen as the answer and stay so firmly seeded in the minds of good people. I know them. Their beliefs in God and country are earnest.

If this kind of political cancer could happen over the last four years when things were relatively benign in economic terms, what happens if, in the near future, we fall into a rip-roaring recession or economic depression? Where do people turn then?

Stop and think about this for a second. The Democrats are in the process of overplaying their hand over the next few years. Straw one. Let's add to this an economy that goes south. Straw two. Someone like Trump comes in offering all the answers to what seriously ails us, and although we will have to give up a few freedoms and a bit of ideology and a value or two, our problems can be solved. Straw three...and one that breaks the proverbial camel's back. This is my nightmare scenario and the reason all of us should be alarmed and on guard. This is the story of Hitler's rise to power as chronicled in Hayek's *Road to Serfdom.*

People have bought into this thinking before. An educated and churchgoing people at the time in Germany.

The Republican Party itself set the stage for Donald Trump over many years. He was just the bit actor who played the role that had been created long ago. Accordingly, we need to examine what went wrong and consider what we might do to calm today's political waters and treat this cancer.

We have to get it right. In the scenario above, the next person to take on Trump's role may have far greater political skill. And what might follow is frightening.

Take the example of the Roman Republic. It had endured for over four hundred years when, from 146 to 78 BC, seeds were sown that led to the weakening and eventual loss of their constitutional form of government. During this time there was a breakdown of unspoken rules of political conduct, disruption to traditional ways of life, rising economic inequality, and increasing political polarization. Most disturbing, what occurred during those years set the stage for the cult of personality that came with Julius Caesar and his dictatorship, and put an end to democracy.

Sound familiar?

Today, Washington is setting a precedent for what will be accepted in the future. We need to pay attention and mold that future into something good and positive. This means a different standard on much more than conservative philosophy. It also means a stand on the truth.

Marine corps four-star general John Kelly, who served as chief of staff to Trump, made an observation that every one of us should find unsettling. He said, "The depth of the president's dishonesty is astounding. The dishonesty, the transactional nature of every relationship, it's more pathetic than anything else. He is the most flawed person I have ever met in my life."[15]

Politics as a whole is a treatise on trust—are you really who you say you are, and are facts as they seem? Teddy Roosevelt noted, "In the long run, the most unpleasant truth is a safer companion than a pleasant falsehood,"[16] and at the core this is what many voters ask for. When trust is lost, regaining it can come slowly. Trust issues are always subject to exploitation in politics, and by its nature, trust is always fragile. The smallest of signals can cause people to turn in a different direction.

Unlike Goldwater, who had a single effective ad run against him, Republicans today have enabled real damage to the party in their embrace of Trump and his behavior. If we want to have any hope of doing more than regaining the House or Senate with the midterm elections, and indeed advancing conservative ideals over the long run, we will have to begin a long, patient walk to rebuild trust with the American people.

For four years, Republicans looked the other way as evidence mounted that President Trump was anything but truthful and had disdain for the very traditions and institutions that conservatives always claimed were vital to maintaining the workings of our government. Even after the events of January 6, over half the Republican members in the House of Representatives—121 members—voted not to certify the results of the Electoral College.

---

15 "Transcripts: The Insiders, A Warning from Former Trump Officials" CNN, October 18, 2020.

16 Theodore Roosevelt, *Theodore Roosevelt's Words of Wit and Wisdom* (New York: Chartwell Books, 2015), 16.

Philosopher Edmund Burke argued that without some measure of morality and virtue and the stability that comes with them, no governmental system could work. Our experiment with Trumpism has reinforced my belief in the merits and applicability of what Burke wrote nearly three hundred years ago.

We would be well advised to look carefully at the ingredients of national destruction that surround us today and realize that staying on this path will surely lead us toward our democracy's downfall. You cannot play with truth and trust in a system that is designed around trust as ours is, and as history has shown, democracy lasts only as long as we work to protect the very virtues, institutions, and traditions that sustain a civilization.

In fact, given the fragile construct of freedom, sustained periods of unrest simply lead to more unrest. The conditions we have toyed with over the past four years—the absence of reason, an abandonment of the vital importance of truth in our politics, and an increasingly combative tone—are the very things that can kill a free and open political system.

If we don't get it right and pull ourselves away from that toxicity, it's not a GOP problem, it's an American problem. Our republic is literally at stake due to the volatility of the political ingredients now being stirred.

Some who believe in American exceptionalism might push back here and suggest our republic's undoing is far fetched. It couldn't happen to us. If this were true, history would read very differently. Our Founders studied history, and what they saw go wrong with other civilizations is what our system was designed to guard against. But it's not an impenetrable wall. We have carved an exceptional place in history only because of the exceptional choices we have made for two hundred years in this fragile experiment of self-governance.

As a party, over the last four years we haven't been making exceptional choices, and here policy gains can never offset deterioration in the tenets of a movement.

I recognize that some feel the idea of our republic being in the balance is totally overstated. They believe that the political waters are calming now that Trump has left office, and that the anticipated GOP gains in the next election are evidence of this. I'd argue that in evaluating progress, we must differentiate between political wins and ideological shifts. The long-term trends of politics run much deeper than any one election cycle and cannot be defined by the temporary gains or losses one finds in the patchwork of different representative bodies across the country, nor in the degree to which Trump still holds a political voice. Rather, those trends are defined by the clarity and consistency of what we stand for as a party.

So how can the GOP ask Americans to trust Republicans after Donald Trump? By changing course and taking little steps. Steps that fit with the Bible's wisdom: "Whoever can be trusted with little can also be trusted with much, and whoever is dishonest with very little will also be dishonest with much."[17] I'd say we must ask carefully, with the right tone, and by recognizing there is no substitute for a governing philosophy and truth.

---

17 Luke 16:10.

WE SHOULD CELEBRATE OUR FAILURE AND USE IT AS A CHANCE TO GET THINGS RIGHT.

There is a silver lining to every cloud. Winter never lasts forever. Out of the ashes, the phoenix rises. And the team that loses on Friday night generally studies the game-day tapes a lot harder on Saturday morning than the team that won. In short, if we make the right choices, the GOP has an extraordinary upside.

Redemption and a second chance underpin stories of faith, and my experiences have shown me that wrongs can be made right. Failure and false turns are part of the human condition, but the important question for all of us lies in what comes next.

There will be three tailwinds to aid Republicans going into the next election: the likelihood of Democrats overplaying their hands, a softening economy, and Trump's weakening hold on the party. As I see it, these things will enable Republicans to win back the White House, the Senate, and the House. But what do electoral gains mean when you don't stand for something? I've known far too many in politics who would bend in any direction just to stay relevant and in the game, but to what end? And even if it works for a politician, it doesn't work for me and you. We are not their career. We want the changes that only standing for something can deliver. So to create lasting change and advance conservative ideals, the bigger question still rests on what the party stands for and the trust it builds in communicating and delivering on its ideals.

WE SHOULD USE THIS AS A CHANCE TO AGAIN EMBRACE DEBATE.

Our Constitution and the democratic institutions and traditions that surround it have always been about creating a robust platform for debate. The party of late has run from this. We have not defended the institutions and traditions that fostered debate. We haven't celebrated it as an American value. We have taken for granted what billions around the world are not allowed in open and free debate. When Liz Cheney spoke on the House floor a final time as the House Conference's third-highest-ranking elected member of leadership, she urged all of us to guard our future here.

"God has blessed America, but our freedom only survives if we protect it, if we honor our oath, taken before God in this chamber, to support and defend the Constitution if we recognize threats to freedom when they arise. Today we face a threat America has never seen before. A former president, who provoked a violent attack on this Capitol in an effort to steal the election, has resumed his aggressive effort to convince Americans that the election was stolen from him. He risks inciting further violence. Millions of Americans have been misled by the former president. They have heard only his words, but not the truth, as he continues to undermine our democratic process, sowing seeds of doubt about whether democracy really works at all... Our duty is clear. Every one of us who has sworn the oath must act to prevent the unraveling of our democracy. This is not about policy. This is not about partisanship. This is about our duty as Americans. Remaining silent and ignoring the lie emboldens the liar… Our oath requires that we love our country…so much we will stand above politics to defend her. That we will do everything in our power to protect our constitution and our freedom, paid for by the blood of so many. We must love her so much we will never yield in her defense. That is our duty."[18]

Cheney spoke much of duty. And given the lives that have been sacrificed to sustain what we know to be the American way, do we not have a duty to protect the constitutional system designed around debate? While she was stripped of her role in Republican House leadership, the question for us lies in what we will do to keep the values and ideals that made this party strong from being further stripped away. This is by no means a Republican or Cheney issue. We would be far weaker as a country without both sides of ideas represented in the national debate, and the solutions offered from both ideologies would be weaker without a contrasting viewpoint. One could argue it's an issue of national security. In a democracy, ideas must be digested and accepted before they can be adopted. This can't happen without healthy debate, which itself can't happen without differing points of view being represented. It's a way of getting to the truth. By and of itself it's of great value, not for what it can produce, but for the way

---

18 Liz Cheney, "Cheney: Our Freedom Only Survives If We Protect It" (speech, Washington, DC, May 11, 2021, Congressman Liz Cheney, https://cheney.house. gov/2021/05/11/cheney-our-freedom-only-survives-if-we-protect-it/

it sheds light on the shadows and uncertainties of life. The French essayist Joseph Joubert observed, "It is better to debate a question without settling it than to settle a question without debating it."[19] In this regard we should celebrate differing points of view because the best collective decisions come because of disagreement and contest. This is what the Founding Fathers knew in Philadelphia in 1787 at our Constitutional Convention, and this is what Republicans need to embrace again in the blessing of reasoned debate.

So where, you ask, in all of this can we possibly find a second chance for Republicans?

And the answer ultimately is that it will be found in ourselves. In what we believe. In what we stand for. Going forward we will have to ask of ourselves and of those who represented us in office these past four years, what were we thinking? Do principles at large and conservative principles in particular no longer matter? Or is it now just about holding and wielding power, no matter the cost? Is it not time to come to our senses and return to the precepts and ideals that once made the party truly great and a positive force for change?

Though many conservatives have been asking these same questions for a while, far too many self-proclaimed Republicans have ignored them—at least, until the events of January 6, 2021. More than any day in recent memory, it wounded the Republican Party, and it wounded the conservative movement.

Is it even possible to find a second chance for the conservative movement at this vital moment in time? Let's explore that possibility.

---

19 Joseph Joubert, translated by Paul Auster, *The Notebooks of Joseph Joubert* (New York: The New York Review of Books, 2005).

3

A SECOND CHANCE FOR THE CONSERVATIVE MOVEMENT

I honestly don't know how something like the federal debt goes from being a major conservative issue to not being on the conservative agenda at all. Outside of absolute desperation, I can't explain how people closely aligned with the Tea Party and what I thought it stood for went from boisterous to quiet on long-standing conservative values like this.

Seriously, how does any movement go from celebrating the likes of Barry Goldwater to embracing someone who had no philosophic mooring?

It was Goldwater who famously said,

> "I have little interest in streamlining government or in making it more efficient, for I mean to reduce its size. I do not undertake to promote welfare, for

I propose to extend freedom. My aim is not to pass laws, but to repeal them. It is not to inaugurate new programs, but to cancel old ones that do violence to the Constitution, or that have failed in their purpose, or that impose on the people an unwarranted financial burden. I will not attempt to discover whether legislation is "needed" before I have first determined whether it is constitutionally permissible. And if I should later be attacked for neglecting my constituents' interests, I shall reply that I was informed their main interest is liberty and that in that cause I am doing the very best I can."[20]

These words are music to my ears, but they in no way fit with what's come of late of the conservative movement. So maybe it's just the times we live in. The book of Ecclesiastes says for all things there is a season. Well, seasons change; times change. Maybe we are just out of the conservative season.

Or maybe leadership is part of it. There was a time when we had leaders on the world stage who brilliantly articulated the merits of conservatism and its ties to human freedom. We no longer have the kind of conservative leaders I remember from my formative years—Margaret Thatcher, Ronald Reagan, Vaclav Havel. Leaders like that don't come along very often.

Or maybe it's simpler stuff.

---

20 Barry Morris Goldwater, *The Conscience of a Conservative* (Princeton: Princeton University Press, 2007), 15.

Maybe there are things we aren't doing that we should be, and maybe things we are doing that we shouldn't…

Let's look at a few ideas.

THE CONSERVATIVE MOVEMENT NEEDS TO GET BACK TO TAKING A CLEAR STAND.

Is this not the beauty of Goldwater's thoughts above? They are clear. They are to the point. They make a stand, and in life you are defined not only by what you stand for but also by what you stand against. The same goes for a movement. A movement disappears when it quits taking clear stands on important issues. Unfortunately, this has been the posture of the conservative movement of late. If not, conservatives would have stayed vocal in their condemnation of the stands that Trump took that were not conservative in nature.

Conservatives legitimately decried President Clinton putting Hillary to work in the Oval Office but said nothing as President Trump relied on an array of family members in projecting the administration's voice.

Conservatives roundly denounced the financial self-dealing of President and Hillary Clinton, and yet nothing was said about Trump's self-dealing and conflicts of interest when the Trump Hotel in Washington became the place for foreign governments to stay and lobbyists to be seen.

There was lots of fanfare and press about draining the swamp, all while swamp creatures like Paul Manafort were brought in to run the show. But the hypocrisy here continued even through the last hours President Trump held office, when he revoked the executive order that he, himself, had signed that barred former officials from lobbying for five years after leaving office. But not a sound was heard from conservatives as the president rescinded his own order!

The list goes on, and it all points to how it's past time for the movement to stand again for a few simple but concrete conservative principles. When you win Wimbledon or the Super Bowl, you don't have to hold a press conference to drum up accolades; the action speaks louder than words ever could. As a movement, conservatives need to go back to embracing actions that say more than we do.

We most decidedly have lost our voice in proclaiming our stand on freedom. Seriously, at the elected level, who do you hear talking about that most precious right anymore? Officeholders speak often about program wins or needs or what the Democrats are doing, but do you hear much about freedom? While conservatives are apt to stand at attention and mouth the words to the Lee Greenwood song "God Bless the USA" and love its lyrics about freedom, who is advancing those same sentiments in political circles? Kevin McCarthy? Mitch McConnell? The crazy but lovable fringe libertarian hung up on legalizing weed?

There is much work to be done here. I still remember Newt Gingrich telling me, "You have to plow the field before you plant it," and there is a conservative harvest out there still waiting for a clear planting.

FREEDOM HAS BEEN MISSING FROM THE CONSERVATIVE MOVEMENT AS BOTH A CLEAR AND A CENTRAL STAND.

If conservatives believe in more human freedom rather than less, how can saddling our kids with $2 trillion in annual deficits over the last four years be consistent with that? How does a schoolyard bully singling out individuals for derision foster freedom for them? How can legislation benefiting only a handful of companies be consistent with a limited federal voice and the liberty found in a free market? Yet conservatives watched and stayed quiet as President Trump did each of these things and much worse.

The real problem was that other people were watching, too, and despite suggestions to the contrary, what happens in Vegas rarely stays there.

Actions have consequences, and as conservatives we irrationally presupposed that Trump's destructive actions would have no consequences, though consistency in doing what you claim you're all about is the cornerstone to building political trust.

Rather than insisting that freedom ring, we have let it slide and by the scorecard of recent elections, the voters know it. So it's worth thinking hard about what we believe as conservatives and how we might consistently act on those beliefs.

The cause of the American Revolution as a movement was fueled by the unifying theme of freedom for its citizens. The movement was much more than a simple coalition of cities, colonies, or ethnic types; it was founded on simple and shared beliefs like "no taxation without representation." In the American civil rights movement, Blacks, Whites, and people of all races joined together through their shared belief in equality. Freedom didn't have different versions—one for Black people, another for White people, a third for other groups. I see nowhere in his letters from the Birmingham jail or in any of Dr. King's other works a desire or an effort to come up with different versions of his message so as to appeal to the many different groups that became a part of the civil rights movement.

In both the Revolution and the civil rights movement, leaders within it stood for something concrete. They said, "This is where I stand, this is what we believe, and if you agree, come join us."

Dr. King warned against the tranquilizing drug of gradualism. The Bible similarly warns of how little progress toward any goal comes from being in the middle, and calls on us to be hot or cold but never lukewarm. Making more noise here and taking a firmer stand means fiercely rejecting efforts to settle for lukewarm on freedom or anything else that matters. Reality is, all healthy political debate eventually moves us toward the middle as ideas are digested and acted upon. But we shouldn't *start* there. It was Trump's firm stands that originally drove his rise as a candidate in the polls. At the time, I remember conservatives feeling the left was brimming with strong philosophical standard-bearers in the likes of a Bernie Sanders or Elizabeth Warren. Meanwhile, conservatives were being philosophically disappointed by an abundance of dealmaking dealmakers at all levels of government. Conservative frustration was palpable, and voters were predisposed toward what they perceived to be strong leadership in Trump.

This was compounded by the fact that prior to the eight years spent in the liberal desert under Obama, the movement had been subjected to a kinder, gentler, compassionate conservatism under the Bushes. To the die-hard conservatives in the mix, it sounded like more of the old lukewarm political notion of being all things to all people. Republican William McKinley's presidential campaign slogan of "A full dinner pail" in 1900 fit the bill of invoking government goodies for all, just as Democrat FDR's promise of "A chicken for every pot" did some years later. More random government stuff did not fit with conservatives' once-firm belief in the need to fight for freedom. Dealmaking just didn't fit with Patrick Henry's "Give me liberty or give me death!"

Trump did recognize the need for a fight. But it was simply for the sake of a fight, not for the cause. It energized his political base but hurt the conservative movement. Fighting toward a philosophical objective was not Trump's strong suit, but it is understandable that after years of someone like McConnell, the MAGA folk and a few conservatives as well felt that any fight was a fight for them. Trump zeroed in on the need for a simple message, but rather than it being about conservative principles, it morphed into a whole lot about him. And although conservatives had many chances to object to this, they did not.

So to grow again, the conservative movement needs to get back a few basic but important things, the most central of which is freedom. And clearly expressing this will be important. In 1982, the international bestselling book *In Search of Excellence*, by Tom Peters and Robert H. Waterman Jr., explored leading companies with records of long-term profitability and continuing innovation.[21] They found eight common themes they argued were responsible for the success of the companies. The sixth theme was "Sticking to the

---

21 Robert H. Waterman, Thomas J. Peters, *In Search of Excellence: Lessons from America's Best-Run Companies* (New York: Harper & Row, 1982).

knitting and staying with the business that you know."[22] By doing so, great companies built great brands, and those great brands were largely defined by not trying to be all things to all people. They stuck to the knitting, the core of what the business was about, and consistently did what they said and advertised.

Accordingly, great brands walk the walk rather than simply talking the talk. And that's where we have gone wrong lately. We have been all over the place, which means if we were a brand, we would be a dead brand. Like Sears after bankruptcy. But here is the cool thing: Sears horribly mismanaged the brand, but their Craftsman tools were still really good. We just forgot they existed, given all the junk we read about Sears. So if we get our ducks in a row and stand for a few things and insist our candidates do, too, we can be back in the business of standing for the single most important thing we can stand for politically—freedom.

THE CONSERVATIVE MOVEMENT HAS LOST ITS PHILOSOPHICAL MOORING AND GONE QUIET IN ESPOUSING ITS ONCE-ANCHORED BELIEFS.

In my opinion, the conservative movement allowed its identity to be too closely tied to the Republican Party, which mistakenly has aimed of late for constituencies rather than philosophy. Big tents do not create movements. Clear ideas create movements, which in

---

22 Robert H. Waterman, Thomas J. Peters, *In Search of Excellence: Lessons from America's Best-Run Companies* (New York: Harper & Row, 1982), 292.

turn create change. It's a chicken-and-egg kind of thing, but one must come first, and for a movement, clear ideas are the beginning.

How does a movement sustain itself when its voice gets quiet from the top as well as from the rank and file? What happened to conservative voters insisting that the candidates they supported, the officials they appointed, and the causes they fought for were all equally clear in embracing an overriding conservative philosophy? That officeholders held loyalties to ideas, not to individuals?

The great success of the popular restaurant Chick-fil-A ultimately lies not in its chicken sandwiches but in its exacting standards—standards that range from being closed on Sundays to keeping the whole restaurant spotlessly clean. The corporate office does not say to a franchisee, "However you want to keep the bathroom is cool." They know a customer's opinion and loyalty to the brand are determined by far more than just the sandwich.

The conservative movement and voters for too long have accepted Republican "franchisees"—individual politicians—that have been weak on philosophic standards. The conservative movement as harnessed through the Republican Party has been very blurry on any kind of philosophical standard at all. I saw it firsthand in the governorship where I allegedly spent much of eight years arguing with Republicans. But the fact was, I was arguing with people like Hugh Leatherman, who for fifty years was a Democrat and then changed his party affiliation... but not his beliefs. The late Democratic National Committee chairman Don Fowler put it best back in 2007. "Ideologically, the South Carolina legislature is no different today from the legislature fifty years ago when it was Democratic. They changed partisan identity because that's the way the political winds were blowing. But it's no different than it was fifty years ago." This same phenomenon of "label only" at the national level made Trump nothing more than the logical extension of the blurry path Republicans had long traveled.

The late senator Ted Stevens of Alaska is one such example. In many ways he personified the opposite of what the conservative movement was supposed to be about, reveling in his ability to secure pork and promote government spending in his district, but he fit right in with the GOP's excuse for government excess in the name of a big tent. His proposal to build the Gravina Island Bridge, more commonly referred to as "the bridge to nowhere," drew nationwide ire. This bridge would have connected Gravina Island and its fifty residents to the mainland…for a price of $398 million. It would have been nearly as long as the Golden Gate Bridge and, to accommodate summer cruise ship traffic, taller than the Brooklyn Bridge. It would have replaced a $2.50 ticket on a ferry that left every fifteen minutes in the summer and every thirty minutes during the rest of the year.

Seriously?

You cannot sustain a movement or build brand loyalty when the customer—that is, the voter—must figure out how the late US Senators Ted Stevens and Tom Coburn, a conservative warrior, could both be franchisees of the same brand.

Saint Augustine called for unity in the essentials, diversity in the nonessentials, and charity in all things. I believe worthwhile movements will build a diverse following, but they must start with a shared agreement on the essentials of that movement. In my view, conservatives lost sight of the importance of insisting on philosophical mooring and anchored conservative beliefs, and in so doing allowed someone to allegedly represent us who eroded the move-ment's strength even further.

THE CONSERVATIVE MOVEMENT HAS IGNORED THE SIGNIFICANCE OF TONE.

Can you imagine the reaction you would get if you used Trump's words or tone in your family or at work? I'd think "I really don't care to hear what you're saying so long as you're yelling at me" would be the normal reaction to verbal hostility.

To believe the movement could expand its following while par-doning Trump's strident and condescending tone was nonsensical. That deafness will cost us because bullying doesn't work for long in life or in politics.

Yet that's the place former president Trump lived and thrived. Worse, his words and tone have given license to rudeness and cru-elty on both the political right and left. The Faustian deal struck between the religious right and Trump in pretending these things don't matter was a huge mistake if one takes the long view in grow-ing our conservative movement. I've seen firsthand how the presi-dent turned off many young voters with his behavior and words. They don't always agree with Mom and Dad, but what they saw in Trump was so at odds with what they had learned from Mom and Dad about treating others the way you want to be treated that young people turned away in droves.

Who can blame them? Politics has become so strident of late. We have lost the humility that allows one to believe in something but be willing to hear another view. Maybe it just requires a renewal of compassion or faith on our part, but whatever is needed to fix this, we need it now.

Ronald Reagan liked to quote French political philosopher Alexis de Tocqueville, who observed that "America is great because America is good. If America ever stops being good, it will stop being great." I still believe the American people are good at heart, but we have lost that goodness in politics. It's been far too long since we had Ronald Reagan talking about a bright, shining city on the hill, and even longer since we heard his tone. Obama was strident. Trump was that on steroids.

All sorts of science point to the way humans react to how we feel in the company of another. We may disguise an emotional response with good, brainy arguments, but as a movement we need to rekindle a warm tone in selling what we believe, and remember Teddy Roosevelt's notion of speaking softly while carrying a big stick.

THE CONSERVATIVE MOVEMENT HAS NOT CHAMPIONED POLICY RISKS ON IDEAS THAT MATTER TO PEOPLE'S LIVES.

In all the debate you have watched lately in Washington, how much of it has been about transformative policy? There are debates on guns and abortion that fire up the base, but inevitably all of that is being read from the same script as last year. The last major policy change came with welfare reform, and when Republican governors such as John Engler and Tommy Thompson first took it up in the 1990s, they were widely criticized. When I was voting on this, crazy articles were being written on the issue as the left and the media rose to defend the welfare system as it stood.

But these governors' perseverance and the tangible and undeniable successes of their programs laid the foundation for the reforms that followed at the federal level. While successful companies may stick to the knitting at the core of their work, they still allow for innovation and change in the way they deliver it. Maintaining distinct levels of government through federalism creates the competition, the back-and-forth, between those differing levels that is key to innovation. Federal welfare reform in the 1990s wouldn't have happened without first being tried and tested years earlier at the state level.

The irony is that change is still happening at the local level. We're just not promoting, chronicling, and embracing it in conservative circles as we were twenty years ago. The degree to which government is functioning and change is happening at the local level was showcased a while back by James and Deborah Fallow. This husband-and-wife team flew a small plane on a one-hundred-thousand-mile journey across the heartland of America and wrote about it in their book *Our Towns.* It illustrates what so many of us know about local things that work.[23] Maybe it's time again to talk less about what's happening in Washington and more about what's happening in Peoria.

---

23 James Fallows and Deborah Fallows, *Our Towns: a 100,000-Mile Journey into the Heart of America* (New York: Pantheon Books, 2018).

Only a fraction of what happens in government should even be happening in Washington, and in thinking of the different levels of government and federalism, it's useful to think about an aircraft carrier. There are no tourists on board, and everyone has a role vital to the ship's mission. The men and women in green run the catapult and arresting gear, those in red the aviation ordinances, in blue the flight-deck crew, and purple the aviation fuel. Having firm, clearly defined roles allows each of them to be and do their best. Without defined roles the crew would be overlapping and inefficient in their efforts. At worst, those on the flight deck might attempt to drive the ship or run the kitchen, which would create chaos.

Our various levels of government today act in a way that I would describe as the opposite of an aircraft carrier. No one seems quite sure of their role. Governments consequently overlap, miss things, duplicate, and waste money. How can a local government function efficiently when in some areas the federal government takes care of local things and in other areas they don't?

So let freedom and federalism ring—and in the process let's take policy risks and celebrate policy wins in the places where government still works.

THE CONSERVATIVE MOVEMENT STALLED AT SAYING NOTHING BUT NO.

If your only answer to your kids was no, how well do you think that would work out for you? So while it's important to argue against things we disagree with, the American people will ultimately respond most to policies that make a tangible difference in their lives. It just makes sense that the word yes can be good too!

In this vein, conservatives need to advance meaningful yeses that serve as alternatives to government's growth and imposition into our lives. Let me give two examples.

On the issues of education and health care, conservatives have largely run for the hills. Jeb Bush really led on educational choice when he was governor in Florida, and when I was governor in South Carolina we tried to follow suit. As a consequence we had a real fight over school choice. But what have you heard about it lately? There are a handful of private businessmen, like my friend Bob Luddy in North Carolina, who are out there pushing the frontier on this issue, but nationally it's quiet. If you are elected and from a nice area, you usually try to keep your head down, because many voters in affluent suburbs think that school choice means hordes of poor will come and take over their nice suburban schools. They occasionally vote no on something outrageous regarding new education spending, and it's a no on a host of other issues advanced by progressives. But beyond that, they remain silent.

How about a yes vote on something truly transformative?

With education, people have largely accepted the simplistic idea of more money being the answer to all its problems. And yet, from kindergarten through high school, education in America is not a market-based proposition. It is a monopoly; accordingly, taxpayers are denied the best price, and students don't get the best service, which in this case means a great education. Too many minorities and poor are trapped in failing schools because our current system is simply school assignment by zip code. If you are wealthy, you can buy the right house in the right neighborhood and get a great public education. If you can't, you simply get to be out of luck.

In the debate on education, years ago I met a very cool man in Minnesota trying to change this, Howard Fuller. He was a forceful voice for school choice. He was a guy with heart and soul who really cared. He had spoken up at the time of our civil rights crisis, and he was speaking up on education when we met. His activism was born of sheer frustration when he was looking for an alternative to what he'd had to deal with as superintendent of schools in Detroit. One day he was assigned teachers who could not speak Spanish to teach Hispanic children English. At that moment, all his frustrations with the system's focus on its union employees and protecting the system rather than the students galvanized. He would again try to make a difference. He became a voice for the urban poor trapped in educational systems guaranteed to fail them.

I remember standing at the back of the Marva Collins Charter School in the inner city of Milwaukee with him, watching children exuberantly recite their school creed. My eyes filled with tears as I saw potential being realized.

They beamed as they exclaimed,

"Society will draw a circle that shuts me out, but my superior thoughts will draw me in. I was born to win if I do not spend too much time trying to fail. I will ignore the tags and names given me by society since only I know what I have the ability to become. Failure is just as easy to combat as success is to obtain. Education is painful and not gained by playing games. Yet it is my privilege to destroy my-self if that is what I choose to do. I have the right to fail, but I do not have the right to take other people with me. It is my right to care nothing about myself, but I must be willing to accept the consequences for that failure, and I must never think that those who have chosen to work while I played, rested, and slept, will share their bounties with me. My success and my education can be companions that no misfortune can depress, no crime can destroy, and no enemy can alienate. Without education, man is a slave, a savage wandering from here to there believing whatever he is told. Time and chance come to us all. I can be either hesitant or courageous. I can swiftly stand up and shout, 'This is my time and my place. I will accept the challenge.'"

The beauty of what I saw was that taking stands, saying yes, and pursuing innovation in things that matter to people are the lifeblood of a movement. Any movement. Ideas always matter, and in my experience good ideas eventually have their day in the sun if people are willing to push hard enough and long enough.

On health care, conservatives have been even worse. We have put forward a lot of no and nothing more. From the time of the Affordable Care Act's inception in 2010, Republicans in Congress have put up more than seventy votes to overturn it.

Okay, point made. We voted no and were against it. It passed anyway. Now what?

When I returned to Congress, I offered the Republican alternative to the Affordable Care Act. It went nowhere because it was safer for Republicans to criticize Obamacare than to offer an alternative. But we desperately need a yes, but laced with conservative philosophy. It's vital because in America we don't have a health-care system, we have a disease-treatment system. The fact that we spend far above what other industrialized countries spend but reap far inferior health results is outrageous, and makes this a critical area where real differences could be made in people's lives. For this reason, when I was governor our administration went to Washington to ask for a waiver that would make South Carolina the first state in the country to offer a statewide option of medical savings accounts. We got it, and there are lots of similar things that could be done by all levels of government to improve people's lives. On education, welfare, infrastructure, immigration, and even programs like veteran's care, there is still much room for conservative creativity.

But guess what we need as a movement to uncover these gems? A whole lot of yes!

The degree to which we aren't there yet was superbly illustrated a few months ago by House Republican Whip Steve Scalise. He's a good guy, and I love him, but when asked about the larger Republican message, he said, "It's not about right or wrong, it's about the focus of our Conference, and focusing on pushing back on the agenda that's being pushed by the Biden administration."

Say what? It's time we all push for constructive and conservative yeses!

WE ARE ALL DEFINED BY THE COMPANY WE KEEP.

If you hang out with an ax murderer, it's probably not going to help your reputation in town. Each one of us defines ourselves by who we choose to associate with or disassociate from. The conservative movement did itself no favors here in putting up with Trump.

This is compounded by the fact that in politics, and in life, not only do words and associations matter, but perceptions often matter even more. Conservatives lost a lot under Trump. He was seen as carrying the conservative mantle, particularly because he outsourced judicial appointments to the Federalist Society. Their appointments were genuinely conservative, and when voters combined these appointments with Trump's tax cuts, his support from evangelicals, and his newfound "conservative" stands on a host of issues, there were plenty of reference points for most voters to label him a conservative...something he never was.

This will prove to be a big problem in getting independent voters to embrace conservative ideals going forward. Many will think "If Trump represents conservatism, I'll pass."

A cult of personality is actually the opposite of what conservatism actually stands for, but most people just go with what they know...or think they know.

And while brands and the perceptions that create them can take years to build, they are fragile and can be lost in a day. And once an opinion is formed, people tend to stick with it. Young people who went through the Great Depression locked into voting for Democrats for the next forty years, and sadly we may have already lost many young people today. The progressivism of Alexandria Ocasio-Cortez, Andrew Yang, and Bernie Sanders has pulled many in that direction.

And as these young people age most will not change political stripes, not only because this is what they got used to but because politics is in part identity—and few people change their identity. On this point, when I talk to Black Republican friends, they have consistently told me how hard it was to switch from being a Democrat—because the voting patterns established by their family and community had as much to do with identity as it did with issues.

People indeed go with what they know. We can't think through every decision, and whether with your soap, toothpaste, or voting patterns, defaults become norms. If conservatism sees any sort of public opinion shift like this as a result of Trump's negative tenure, we are due for a long time in the desert.

WE NEED TO REMEMBER THAT WE HELPED LIGHT THE MATCH.

A friend once cynically likened politicians to the owner of a gas service station on a lonely stretch of road. Hungry for more business, the owner sprinkled nails on the road, yet when the driver limped into the gas station, he was more than courteous and helpful in fixing the tire. The driver leaves the station genuinely appreciative of the fine job done fixing the tire but totally unaware of the fact that were it not for the owner, the problem would not have occurred.

Is this not where conservatives have been in looking the other way as the last four years made our climb in advancing conservative ideals tougher? Seriously, the damage done by a now-unchecked march toward progressive policy may create a financial debt crater so deep that we can't climb out from it. This march was aided and abetted by Trump's torching of the two Georgia Senate seats, and the consequences in this shift of power will last far longer than the ever-changing composition of the Senate itself.

The surest route to killing a civilization is financial ruin, and a political landscape that doesn't include true conservative philosophy as a check against those who would significantly expand government is guaranteed to get us there, especially given the tipping point we have now arrived at in our national finances. But Trump drove conservative representation down, not up—this is where we helped sprinkle nails along the road by not speaking up against him on spending and doing things that politically hurt the conservative cause.

Consequently, there is an explosion of government spending coming our way. Financially, Biden is a wreck. And the reef that would sink our ship of state is frighteningly close. Consider this. Our country's net worth relative to the economy is at a level we have never seen before over my sixty-one years of life. The closest reference point would be the 1920s, and we know how the stock market crash of 1929 and the ensuing Great Depression changed things. Based on the buildup of debt, we are at an economic and political tipping point that no one in Washington seems to acknowledge. Yet Biden now is working with Nancy Pelosi, Chuck Schumer, and the progressive wing of the Democratic Party to blindly recalibrate many of our default policy settings on taxes and spending. It will make things worse if enacted, but sadly the conservative movement is party to this inasmuch as we looked the other way with Trump.

IS THERE A WAY FORWARD?

I think so. What the conservative movement lost under Trump is something of a riddle. On one level we lost nothing. At the end of the day, Trump was a transactional populist, not a conservative at all, so it would be hard to imagine how conservativism lost anything from his time in office. But for all the reasons just mentioned, we did lose a lot, and so the question lies in our path forward. A few things stand out.

We need to find our voice again, and real voice comes with authority: This is not the appointed or elected sort but rather moral authority. Being authentic. Walking the walk. Being real. In fact, only if you do right the right thing will you earn the authority to talk about what's right to do. In this regard trust is simple and straightforward. Do you do what you say you are going to do? If so, people trust you. Every trustworthy action builds on itself. Trust is additive. Trust in smaller things leads to trust in greater things.

We have examples to pull from here. Who do you know of that took greater risks for freedom than Abraham Lincoln? He had authority because he was both real and consistent.

Ronald Reagan was similarly unwavering in his stand against communism and in his belief that freedom was a universal birthright. Reagan stated eloquently what we should be hearing from conservative circles today.

> "Freedom is the right to question and change the established way of doing things. It is the continuing revolution of the marketplace. It is the understanding that allows us to recognize shortcomings and

seek solutions. It is the right to put forth an idea, scoffed at by the experts, and watch it catch fire among the people. It is the right to dream—to follow your dream or stick to your conscience, even if you're the only one in a sea of doubters. Freedom is the recognition that no single person, no single authority or government, has a monopoly on the truth, but that every individual life is infinitely precious, that every one of us put on this world has been put there for a reason and has something to offer."[24]

Unequivocal and clear as Reagan was, this is where we should be again as conservatives.

We also need to be careful to whom we hitch our wagon. The ultimate test of politics always lies in what actions you take to support your beliefs. If you claim to be a conservative but vote the other way, people will care little about what you have to say on conservatism. Your actions don't match your words. This is where I believe the conservative movement has been trashed by the Republican Party. Politicians said one thing and did another, and this is deadly for both a brand and a movement.

Leaders kept saying they just needed a little more power, and then they would deliver. Meanwhile, conservatives at home were saying, "Something is wrong here. First you needed the House. We conservatives got it for you. Then you needed the Senate. We got it for you." But then Republican leaders claimed to need the White

---

24 Ronald Regan, "Moscow State University Address" (speech, Moscow, Russia, May 31, 1988).

House in order to deliver—which was not what they had promised when they harnessed those of us in the grassroots to work hard for a Republican House and Senate.

And that is why it was so easy for a self-proclaimed nonpolitician and businessman to step forward and offer something different. People bought the idea that different might be better, and we got a more strident, vigorous, and at times flamboyantly entertaining form of philosophical nothingness than we'd had over the preceding years of Republican malaise. Trump was elected in part because he was seen as "real." He wasn't your stereotypical perfect, camera-ready politician, and people loved him for this. And in fairness, he never really tried to hide his true personality. It always came out in spades. But what worked personally for Trump did not work for the conservative cause. As a measure, tumbling Gallup polls illustrated the damage as polls now show adults under the age of thirty-five more likely to identify as liberal than conservative, and falling numbers for the population at large for those who would identify as conservative. Further proof was the Republican Party's historic drubbing in its trifecta of losses during the 2019 election.

We need to always remember to separate the tactical from the strategic, the need of the day from the cause and mission. Being all things to all people never works. It was a fundamental mistake when conservatives went along with the Republican Party in connecting wildly different political coalitions. The cobbling together of defense and traditional-value advocates, with a few spending-and-debt hawks thrown in for good measure, might make the Republican Party work for a while in Washington, but it sure doesn't give fuel to a conservative movement.

This approach only works at the tactical level and in the short term, as in moving a bill through the House or Senate. Trade-offs and compromises are part of the grease that makes any legislative system work. When some political figures take what works at the tactical level and try to apply it to the strategic level, they mistakenly assume this is leadership. It is not. Instead, it illustrates the difference between management and leadership. When mismatched coalitions are formed in the world of politics, it totally misses what builds a true political movement: unity around a few core issues.

Trump did get this part. He had a few simple ideas. Build the wall. Blame the Mexicans. Blame the Chinese. Make America Great Again. But while simple, these were not the unifying themes of a movement—they were a listing of fears.

We need to start making noise again. But not noise for noise's sake, and not with policy papers. Instead we need to be distilling complex ideas into one word or phrase that captures the direction of where everyday people are trying to go in dealing with their needs, honoring their beliefs, and in advancing their dreams.

Here we also need to honor those who were not remembered for what they promised but rather for what they asked of each of us as Americans. For conservatism to grow again, it must ask for sacrifice toward our greater good of individual liberty and a free republic.

We need to trust what we know, and the Founding Fathers' system, again. It's time we return to what Edmund Burke described as "a trust in experience and in the gradual improvement of tried and tested arrangements."[25] Our thinking works because principles as diverse as the separation of power, private property, or financial prudence have indeed been tested across the pages of time—and they worked.

Didn't *conservative* once mean taking deliberate steps not to discard the collective wisdom of those who have come before us? Wisdom and traditions matter. What has worked matters. Through political norms, time-honored ways of doing things are institutionalized and memorialized. Wisdom does not blindly discard the good with the bad in the traditions and institutions that have served our country well.

The same holds true on trusting our system. In thinking about our approaches to ideas, a person or object can be a problem but not *the* problem. Donald Trump was certainly a problem, but in questions about him, we must ask whether we trust the system to dispense with him as a counterfeit to conservative ideals. Though the system is delicate, it's not yet broken, and accordingly I believe in the sensibilities and decency of who we are as Americans, the strength of our institutions, and the system of balanced power designed by our Founders to prevail over even the most forceful of personalities.

Though he may have rankled our sensitivities on a host of fronts, upset our beliefs, and undermined institutions we hold dear, he did not sink what the Founding Fathers gave us. He diverted, divided, and distracted us, but will surely prove to be no more than an

---

25 Anthony O'Hear, Edward Craig, ed., Routledge Encyclopedia of Philosophy (London: Routledge, 1998).

insignificant irritant in the pages of time. Self-absorption does not fit with greatness or lasting change. Meaningful change only comes in a life built around something bigger than self—be it in principles, ideals, or focus on others. Leaders like Gandhi, Mandela, Lincoln, or Jefferson were not perfect, but all were capable of moving far beyond personal needs in their expression of ideas.

That Trump was incapable of this was his fatal flaw, and should allow each one of us who found many of his actions distasteful to breathe a little easier, knowing that there is a short half-life to efforts that begin and end in one personality. What we have just been through is what the Founders defined as the "turbulence and follies of democracy." Occasional periods of going sideways are baked into our political cake.

So where does all this leave us?

With conservatism as a place in our history, it should be part of our future. The principles that build toward individual freedom need to be recelebrated and restored. If the conservative movement can find the will to move on from where we are today, a second chance and renaissance for America and the ideals that made it great can be ours.

Let's take that second chance.

4

A SECOND CHANCE
FOR AMERICA

America today is also at a crossroads, but we have been here before, many times. Our country could have gone in very different directions at the time of the Revolutionary War, the Civil War, the Great Depression, the two world wars, the turbulence of the civil rights movement, Vietnam, and more.

But we didn't.

We managed as a country to maintain balance and work through the pains that came in each of these chapters of American life.

We also know that the well-worn and easier path before us is a path toward decline. We are seeing it today in American politics. This breaking of the norms and institutions that undergird open political systems has been seen many times before in history. While nothing lasts forever, our present path is one that will surely speed our demise. America has been able to make it through almost 250 years, a respectable number as democratic systems go, but that is a long way from the Roman Republic's five hundred years.

Whichever path America chooses from here, is our choice. Free will is tough. It means you and I have a responsibility in sustaining our birthright of freedom. What is granted at birth is not guaranteed for life, and its difficulty was perfectly expressed years ago in the movie *The American President*. Michael Douglas plays the role of president and in a great scene he says simply, "America isn't easy. It's advanced citizenship. You gotta want it bad, because it's going to put up a fight. It's going to say, 'You want free speech? Let's see you acknowledge a man whose words make your blood boil, who's standing center stage and advocating at the top of his lungs that which you would spend a lifetime opposing at the top of yours.'"[26]

Indeed these sentiments are right. If you look on the back of a dollar, you will see the Great Seal of this country. There is a pyramid in the center, the top of which is elevated and filled with the all-seeing eye of God. Above it are the words *Annuit Cœptis*— "God Favors Our Undertakings." Below that, it says *Novus Ordo Seclorum*—"New Order of the Ages." The pyramid traditionally represents the Israelites' exodus from Egypt and tyranny into God's Promised Land. The Founders believed our Promised Land to be the dream that is America. At the bottom of the pyramid is MDCCLXXVI, the roman numeral for 1776, the year the American Dream began.

---

26 *The American President*, directed by Rob Reiner (1995; Burbank, CA: Warner Bros. Pictures).

The interesting tension built into the seal is between the all-knowing eye of God at the top and the New Order at the bottom. One was the idea of God's providence, his eye and plan favoring our country and the Founders' remarkable undertaking; the other, the New Order of our society, the revolutionary idea that the American system was to be built on reason and individual responsibility rather than an autocratic regime. In 1776, this departure from a king's edicts, with ordinary citizens elevated to being the reservoir of political power, was indeed revolutionary, the basis for a whole new political order.

God's grace has undoubtedly shone on our undertakings, but our country's destiny, by the design of those who started it, will always be driven by the choices we make as a nation of individuals. Those who insist on the notion of American exceptionalism dismiss both our history and the very construct of the Founders' design.

In explaining the idea of needing to do our part, historian Niall Ferguson framed it interestingly. He said America's exceptional place in the world originally came about because of our country's belief in competition, science and technology, property rights, medicine, consumerism, and a strong work ethic.[27] These beliefs resulted in ways of doing things here that were very different from the rest of the world.

But what happens when other countries catch up and apply these same ideas? What happens when one culture's behavior is not that much different than another's? Can you have different results if your actions mirror those of your neighbor?

---

27 Niall Ferguson, Civilization: The West and the Rest. (New York: Penguin, 2012).

Unlike those in so many other parts of the world, American government from the beginning was decentralized, often with fierce competition between state, local, and federal powers. In contrast, what we have seen lately under both Republican and Democratic governance is a growing federal sphere. And when business must fear a presidential tweet or arbitrary pronouncements on what they can and can't do, that administration is undermining the basics of limited government that allowed America's collective growth. The closest we have ever gotten before to this sort of government control came under FDR during World War II, but times were a bit different as we were fighting the Germans and Japanese for our very survival, and the war effort was central.

A connected world and globalization have also favored the United States, but things are now moving in the opposite direction. Niall Ferguson put it this way: "By 1910 the world had been economically integrated in a way never seen before. The different bonds that linked it together—railways, steamship lines and telegraphs—were almost entirely Western-invented and Western-owned. The West literally shrank the world."[28]

The technology revolution of the last fifty years shrank it still further. It used to be that if you were the brightest person on earth but were born in Burma, there was no way to export the value of your intellectual prowess. Unless you immigrated, you were forever locked into a diminished economic state. You could love your wife and kids and enjoy the neighbors, but economically you would be a second-class citizen. Now with the internet, for the first time

---

28 Civilization: The West and the Rest by Niall Ferguson (See page 97 citation)

in the history of man, you can monetize your intellect globally. This changed and shrank the world even as it further expanded America's place in the world.

But today we are riding a wave of nationalism that threatens the connectivity that has driven world commerce. Where before we were committed to building a railroad or a canal or an internet platform, today's most popular sentiment revolves around building a wall. Where working was once seen as an essential value, now many people are happy being paid not to work.

The American system was built on a constitutionally mandated limited and predictable federal government. Our system was further insulated from populous shock by institutions and traditions that protect the balance of power our Constitution demands. Integral to this form of government was Adam Smith's so-called invisible hand—a robust free market economy driven by the independent decisions of millions acting in their perceived best self-interest.

Again, the Constitution states in the Tenth Amendment that "the powers not delegated to the United States by the Constitution, nor prohibited by it to the States, are reserved to the States respectively, or to the people."[29] This provided a role for state and local government, but even more significant, for business and commerce and a robust civil society made up of organizations like Habitat for Humanity, the Rotary Club, or church groups working in unison with a market-based economy to solve problems that in many other countries are handled by the government.

---

29 U.S Constitution. amend. X.

Now we have government that never leaves us. It's on Twitter. It's on social media. It's in nonstop media coverage. It regulates large parts of our lives. It takes big parts of what we earn. It borrows from our future at frightening levels.

There was nothing limited about the last four years, and we are set to see levels of government over the next four years that are unprecedented in history. What President Biden has already proposed represents a radical shift in the way we reward and treat financial and human capital, and the work associated with both. How can any of these things make America great again?

If we dream of truly doing so, I suggest we go back to the things that actually make us great. This is not our present course. We have been off course for some time, but the rate of destructive change has been accelerating.

Consider the contrast on budgets and spending. Spending began its upward run under Obama and Bush, and went wild under Trump and now Biden. Some say we are now over $60 trillion in debt, and generational accounting paints a gloomy picture for our children. As conservatives we should be leading efforts to stop this. Government programs have been likened to the closest thing to eternal life and have a way of lasting and growing far more than we do.

More seriously, Scottish historian Sir Alexander Fraser Tytler warned in the 1800s that a democracy would end when voters discovered they could vote themselves goodies from the public treasury. The whole of his most sobering quote is worth pondering.

"A democracy cannot exist as a permanent form of government. It can only exist until the voters discover they can vote for themselves largess from the public treasury with the result that a democracy always fails under loose fiscal policies and is generally followed by dictatorship. The average age of the world's greatest civilizations has been 200 years. These nations have progressed through this sequence from bondage to spiritual faith, spiritual faith to great courage, great courage to liberty, liberty to abundance, abundance to selfishness, selfishness to complacency, complacency to apathy, apathy to dependency, and from dependency back again into bondage."[30]

In his book *The Decline and Fall of the Roman Empire*, Edward Gibbons wrote of the citizens of Athens, "In the end, more than freedom, they wanted security. They wanted a comfortable life, and they lost it all—security, comfort, and freedom. When the Athenians finally wanted not to give to society but for society to give to them, when the freedom they wished for most was freedom from responsibility, then Athens ceased to be free and was never free again."[31]

It all sounds frighteningly familiar.

Unless we are deliberate about protecting the institutions and norms vital to sustaining our democracy, while simultaneously curtailing the spending, debt, and ensuing taxes that stifle individual effort and initiative, America will go the way of Athens, Rome, and other failed republics.

---

30 Elmer T. Peterson, "This is the Hard Core of Freedom" Daily Oklahoman, 9 December 1951.

31 Edward Gibbon, The History of the Decline and Fall of the Roman Empire. (London: Alex. Murray & Son, 1869).

In their book *This Time Is Different,* economists Carmen M. Reinhart and Kenneth Rogoff chronicled the last eight hundred years of government spending and ensuing financial crises.[32] They catalog over 250 financial crises in sixty-six countries, and their conclusion was straightforward—that bad financial choices lead to bad financial consequences. History has shown that there are no exceptions to this. It's just a matter of when and how long before consequences come. We all know at a gut level this is true. What is alarming about Reinhart and Rogoff's work is that it shows that in every instance when civilizations have spent beyond their means and borrowed, its citizens have paid the bill with their currency falling, or through inflation.

In Europe from 1400 to 1850, the average silver content of the top ten currencies fell from about nine grams to one, and their analysis shows a remarkable correlation between too much spending and a falling currency across an amazing array of different countries.

Furthermore, according to Reinhart and Rogoff,

> "The lesson of history, then, is that even as institutions and policy makers improve, there will always be a temptation to stretch the limits. Just as an individual can go bankrupt no matter how rich they start out, a financial system can collapse under the pressure of greed, politics, and profits no matter how well regulated it seems to be. Technology has changed, the height of humans has changed, and fashions have changed—yet the ability of governments and

---

32 Carmen M. Reinhart, Kenneth S. Rogoff, *This Time is Different: Eight Centuries of Financial Folly* (Princeton: Princeton University Press, 2009).

investors to delude themselves, giving rise to periodic bouts of euphoria that usually end in tears, seems to have remained a constant."[33]

No one should really be surprised by Reinhart and Rogoff's lessons about the mismanagement of government spending, debt, and financial markets. But they even went on to say,

> "As for financial markets, we have come full circle to the concept of financial fragility in economies with massive indebtedness. All too often, periods of heavy borrowing can take place in a bubble, and last for a surprisingly long time. But highly leveraged economies, particularly those in which continual rollover of short-term debt [*exactly what America is doing today*] is sustained only by confidence in relatively illiquid underlying assets, seldom survive forever, particularly if leverage continues to grow unchecked. 'This time may seem different.' but all too often a deeper look shows it is not. Encouragingly, history does point to warning signs that policy makers can look at to assess risk—if only they do not become too drunk with their credit bubble—fueled success and say, as their predecessors have for centuries, "This time is different."[34]

---

33 Reinhart, Rogoff.
34 Reinhart, Rogoff.

On this point, one of our country's Founders had remarkable foresight. In the struggle between Jefferson and Hamilton on the appropriate size and scope of our federal government, Jefferson wanted an amendment to the Constitution to prevent borrowing. Given the academic work of Reinhart and Rogoff and what we're experiencing now with the national debt, we would indeed have been fortunate if his thinking had prevailed.

Somewhat surprisingly, former Federal Reserve chairman Alan Greenspan wrote in his book *Gold and Economic Freedom,*

"The abandonment of the gold standard made it possible for the welfare statists to use the banking system as a means to an unlimited expansion of credit. They have created paper reserves in the form of government bonds which—through a complex series of steps—the banks accept in place of tangible assets and treat as if they were an actual deposit, i.e., the equivalent of what was formerly a deposit of gold. The holder of a government bond or of a bank deposit created by paper reserves believes that he has a valid claim on a real asset. But the fact is that there are now more claims outstanding than real assets. The law of supply and demand is not to be conned. As the supply of money (of claims) increases relative to the supply of tangible assets in the economy, prices must eventually rise. Thus the earnings saved by the productive members of the society lose value in terms of goods. When the economy's books are finally balanced, one finds that this loss in value represents the goods purchased by the government for welfare or other purposes with the money proceeds of the government bonds financed by bank credit expansion.

In the absence of the gold standard, there is no way to protect savings from confiscation through inflation. There is no safe store of value. If there were, the government would have to make its holding illegal, as was done in the case [of] gold. If everyone decided, for example, to convert all his bank deposits to silver or copper or any other good and thereafter declined to accept checks as payment for goods, bank deposits would lose their purchasing power, and government-created bank credit would be worthless as a claim on goods. The financial policy of the welfare state requires that there be no way for the owners of wealth to protect themselves.

This is the shabby secret of the welfare statists' tirades against gold. Deficit spending is simply a scheme for the "hidden" confiscation of wealth. Gold stands in the way of this insidious process. It stands as a protector of property rights."

While this sounds good, Greenspan, Bernake, and the like all fell prey to staying relevant during their time in power while running the Fed, and that which they had preached earlier went out the window.

Under the category of other influential thinkers in this same vein, consider what John Maynard Keynes wrote. "Lenin was certainly right. There is no subtler, no surer means of overturning the existing basis of society than to debauch the currency. The process engages all the hidden forces of economic law on the side of destruction, and does it in a manner which not one man in a million is able to diagnose."[35]

So where does this leave us? I think it's with the Dos Equis beer commercial wherein they simply say, "Stay thirsty, my friend." We need to do many things to strengthen America's hand and our way of life. We must yearn for it. It will take effort. And as one goes down the list of issues that range from immigration, infrastructure, and education to our changing culture and increasing loss of moral compass, I simply think we need to start with the things that will have the biggest effect. We can't pay for any of government's needs if our currency and economy collapse. Similarly, our government doesn't work without maintaining the balance of power that our Founding Fathers set in motion. Finally, retreating to live within the walls of America does not fit with the outward-looking optimism and zest for competition that had so much to do with building this great country.

So are these ideas exhaustive? Absolutely not. But I think they are the right place to start.

Let's look at some concrete things we can choose to turn to, or return to, if we want to make the GOP, the conservative movement, and America stand for something truly great.

---

35 John Maynard, *The Economic Consequences of the Peace* (1919), 104.

PART TWO

★ ★ ★

WHAT WE CAN DO

5

NINE THINGS WE CAN DO FOR THE PARTY AND THE MOVEMENT

Whether we like it or not, Benjamin Franklin's notion at the time of our Revolution, that "we must, indeed, all hang together or, most assuredly, we shall all hang separately," fits. Remarkably, America has but about 4 percent of the world's population though it harvests over 20 percent of the world's income. Billions around the world would like to take our place, so what happens next is neither theoretical nor unimportant. Getting political debate recentered in our country is key to sustaining all that we have come to enjoy as Americans.

If one believes that ideas are made better through contrasting opinions and perspectives, we need the strong views of Republicans, Democrats, and Independents. Here are a few ideas for Republicans and conservatives that will also help Democrats and Independents. Iron sharpens iron, and as Americans we are better off when all political philosophies are at the table, and robustly so.

ONE: REEMBRACE TRUTH.

Truth is the foundation of trust. If you don't have this, you don't have anything when you are dealing with others, and in our case, we have over three hundred million "others" to deal with in America. As I was writing this, the Republican Party was having quite a stir on this issue after Liz Cheney's stand not to whitewash and repeat Trump's lies. But all the controversy surrounding the election comes down to something quite simple. What is the truth, and will we stand up for it?

What we are playing with as a party can be lethal for a democracy. Joseph Goebbels, Hitler's propaganda minister, is alleged to have said, "If you tell a lie big enough and keep repeating it, people will eventually come to believe it. The lie can be maintained only for such time as the State can shield the people from the political, economic, and/or military consequences of the lie. It thus becomes vitally important for the State to use all of its powers to repress dissent, for the truth is the mortal enemy of the lie, and thus by extension, the truth is the greatest enemy of the State."

Though Goebbels lived this philosophy, whether he actually said it is disputed. What's not disputed is what Hitler himself wrote in *Mein Kampf.*

> "In the big lie there is always a certain force of credibility, because the broad masses of a nation are always more easily corrupted in the deeper strata of their emotional nature than consciously or

voluntarily; and thus in the primitive simplicity of their minds they more readily fall victims to the big lie than the small lie, since they themselves often tell small lies in little matters but would be ashamed to resort to large-scale falsehoods. It would never come into their heads to fabricate colossal untruths, and they would not believe that others could have the impudence to distort the truth so infamously. Even though the facts which prove this to be so may be brought clearly to their minds, they will still doubt and waver and will continue to think that there may be some other explanation."[36]

Hitler's thinking was documented in 1943 by our government. At that time the Office of Strategic Studies, our precursor to the CIA, produced a 165-page document entitled "A Psychological Analysis of Adolf Hitler." Shared with American and British war planners, it considered him weak and a bully but underscored his belief in big lies. It said, "His primary rules were: never allow the public to cool off; never admit a fault or wrong; never concede that there may be some good in your enemy; never leave room for alternatives; never accept blame; concentrate on one enemy at a time and blame him for everything that goes wrong; people will believe a big lie before a little one; and if you repeat it frequently enough people will sooner or later believe it."[37]

---

36 Adolf Hitler, *Mein Kampf* (Boston: Houghton Mifflin, 1999), 134.
37 Walter C. Langer, *A Psychological Analysis of Adolph Hitler: His Live and Legend* (Washington D.C.: Office of Strategic Services, 1944), 38.

Mark Twain's notion that history doesn't repeat itself but often rhymes, eerily resonates here, and I find words about a big lie a horrific reminder of the importance of truth in any political system—and especially ours.

Facts used to be stubborn things in America. They actually used to exist, and I still remember my high school teachers, Mr. Hincher and Mrs. Spears, drilling this into me at school. "Alternative" facts are not to be taken lightly; they represent madness. If I don't trust you, and if we can't even agree that there are things we legitimately disagree on, what are we doing? A debate between conservative and liberal answers to the problems that ail us can't even begin without actual facts to debate. Without facts and objective truth, debate is lost. Trust is lost. Our system grinds to a halt.

We end up with Republican state lawmakers recounting Arizona's Maricopa County ballots from the 2019 presidential election nearly six months after former president Trump lost.

The almost $2.1 million ballot audit is the result of a subpoena by Republican state senators who sought the recount to examine unsubstantiated claims that fraud or errors tainted President Biden's win. We end up with this doubt metastasizing in Georgia, Michigan, and New Hampshire.

I recognize Trump is not the first official to tell a lie, but he was the first ever to suggest a US presidential election result was a lie. The big lie here is different because it was not a claim about himself but a claim about our constitutional process. We have endured Obama's claim that "If you like your health plan, you can keep it," George H. W. Bush's "Read my lips," Clinton's strong words that he "did not have sexual relations with that woman." Lies are as old as time, and unfortunately these are undoubtedly not the last presidential lies that will be told. But the new claim that a process enshrined in the Constitution is a lie represents a path we should not travel. When people cease to believe in our system, it will cease.

With the party and the movement, healing and moving forward start with telling and demanding the truth.

TWO: REEMBRACE REASON.

Just as you can't have a debate of ideas without facts, neither can you have a debate without reason. Our Founders gave us a reason-based republic, and two of its underpinnings are faith and common sense. Their idea of reason was built on the common sense of the farmer, not of the aristocrat or the intellectual. In a time when many were tired of political correctness, Trump's common-man language had great appeal. But it wasn't reasoned. It was authoritarian. "Do it because I said so" has a short half-life in the system of checks and balances the Founders created.

For officeholders, reason should also mean looking past the next election and beyond one's immediate self-interest. Carefully considering what a decision means for our descendants requires a kind of leadership sorely lacking in today's politics. But I believe it's precisely the thing that people would respond to. The fact that in the red state of Tennessee, Vanderbilt University launched the Project on Unity and American Democracy—which they describe "as seeking to counter America's drift from evidence and reason toward ideological certitude and reflexive partisanship"—says everything about how much our party needs to champion reason in our ideas and policies.

If not anchored in reason, politics pulls us in all sorts of truly unreasonable directions in order that policy makers can get what they want. For example, would you believe a political body would create a "thirteenth month" to enable more spending? Remarkably, our legislature did just that in calculating the budget revenue in South Carolina. I fought against this while governor but—remarkably—lost. How is that for reason? If bringing in money to spend was as easy as creating an artificial new month to the year, businesses and families would have done so a long time ago.

In another insane move, South Carolina legislators decided to arbitrarily increase the assumed future rate of return for the state's pension fund so they could increase the payout to retirees. During the fight I pointed out mathematical flaws in their assumed rate of return. I highlighted Warren Buffett's opinion in his letter to shareholders that year. And none of it mattered with a debate centered on anything but reason. Buffet described political reasoning perfectly when he said this about pension managers' projections of 8 percent returns, "If they are wrong, as I believe they are, the chickens won't come home to roost until long after they retire. Public pension funding is woefully inadequate. Because the fuse on this time bomb is long, politicians flinch from inflicting tax pain, given that problems will only become apparent long after these officials have departed. Promises involving generous cost-of-living adjustments are easy for these officials to make…those promises will be anything but easy to keep."[38]

South Carolina is hardly unique in making unreasoned political decisions. When I was governor, our state's unfunded retirement liability was more than $10 billion, and when one added in the health-care liability, it doubled. With more than $20 billion in unfunded political promises, any reasonable fiduciary would very soberly assess the problem and begin to deal with it. Regrettably, this is not the way of politics. You see the issue in a state like South Carolina, and you see the same issue in Washington where entitlement spending is at a much grander level.

Having some understanding of finance and math, I have always found these types of things maddening. There is never any "reason" involved. We are left with policy makers who embody the proverbial see no evil, hear no evil, speak no evil, which saves them from making the difficult decisions.

Getting the vote today is clearly more important to most office-holders than the financial viability of the system tomorrow. The tools of government often are arranged so as to disguise or shelter political figures from the consequences of rigorous, reasoned debate. Approximately 95 percent of all bills passed in the South Carolina House and Senate during my eight years as governor were passed with individual votes unrecorded. How can you have any kind of accountability in a political system that doesn't mark for history where a house or senate member stood on an issue? When

---

38 Warren E. Buffett, *Chairman's Letter* (Berkshire Hathaway Annual Report: 2007).

you then ask about a vote, it allows a back-slapping politician to simply smile and say, "I was with you!"

Amazingly, we aren't even talking about political hyperbole or exaggeration, we are just talking about what I saw in a political body's bizarre approach to fairly straightforward numbers. For me, it underscores the desperate need for reason in deciding all issues. Part of the Founders' embrace of limited government was grounded in their observation of what I had also witnessed, that government can be all too tempted to throw out reason when facing difficult issues. Reason is not the default commodity the government trades on, so our republic all the more desperately needs people who will embrace and demand the notion of reason as they approach government and its challenges.

THREE: REEMBRACE SCIENCE.

The ability to reason is the greatest part of what separates humans from the many animals with which we share our planet. Animals act solely on instinct, but we have a choice in whether we employ reason, within ourselves and in interacting with others.

Reason applied to the physical world around us is my definition of science; thus, to reject science is to reject reason, the very thing our Founding Fathers considered foundational to democracy and our way of life.

As Republicans, we have simply lost our minds on the issue of science. How can there be any logic in trusting with our lives the science behind the miracles of modern medicine, but when that same science is applied to our planet, it's fake science? We should embrace science, wherever it might lead, and then look for conservative solutions to fix the problems science uncovers. It's pretty amazing to think of Benjamin Franklin venturing out in a thunderstorm and flying a kite in his pursuit of understanding and science. What a contrast with today's rejection of science from many senior Republicans. Like math, science is only as good as the validity of its inputs, but where we find science we disagree with, we should challenge its assumptions rather than discard its worth. Having learned the Socratic method in grad school, during my governorship my veto sessions with my staff became fairly robust. We would sit in a circle in my office, and one person would present the argument for the veto, and it was everyone else's job to rip it apart. We probably overdid it as these sessions sometimes became most intense. Occasionally some staffer would unwisely take the approach meant for the team to some unsuspecting visitor acting as a plaintiff for some need from state government. But this is the way we should challenge what we don't agree with in scientific issues. Every claim deserves a challenge, and dismissing an issue as "fake news" or "fake science" does not meet this standard. John Adams believed in healthy debate rather than dismissive pronouncements, and we should too.

FOUR: REEMBRACE MATH.

Milton Friedman once observed that the ultimate measure of government was what it spent. Yet Republicans have joined the race of upward spending with the Democratic Party, and in doing so we have robbed themselves of what was once a distinct difference between the parties. If both parties have abandoned watching out for my financial future, what difference does it make who I vote for? This is what many think as they compare Democrats and Republicans. Our collective financial amnesia brings us one step closer every day to the most predictable financial crisis in our history as we have been adding about $1 trillion a year to the debt. Most Republicans give lip service to cutting spending but then go on to vote for every appropriations bill presented, and Democrats seem to have abandoned any pretense of interest at all in this issue.

Consider the following quote. "The budget should be balanced, the treasury should be refilled, public debt should be reduced, the arrogance of officialdom should be tempered and controlled, and the assistance to foreign lands should be curtailed lest our country become bankrupt. People must again learn to work, instead of living on public assistance."

If you had to guess, who would you say was the person who said this? Were they talking from the US Senate floor, the House floor, the White House, or as part of a television interview on CNN? Was the person even speaking from America? Or could it have been a candidate from Europe? Was the statement made in the last few years? By Ronald Reagan? Or was it maybe Abraham Lincoln?

The answer is no to all the above. It was Marcus Tullius Cicero talking about Rome and the Roman Republic in 55 BC. He wore many hats as a Roman philosopher, statesman, lawyer, political theorist, and Roman constitutionalist. He was elected consul in 63 BC, and during the chaotic years that marked his time in politics— that is, the civil wars and the dictatorship of Julius Caesar—he championed a return to the principles that had made the Roman

Republic great. It's something we Republicans might want to consider today.

Sadly, it hasn't been our path for a while. In 2008, no doubt because of my fiscal outspokenness, I was asked to testify before the Ways and Means Committee in Congress on the stimulus bill then beginning its quick journey through Congress to passage. It was pint size relative to recent stimulus bills but a big deal at the time given its unprecedented scale and precedent-setting nature. As a testament to the way things have changed, back then it wasn't just me—many voters got excited about it. The hearing was titled "Economic Recovery, Job Creation, and Investment in America," and there was the usual lineup of plaintiffs who were to ask for, argue for, and make the case for the stimulus package. I was seated immediately beside Governor Patterson of New York. After pondering the political or academic positions my fellow witnesses held, I quickly surmised I was the only person there not asking Washington to take care of things for them.

Committee rooms are designed to be somewhat intimidating for those who testify. The room is ornate, and just its decoration and lighting are there to remind you that you stand before those who hold power. These effects are amplified by the superior demeanor too many in office hold, and the way you literally speak and look up to members who sit in an elevated semicircle before you. While you speak, they don't always listen, as they are preparing their next point and an array of staff members are feeding them talking or rebuttal points. My talk that day began slowly.

"Chairman Rangel, Congressman McCrery, and members of the committee: I thank you for this chance to testify before your committee.

I'm here to beg of you not to approve or advance the contemplated $150 billion stimulus package for the effects that it would ultimately have in the state that I represent, and in turn all states across the country and the nation as a whole. I applaud the sentiment behind it and your intentions in trying to help the American public given the enormity of the financial collapse before us, and I understand the supportive position staked out by many of my fellow governors by a letter from the National Governors Association this Monday as well. Still, I feel it's incumbent upon me to stand up and speak now, or perhaps forever hold my peace, and with the greatest respect I'd submit that I don't think this is the course to be taken.

I'd ask that you, as leaders at this crucial juncture in our nation's story, do three things: one, recognize that the current avalanche of bad news can be traced back several years to oftentimes poor financial decisions that snowballed out of control; two, consider that this $150 billion salve may in fact further infect our economy with unnecessary government influence and unintended fiscal consequences; and three, accept that there may be better routes to recovery than a blanket bailout, including offering states like mine more in the way of flexibility and freedom from federal mandates instead of a bag of money with strings attached.

The situation we're now in did not develop overnight, and in the same way it won't be cured by morning. As the old saying goes, the first step to getting out of a hole is to quit digging."

About this time all hell broke loose. Chairman Rangel tuned in to the fact that I was speaking against his legislation. A back-and-forth ensued, and it foreshadowed a larger conversation that would go on in South Carolina for another eight months.

As an aside, it's interesting to note as our nation runs down the path of never-ending stimulus that history says this will not work. FDR's own Treasury Secretary, Henry Morgenthau, weary of the Keynesian spending, wrote in May 1939, "We have tried spending money. We are spending more than we have ever spent before and it does not work. And I have just one interest, and now if I am wrong somebody else can have my job. I want to see this country prosper. I want to see people get a job. I want to see people get enough to eat. We have never made good on our promises. I say after eight years of this administration, we have just as much unemployment as when we started. And enormous debt to boot."

All sorts of history show the ways in which too much debt and spending doesn't work, and even carries with it the capacity to kill governments and the freedoms they were designed to protect. Can we learn from history and as a party be consistent in our stand for the math that limits debt? The possible consequences are dire, and as Spanish American philosopher George Santayana warned in the early 1900s, those who don't learn from history are destined to repeat it.

FIVE: REEMBRACE ACCOUNTABILITY, BECAUSE THERE IS NO CLEANING LIKE SELF-CLEANING.

Accountability is what we all say we want in government, but too often we only insist on it for the other side.

I think accountability rests on two foundations. The first part is structural. Do we really believe in and act on this notion of federalism, of power and authority resting in different levels of government? The competition for power between the various levels of government helps create accountability and is vital. When federal, state, and local government actors compete for power and bases of power, good things happen. The same holds true for structural divisions of power found in things like the law or private property rights that restrain the capricious nature of government and those who run it. My experience has been that the more divided the powers of government, the better the foundation for freedom.

The second part lies in recognizing what ultimately creates accountability, and that's the fact that real change can only come from within. Others can attempt to hold us accountable, they can check our prerogatives, but they can't change us. It's an internal process, and both parties are horrible at it. The most religious of Democrats I knew in the early 1990s contorted themselves to explain why Bill Clinton's behavior with Monica Lewinski didn't matter. Republicans in the House and Senate did the same in coming up with a litany of excuses for explaining away President Trump's many bizarre behaviors. But worrying about that log in your own eye before you worry about the splinter in someone else's means building trust in less sensational things that often don't make the headlines.

Take President Trump's self-serving pardons as an example. We should all be aghast, particularly as Republicans. If we care about what the Founders created in checks and balances, if we care about the idea of an independent judicial system, or even in the idea of right and wrong, we should care deeply about what's occurred. President Trump certainly lived by the notion of going big or going home, but the scale of those pardons undermines, and is corrosive to, the very nature of justice and our justice system in the United States.

No system designed by man is perfect, and accordingly, the Founders built into ours this last-gap measure to right a judicial wrong. Trump took that system and twisted it to do nothing more than reward people who had been loyal to him and to quiet those who might hurt him. Certainly a few legitimate pardons were thrown in, but they mainly served as cover for his injustice of letting people escape from the lawful workings of our justice system.

And this is poison.

Has poison entered our system previously through unjust pardons? Absolutely. President Clinton pardoned Marc Rich. It was pure cronyism and pay-to-play politics, and it was wrong. There have been other abuses as well, but nothing remotely on the scale of what unfolded with President Trump.

If you look at the overwhelming majority of pardons in recent history, they were used as intended by the Founders in righting a wrong or what that administration perceived as a wrong. In recent political history there have been about 450 pardons per president. The Justice Department actually has a process to bring them forth, and through the Ford, Carter, Reagan, and Clinton presidencies, there were a little over four hundred pardons per president. The Bush presidents came in low at seventy-seven and two hundred pardons, respectively, and Obama set a new record at 1,927 pardons. But they were a matter of policy. There was no personal connection as Obama commuted sentences for a large number of nonviolent drug offenders. In many cases they had served fifteen years of a twenty-year sentence, and he commuted the last five years of their sentence. One could have a long debate on the fairness of very different sentencing guidelines between crack and cocaine, but no one can dispute that commuting the penalties that came with this difference is based on policy.

As opposed to the very unusual way President Trump used pardons.

He set a strong precedent for nothing more than tribalism—I'll cover for you if you cover for me. It makes a mockery of the process that has operated for more than two hundred years. It undermines the legitimacy of those who work as dedicated professionals in law enforcement, the courts, and the judicial system when every four years a new "king" can toss aside their thousands of hours of work and the supposed process of law under which they serve.

It also makes all of us who attempt to play by the rules suckers. Why don't we all do insider trading? Or if in elected office, why don't we use our campaign accounts as personal slush funds, as a now-pardoned California congressman did? If those in favor with the king can get away with it, why can't we? At some level it sends a signal to good people across our country that the way to success is not by working hard and playing by the rules but by bowing before the king. Brownnose a bit, and you, too, can be absolved of your sins and skip the consequences that might come to those who stupidly don't. That is exactly what the Founders designed our entire system to guard against…but here we are.

What's at play goes to the core of what we try to teach our children about consequences and living by the rules. I'm not a lawyer, but I know through experience and at a gut level that this is not just. What we accept as right and wrong as individuals defines right and wrong for society. But there was not a peep from Republicans that the way Trump was doing these things ran counter to conservative precepts.

It's all about self-cleaning. Republicans can't do it for Democrats, and Democrats can't do it for Republicans.

It's time to stop looking the other way and instead look in the mirror.

SIX: GET SERIOUS ABOUT TERM LIMITS.

People respond to incentives. Our entire tax policy gives definition to a host of incentives. Much of government funding in general is built around incentivizing certain behaviors and discouraging others. If a state passes a seat belt law or toughens DUI penalties, they are rewarded in federal funding. To suggest people and institutions don't respond to incentives is preposterous, yet many in politics promote the lie that says how long they stay or hope to stay in politics doesn't affect their point of view or voting behavior. Really? The reality is that if a given political decision jeopardizes what they plan on doing for the rest of their professional life or jeopardizes the next step in their political career, they will be averse to taking that risk. Risking the rest of one's career is a big decision, but risking a few years that one might offer in helping one's community is quite different. These two ways of thinking lead to very different appetites for political risk. Yet to solve the problems of the day, we need more political risk-taking, not less. Everyone plays it so safe these days. How else do you explain the level of silence on things that should clearly register as outrageous or unacceptable?

This is exactly why we need term limits.

My old friend and congressional colleague Tom Coburn used to talk about how term limits would also impact spending because of the unholy alliance between lobbying interests and officeholders needing to raise money to sustain political careers. There are many reasons term limits amount to the lynchpin reform needed to help fix Washington, but let me give you a story that illustrates the corrupting influence of too many years in office. And by corrupting, I'm not talking about illegal behavior, I'm just talking about rot to the soul and the arrogance that can creep in and distort perspective.

Political hubris isn't necessarily the obvious kind that one wears on one's sleeve. Many people in politics have fairly pleasing outward dispositions. Instead it rests in politicians beginning to think more highly of themselves and their motivations than they ought to, and next thing you know, they are telling you what's best for *your* life.

I am struck by the nearly invisible way in which this danger starts. First come the solicitous comments from friends back home. They mean well. They are proud of you, their hometown boy or girl who grew up with them but now can be seen on the five o'clock news. Pats on the backs at the local grocery store increase. There are TV, radio, and newspaper requests for your perspective. That's kind of fun; everyone loves to offer their opinions, and it's a luxury not afforded in many lines of work. I remember early on being asked my opinion on the situation in several of the former Soviet republics. I wasn't even sworn in yet, and Soviet republics sure hadn't been part of the campaign debate, and yet the national news media wanted my perspective. Over time all this attention can be corrosive, and it's certainly a nudge that leads many to fall prey to thinking more highly of themselves than they should.

But let me give you a story that illustrates including this concept.

I still vividly remember my first exposure to the pomp and ceremony that came with being a member of Congress. I don't know that it would catch my attention these days as it did when I first started, but back then as a congressman-elect, it really jumped out at me. I remember driving my beat-up Honda Accord hatchback and arriving at Charleston Air Force Base for an official ceremony, a little embarrassed and reticent about the car's condition. I had caulked over holes in its roof where it leaked with every rainstorm, and the mixture of its light blue exterior, rust, and white caulk was not the sort of thing you wanted noticed by impeccably dressed airmen. Turns out I didn't need to be worried. I was greeted at the gate by smartly dressed military aides who said I was to leave the car and ride with them. Riding out toward the flight line alone in the back seat of an Air Force vehicle, I wondered why the members of Congress couldn't ride together. I remember being recognized by name at the beginning of each of the speakers' remarks and wondering, why not mention everyone's name if you're going to mention mine? Over time the skittishness subsided as it became normal to hear my name singled out at events, and then as the years went by, I became slightly bewildered if I was not recognized. The thought that went through my head in the rare instances I wasn't recognized was, I made the effort to come all the way over here, and they are not even recognizing me?

I remember being in a holding room before going onstage and waiting for South Carolina's US Senators Strom Thurmond and Fritz Hollings to arrive from Washington. They arrived in a magnificent light-blue and white Gulf Stream jet emblazoned with the words "United States Air Force." I'd never seen one before except in magazines and movies and wondered what it would cost to fly down and back from Washington for the afternoon. After the senators walked inside, military personnel went over seating diagrams and speaking order, and while they did so, Senator Thurmond asked for lemonade without ice. I then watched two full-bird colonels heed the call of duty and strain lemonade with their fingers to catch the ice, but in the process they sluiced more than a little lemonade down their starched sleeves. The whole scenario didn't seem normal to me. In the real world, someone would have suggested that anyone who did not want ice could pull ice out of their own lemonade.

The point is, if someone is singled out for special attention long enough, nine out of ten times it will begin to go to their head. When compared to most jobs, politics, which some consider the "plain-looking man's version of Hollywood," offers unusual temptations on this front.

Yet another reason term limits make a whole lot of sense.

Even before I got to Congress, I had begun to get clues as to what made elected office so addicting for many, and why so many became tone deaf to the real concerns of the people they were supposed to represent.

On November 13, 2003, less than two weeks after my first election to office, I was asked to join two other young soon-to-be congressmen on the CBS news program *Eye on America.* For someone new to national news exposure, that kind of experience was odd. It again leads to phone calls from former classmates that you haven't talked with in fifteen years. These old friends are not trying to do you a disservice, because they are genuinely proud of your accomplishment, but in fact they are. Those calls represent just the beginning of Washington's unseen influence that in subtle ways exploits the different weaknesses in each of us elected to work there.

It is a very human system, and because of the scale of the institution, the temptation to fall victim to our own hubris is supersized compared to a normal workplace. The average person goes about their work doing the best they can and sure doesn't get phone calls from the other side of the country complimenting them on that work. The human spirit is so susceptible to this stroking of the ego. Knowing these dangers, I tried hard to remind myself that my opinion was no more valuable than another's. This, along with my somewhat Depression

Era frugality, was a big part of the reason I slept in my office over the twelve years I was in Congress. It's also the reason I did things like drive a ridiculously worn-out twenty-year-old Honda hatchback while in Congress. But try as I might, I, too, wound up thinking more of myself than I should have.

No one is immune. Movie stars often become head cases because they live in a world of constant adulation. That's not the reality with politics—at best half love you and the other half dislike you—but there is certainly enough of it to cause one to lose perspective. The healthier notion that holding office is never about you, that power is simply loaned to you for a few years, and that you can sometimes take political risks in order to serve the greater good would all be enhanced with term limits. Immanuel Kant once observed, "The possession of power inevitably spoils the free use of reason."[39]

There are just too many things that can go wrong by officeholders staying in the spotlight, and that is a big part of why we need term limits now.

SEVEN: FOR THOSE OF US WHO CONSIDER OURSELVES CHRISTIAN, LET'S REALLY TAKE A DEEP DIVE ON THE GOOD BOOK'S TEACHINGS ON HUMILITY.

I realize the so-called fruits of the spirit—patience, kindness, and gentleness—are hardly considered selling themes these days

---

39 Immanuel Kant, Perpetual Peace and Other Essays. (Indianapolis: Hackett Publishing Company, Incorporated, 1983).

in politics. Everyone wants a fighter against the other side. But Lincoln said in his first inaugural address, "We are not, we must not be, aliens or enemies but fellow countrymen and brethren."[40] Divisions were extreme back then, but his tone was conciliatory in trying to bridge our country's divides. He was elected with far less than a majority, and as he prepared to speak at his inauguration, seven Southern states had already seceded from the Union. Cavalry patrolled all the capital's major intersections, and army sharpshooters were stationed to guard against Confederate sympathizers. Lincoln had the humility it took to gather a team of rivals—three of his cabinet members had run against him—and yet on that day he conveyed hope and empathy.

We have come a long way, because today we have replaced the strength found in reconciling conflicting personalities and political factions with a White House most recently staffed at the senior level by family and folks with little room for conflicting opinions.

Humility has worked in the past. If it worked for Lincoln, could it not work for us?

But it's ultimately an act of faith. One would think this would resonate with evangelical Republicans, but instead, many left church for Sunday while their political faith rested with others more strident the rest of the week.

What if we went back to the basics? What if we truly believed that God had purpose in all things and that Western civilization's future did not rest on how hard we opposed the other side? Resist,

---

40 American Literature: A Journal of Literary History, Criticism and Bibliography. (Durham: Duke University Press, 1939).

yes, but is your opponent really Satan's new form? Might we not be able to turn down the volume just a touch?

Republicans once believed that God was the author of the original foundation of our nation's promise and all its blessings. And those blessings flowed straight to the individual, not down through the state. Our rule of law was predicated on the belief that power flowed upward in our political system. Our government was set in place to protect this order, and even the power to create laws in the first place was a power in the American system that came from God to man and then was loaned by individual citizens to the state. Our foundational belief as Americans was that power did not flow from government and the top down, but from the bottom up. To really understand American history and the foundation of our republic, one has to understand this. It should make political activity a noble and moral cause about service, and not the self-promotion it too often becomes.

This greater belief about the origin of political power in the American system galvanized people and sparked action. It led to a band of brothers in the form of the Founders coming together of their own volition and free will. Without a formalized federal government and without a formalized Constitution, they pledged their lives, fortunes, and sacred honor in banding together. The power of their beliefs and extraordinary commitment allowed them to join with ordinary citizens of all walks of life to miraculously defeat the most powerful military force in the world at that time.

This in itself was remarkable, but from that starting point they codified the revolutionary thought that all men were created equal and endowed by their creator with certain unalienable rights—life, liberty, and the pursuit of happiness. But the really big kicker was that the individual was to be the sole repository of political power in the American system, and that any government, be it state, local, or federal, had legitimacy only inasmuch as there was consent by the governed.

This storyline, our political lineage, makes our citizenship a most sacred political birthright. Might it not be time to remember that our entire political system is predicated on power far bigger than Washington and our own worldview? If we did, would our political actions contain a touch more humility?

EIGHT: EMBRACE THE POWER THAT COMES WITH DIVERSE BACKGROUNDS AND PERSPECTIVES.

You can't forge politically meaningful solutions for 330 million people if everyone comes from only one perspective in forging those solutions. The first cousin to humility is the ability to embrace the strength and power that come with measured debate and bouncing ideas back and forth. You can't refine ideas and make them better if everyone simply agrees. The term *groupthink* has often been used to describe John F. Kennedy's disastrous invasion at the Bay of Pigs in Cuba. A lot of smart people in the room, all with the same perspective and no real dissent, led to many men dying that day.

That was why I tried to go the extra mile as governor to surround myself with differing opinions and perspectives. I had the state's first African American chief of staff and more minorities in my cabinet than any other in our state's history. I did things like staying in close touch with Lonnie Randolph, then head of the NAACP in our state, not because these actions were helpful politically—South Carolina is a deeply red state—but because I believed it helped us to make better decisions for the millions who made up our state. Colin Powell had always described affirmative action not as set-asides but in being affirmative by trying to include the perspectives of others. I did, and I firmly believe it works.

NINE: TAKE A SERIOUS LOOK AT THE IDEA OF THE REPUBLICAN PARTY AS A BRAND.

To be a good brand, the customer must see consistency in the service or product offered. But let me try one more take on this, given its importance. Americans need some degree of certainty on what the Republican Party stands for if we are to find our way forward. We may find temporary electoral advantage by being better than the Democratic Party on financial or cultural matters, but if there is no consistency on what the Republican brand stands for, any gains and voter commitment will be short-lived.

Our party doesn't have to be perfect. Business partners, fellow church members, and even family let you down. That's life. But you know where they are coming from, and there is nevertheless enough consistency to keep you connected. With the exception of dysfunctional relationships wherein the roller coaster is the attraction, people don't stay attached to causes that vacillate. Consistency is part of what makes it a cause. Can you imagine contributing to the Sierra Club, but then on every third day the club decides they aren't really for land conservation or fighting pollution?

Yet that's where we are. As a nation and as a party. As a party, our inconsistencies in doing what we said we were about had much to do with Trump coming to power. Then he supersized the fissures. Unfortunately, what's happened over the last four years in the party had real implications for our nation. Are we the country of Reagan's "tear down this wall," or are we the nation of Trump's praise for Putin and Kim Jong-Un?

Dorothy's words to Toto upon arriving in the land of Oz, "We're not in Kansas anymore,"[41] fit here, and while the seeds of today's conflicting messages have been around for some time, Trump has exponentially increased them.

The significance of what's occurring here was captured in a column Thomas Friedman wrote years ago entitled "Never Heard That Before."

> "As a political barometer, the Davos World Economic Forum usually offers up some revealing indicators of the global mood, and this year is no exception. I heard a phrase being bandied about here by non-Americans—about the United States—that I can honestly say I've never heard before—political instability. Political instability was a phrase normally reserved for countries like Russia or Iran or Honduras. But now, as an American businessman here remarked

---

41 The Wizard of Oz, directed by Victor Fleming (1939; Hollywood, CA: Metro Goldwyn Mayer).

to me, 'People ask me about political instability in the US We've become unpredictable to the world.'[42]

In the article, he went on to talk about the political risks inherent in dealing with the major issues of the time while under that shadow. Friedman told of some participants asking if the Beijing consensus was replacing the Washington consensus—a phrase that had emerged as a term after the Cold War to mean the free market, free trade, and globalization policies promoted by America. Sadly, our country is still sending conflicting signals on where we are going and what we stand for, and this is not good for the Republican Party, our nation, or even much of the world, because it takes actions based on American signals of where we may go next.

On the other hand, clarity here can be powerful. Consider Hong Kong prior to China taking over a few years ago. It was originally a far-off territory of the British Empire, but it exploded economically because of the way policy leaders embraced the building blocks of certainty and consistency. Hong Kong was recognized as one of the freest economies in the world and was even called "the world's greatest experiment in free market capitalism" by Milton Friedman. The basics of a market economy, a free port, the English rule of law, private property rights, and a transparent tax system were all there, but it was consistency and predictability that really made investment thrive.

Maybe when thinking about American political investment, consistency might be a good place to start?

---

42 Thomas L. Friedman, "Never Heard That Before" *The New York Times*, January 30, 2010.

6

EIGHT THINGS WE CAN
DO FOR THE NATION

I rish poet William Butler Yeats's poem "The Second Coming" was written amid the chaos of World War I, which inspired his description of a world coming apart. With a passionate intensity that fit his times, it seems also to describe forces at play in America today. His prophetic words underscore the importance of each one of us taking active steps to ensure America is still here for our children.

> Things fall apart; the centre cannot hold;
> Mere anarchy is loosed upon the world,
> The blood-dimmed tide is loosed, and everywhere
> The ceremony of innocence is drowned;
> The best lack all conviction, while the worst
> Are full of passionate intensity.
> Surely some revelation is at hand.[43]

43 William Butler Yeats, Richard J. Finneran, ed., The Collected Poems of W. B. Yeats. (Hertfordshire: Wordsworth Editions, 1994).

With Yeats's description of things falling apart in mind, I offer a few suggestions for ways each of us can better our nation.

ONE: CULTIVATE A CULTURE OF TOLERANCE.

Our original settlers came here for religious freedom. They had seen firsthand the horrors of government-mandated religion and wanted something different. And so in a place like Charleston you have not only the second-oldest synagogue in America but churches of similar vintage for Protestants, Catholics, and more. There was room in our culture to hold differing opinions on something as important as one's faith and beliefs in life and an afterlife. Back then, we could live and let live. Today we can't even agree to disagree on something as fundamental as politics.

These issues can't all be solved in the political sphere. It will mean a larger return to faith because inasmuch as love is the core message of the New Testament, intolerance is hard to fit with it. Regardless of one's religious views, part of what made this country was our spiritual foundation. Whether on a penny or a dollar, the words "In God We Trust" meant something more than a declaration of collective beliefs. It represented a faith in powers far bigger than the sum of one's individual hopes, dreams, and fears. It meant there were bigger forces at play to avenge wrongs. There were bigger forces at play than the political debate du jour. And that truth was bigger than an individual's viewpoint.

All of these elements helped in forging the collective humility that de Tocqueville observed in his travels across America in the early 1800s. But we are testing new boundaries today. As president, Trump embraced intolerance and a very casual relationship with truth, and his supporters and detractors alike took signals from his behavior. During a town hall meeting back home at the time of the health-care debate, there was a man near the front row seemingly trying to set new records in being obnoxious. I didn't know him personally but knew him by reputation through friends. At the meeting's conclusion, I went up and introduced myself and politely said that whatever our back-and-forth had been did not fit with how my friends had described him. His reply was fascinating. "If the president of the United States can say anything to anyone on any subject in any tone, why can't I?" He kind of had a point, was all I could think at the time, but using someone else's poor behavior as license for our own is probably not the best way forward. There is a better path forward if we simply think about how we might embrace others and their ideas, and as well as what we say and how we say it.

TWO: ARTICULATE A CLEAR NATIONAL VISION.

This is what a good constitution does. Our is good, but the question lies in whether we hold on to it. The preamble of our Constitution says that it was formed "in order to form a more perfect Union, establish justice, insure domestic tranquility, provide for the common defense, promote the general welfare, and secure the blessings of liberty."[44] Each of these things is foundational to individual lib-

---

44 U.S Constitution. pmbl.

erty because the pursuit of happiness is different for each one of us. There is no collective idea of happiness. One man's heaven is another man's hell. Some love reading and sitting by the fire others love roaming the outdoors. All of this makes it that much more important we keep in place the safeguards fundamental to liberty that are detailed in the Constitution and made stronger by the institutions and traditions that have protected it over the years.

There are two important components to maintaining a national vision. One is through the institutions we are blessed with, and here the executive branch is paramount. Unlike Congress, which has 535 members who all consider themselves captains of the ship, the executive branch speaks with one voice, not the cacophony of differing voices that make up most legislative bodies. It's incumbent upon each one of us to insist that the White House does not play to our fears but points to what it sees as true north, just as Kennedy and Reagan did so eloquently. We should insist the person with the highest pulpit uses it…hopefully wisely.

Two, we ourselves should keep pushing toward what we see as true north. The Bible says, "Where there is no vision, the people perish."[45] That is true in any human enterprise. If you are not aiming somewhere, then any road will take you there. The importance of our Constitution is that it gives us a road map, but we must stay refreshed in reviewing that map, and insist on leaders who will consistently point to the course it prescribes. As governor, I clashed with the head of Senate Finance, Hugh Leatherman. Initially I tried going to his office and paying due respect; then we tried

45 Proverbs 29:18.

140

meetings and social events—but none of it worked. I could have had ten thousand meetings with him, and it would not have made a difference. At the end of the day, we just wanted to go in different directions.

Have a vision. Work to maintain it. Hold it dear. It's part of the puzzle in restoring our country.

THREE: RETURN TO SUSTAINABLE SPENDING.

Not only does liberty need structural safeguards like those found in the Constitution, but it also needs financial safeguards. The Founders were deliberate about limiting federal financial dealings because they had studied the ways in which financial whim was a threat to a republic and the liberty it was meant to protect. Limited government is important because unlimited government doesn't last. There are no exceptions here. Limited government is important because countries without limits are often most threatened from within.

With the exception of the Civil War, every threat to our country's existence has rested in some form of external challenge—what were the Japanese, the Germans, the Russians, or some other group going to do to us? Yet in relative terms, external threats are among the easier problems in life to deal with. The really difficult challenges are internal, and this is true for individuals just as it is for families, businesses, and governments. This reality makes all the more chilling Karl Marx's belief that democracies fail, and would always fail, under their own weight rather than challenge from the outside. Herb Stein, chairman of the Council of Economic Advisers under presidents Nixon and Ford, once made the profoundly logical observation that "if something cannot go on forever, it will stop."[46] Most of us recognize that unsustainable things come to an end, yet for some reason very few in politics are willing to act on this basic premise. All of this makes limited government, and the sustainability that comes with that limitation, all the more important today.

An interesting example of the linkage between military and economic supremacy lies in Paul Kennedy's exploration of British wartime expenditures and revenue in his book *The Rise and Fall of Great Powers*. Between 1688 and 1815, Britain spent £2,293,483,437 on wartime expenditures. During the same time, governmental income was £1,622,924,377. The balance was made up of loans that represented about a third of all Britain spent. Kennedy argued that Britain's financial strength was the most decisive factor in her victories over France during the eighteenth century. Britain's financial strength enabled it to borrow and consequently do things militarily that would have been impossible without it.

But like all things, borrowing has its limits. Any nation can be crippled when it gets too far ahead of itself on spending. In our case, other countries have a degree of influence in what America does next in ways that would have never been possible without America falling into the role of the biggest borrower on earth.

Probably the best recent example of this vulnerability occurred to the British during the Suez Crisis of 1956. In that year, Egypt nationalized the Suez Canal. Britain organized its retaking with Israel and France, and consequently Britain supported Israel's invasion of

---

46 A Symposium on the 40th Anniversary of the Joint Economic Committee: Hearings Before the Joint Economic Committee, Congress of the United States, Ninety-ninth Congress, First Session, January 16 And 17, 1986. (Washington: U.S. G.P.O, 1986).

the Sinai. As British and French forces engaged militarily, President Eisenhower disapproved. Unfortunately for England, although it still had a capable military, it relied on America financially. It specifically needed America's help to maintain the value of the British pound. It also needed oil, which the Suez Crisis stopped from flowing. But instead Eisenhower instructed his Treasury Secretary, George Humphrey, to sell the pound, which would in turn harm the British economy, given its heavy debt load. Eisenhower also throttled American oil sales with the intention of throttling their military action. These things forced British action. Consequently, some consider this event to mark the end of the British Empire. Most telling was that it came not at the hands of an enemy but of its closest ally, the United States. In the same way Britain was dependent on America, America has now become dependent on other countries to finance its spending. Winston Churchill's foreign policy aide years later told US Secretary of State John Foster Dulles, "The British action at Suez was the last gasp of a declining power... Perhaps in two hundred years, the United States will know how we felt."

If we could only be so lucky. Unfortunately we don't have two hundred years.

FOUR: FOLLOW FEDERALISM.

Another part of preserving liberty and sustaining the government we have rests in federalism. Federalism is critical, not just in limiting and sustaining government but in forging government solutions for problems. We have different levels of government for tackling different problems. Local government shouldn't handle national defense, and the federal government shouldn't handle picking up the garbage each week in front of your house. Unfortunately, this is not what always happens. Our federal government is increasingly usurping local power.

As in my previous example of an aircraft carrier, without defined roles, government functions would be overlapping, missing elements, or inefficient. In our various levels of government today, no one seems quite sure of their role, so many do too much or not enough. The situation is to our detriment, both as taxpayers and government customers, and it's the basis of a fair bit of today's financial chaos in government spending.

As an example of the danger of the blurry lines between state and local government and our federal government in Washington, each year the Department of Defense gives away billions in surplus material to other federal, state, and local government agencies. I fought this program both in Congress and as governor, because from an accounting standpoint alone it overstates the cost of the federal government and understates the cost of local government. But accounting is the least of the issues involved. Local sheriffs end up with all sorts of equipment that is improperly valued—do you really value free stuff? And it also encourages the militarization of local law enforcement. Do small town forces really need an armored personnel carrier?

The origins of the program behind giving away helicopters and other things made a lot of sense seventy years ago, because in the wake of World War II we had all kinds of surplus military equipment that needed to be disposed of. But the war is now long past, and we see yet another illustration of Ronald Reagan's idea that the closest thing to eternal life is a government program. The program has grown as we give away more and more each year. By the Department of Defense's own estimates, they give away a few hundred million a year through this program, but this assumes a helicopter is worth $1. If it's worth more, you can do the math on how official estimates obscure the real cost of the program.

To give you an idea of scale, the Law Enforcement Support Program takes five thousand orders a day, and in that process gives away all the things local law enforcement agencies really don't need, like aircraft and helicopters or machine guns and grenade launchers. It also gives away new stuff that ranges from wristwatches to lubricating oil. All these things have a market value and could be sold at open auction, and consequently these funds could be used by the Department of Defense for procurement or training. At a minimum, if we are to make good decisions in government, they need to be based on reality. Getting a free airplane is not, and as said, the program overstates the cost of defense while understating the expenditures of the receiving government entity.

To give an idea of the kind of excesses that occur, *60 Minutes* did a special a few years ago about a small rural county in central Florida that had been given twenty-three helicopters, an armored personnel carrier, and two King Air airplanes, among other things. As it turned out, that county was using those items as a revenue source. They would keep the stuff for a couple of years, and then they would sell it, making millions of dollars for the county.

I remember as governor dropping by to see a sheriff in a rural South Carolina county. I was told he was not in but was out taking helicopter lessons. It happened to be that the county had gotten several helicopters through the program, and while the sheriff's efforts could be attributed to fun, adventure, or a lifelong dream of being able to impress his neighbor by landing a helicopter in their yard, there was no way they could be tied to his county's needs, based on what our state already provided small counties in aviation support through the State Law Enforcement Division.

In other instances, the equipment sat idle. I remember flying into a small county airport in South Carolina and landing next to a number of large air force and navy airplanes and asking the pilot what the trouble was with these planes. He explained the county had accepted them not because they had any use for them—the equipment had been sitting there for years—but because they could not afford *not* to take it since it was free.

One last thought on the practical application of federalism. There is a movement today to further federalize local police actions. This is a mistake. Washington does not need to set all standards, and doing so sure doesn't fit with local control and self-determination.

For example, when I was last in Congress, there was a measure to expand federal criminal laws against harming or attempting to harm police officers. It passed, but I was one of ten Republicans to vote against it because the bill's details ran counter to the larger concept of our alleged belief in federalism. In this regard the details are instructive. Like most everyone, I agree with strict punishments for those who would harm or kill police officers. On that basis alone, I would have liked to support this bill, but it codified beliefs about federal power that weakened local power, and for that reason I voted against it.

There were already very strict laws on the books, both at the federal level and in all fifty states, designed to prevent harm to officers. This bill would have done nothing to meaningfully improve law enforcement safety or achieve greater levels of justice. But the bill's scope furthered the dangerous federalization of criminal law and, by including state and local law enforcement, breached the Tenth Amendment's exclusive reservation to states of the authority and responsibility to prosecute offenses against their officers. And by allowing the federal government to supplant the local understanding and administration of justice, it would allow someone to be prosecuted twice for the same crime, as the bill specifically allowed for federal prosecutions even when a verdict had already been handed down in a state prosecution. Finally, by creating a separate crime for offenses against law enforcement, the bill violated the Constitution's guarantee of equal protection by giving police officers greater protection under the law than was afforded people in other lines of work.

Here is what's interesting, though. Amazingly few in Congress would even have looked at the bill's exacting details. A quick poll would have shown that it was seen as pro–law enforcement and therefore a good thing. But if we are going to save our nation, we all need to look a bit deeper at our legislative actions and evaluate them in light of the importance of federalism.

FIVE: PROTECT PRIVATE PROPERTY RIGHTS.

Collectivism doesn't work. We all know it, but our politics are driven toward it these days.

Reality is you don't cut your neighbor's grass, and he or she doesn't cut yours. You attend to your own things better than others who have no stake in them, and in a communal setting frugality is punished and spending is rewarded. Every one of us has been to that group dinner at a restaurant where the person organizing it yells across the table, "Go ahead and order, and we'll just split it evenly when we get the check." If you order the hamburger basket and water while the guy beside you orders lobster and wine, you become the dinner-table philanthropist. If you do it often enough, you might legitimately become irritated that no one else showed the restraint that you did in placing your order. So what do you do after a few of these dinners? You probably order just a bit more because you've now learned the lesson of collective purchases.

Collective purchases are another part of what makes government inefficient. In the formula within government, thrift is punished. The dollar you save accrues to the benefit of others while the extra dollar you spend only costs you a small portion of the whole. Proof of this comes in the last month of yearly spending in government budgets where "Use it or lose it" is the rule.

Private property rights incentivize the decisions vital to a civilization's well-being, whereas collectivism pulls us in the other direction. Yet that is where today's legislation is taking us. The progressive wing of the Democratic Party is hardly moving us away from collectivism, and even on the right, not so long ago President Trump was dictating the deal points of Carrier Air Conditioning's next move and threatening the likes of Ford and GM. A few years before that, President Obama was attempting by executive order to define a ditch on family farms as navigable waters of the United States. President Biden is now joining Trump in redefining the role of landlord. All these things point to the ways in which property rights are under assault. This right—mine is mine and I'll watch out for it—is a basic tenet of conservatism and fundamental to what made our country great.

One of the Ten Commandments is that we should not steal, and this same principle was also applied to the last clause of our Fifth Amendment, which reads, "Nor shall private property be taken for public use without just compensation."[47] A great example when I was governor was an idea we called the Conservation Bank. State senator Chip Campsen authored it, and we gave it vital support. If South Carolinians wanted open space, rather than taking it by regulatory edict or governmental eminent domain, paying for it was reasonable. The Conservation Bank was instrumental in protecting over 254,000 acres in my home state, more land than any other administration in South Carolina history had set aside for conservation. It proved to be a win-win, applauded by both the Sierra Club and private property rights organizations.

This is the kind of straightforward thinking we need at the federal level when it comes to private property rights. Private property rights have always been key to unleashing initiative. If there is no personal benefit because of your effort, then why bother making the effort? And we often store the fruits of those efforts as physical or intellectual property.

With private property comes the right to use and transfer, and the right to any income from the property you own. I think the stimulus packages of Obama, Trump, and Biden have challenged

---

47 U.S Constitution. amend. V

this notion, and it was also threatened in 2005 with the *Kelo* decision, a 5–4 Supreme Court decision that held that the Town of New London, Connecticut, could condemn property to aid in economic development. It meant government could take your home and give it to another developer because doing so would create jobs and more tax base. The decision was met with outrage, and some states— including South Carolina while I was governor—passed laws to prevent this action. And yet when this same principle was broken to advance stimulus packages, officeholders managed to look the other way. Real ownership means not just upside but downside too. Collectivism is the dreamy world of unlimited upside with no theoretical downside. It's kind of like heaven—without the dying part.

In the case of Chrysler, one of the Obama auto bailouts during the economic storm that started in 2008, officeholders again looked the other way. It was an assault on both private property rights and the rule of law, and underscored how important it is that we stand firmly for the building block of limited government.

It's worth digging a little deeper. Let's assume that in 2008 there really was systemic risk to the financial system and that all those bailouts were justified. Earlier that year Obama had said to UAW members, "I stand with you." He went on to ask them to stand with him in the election. They did, and all too soon he was returning the favor, at significant cost to a few of the principles that made our country great. In the Chrysler deal, standing with the UAW meant standing against private property rights and the rule of law. Obama's kind of thinking is lethal for our country's economic system over time.

The ordering of debt in business works the same way it would on your home. In buying your home, if you take out a mortgage with the local bank, that bank is in the first lien position. If you subsequently needed more money and went to a second bank to add more debt to your home, they would do so understanding that they are in the second lien position. In financial terms, this position is riskier because if you defaulted, they wouldn't get paid until after the first bank's loan had been repaid. If there was still more equity in your home, hypothetically you could go and get a third mortgage from yet another bank. This third lienholder position would be viewed as still more risky, since in the event you defaulted, banks one and two would need to be repaid before bank three could get a dime. So the mortgage in the third position would command a higher interest rate because of the greater risk of being third in the financial pecking order.

For two hundred years everyone has understood this system and the risks entailed in the different lienholder positions. Private property rights mean that there are rules to the game. We know them and can order our priorities and finances accordingly.

What was remarkable about the Chrysler decision was the way in which Obama literally and figuratively said that he did not stand for the differing lienholder positions and the private property rights and rule of law principles they embody. In this case, the banks in the first lien position—the most protected spot based on the rules of the game that came with private property rights—got about thirty cents on the dollar while the UAW—which was in the fourth and bottom unsecured position—got nearly full recovery value for their $10.6 billion retiree and health care claims.

Fortunately, many of the independent investors who didn't have a government gun pointed to their head did balk. The reasoning of these holdouts was expressed by Oppenheimer Funds, which said the government "unfairly asked our fund shareholders to make financial sacrifices greater than those being made by unsecured creditors."

What this meant in plain English was that the Obama administration was breaking America's two-hundred-year commitment to the rule of law and private property rights. Sadly, this sort of government power has grown to be the tolerated rule rather than the exception. But it really got me ginned up as governor, even though I wasn't in Washington, where I might have had some effect on what was transpiring.

Things like this are a horrifying departure from two vital keys to our society's ability to build wealth and two of the most basic principles that made this country great. It's also a reminder of why we need to insist on private property rights. What's yours should be yours, and private property rights mean the whims of government can't take it away.

SIX: TRUST TRADE, NOT TARIFFS.

A bias toward free trade has made America the economic envy of the world. After World War II, our country set up a trading system designed to lower tariffs and facilitate trade, and it worked. This was a major contributor to our economic climb, and the numbers are staggering. World GDP per capita is about $18,000, but ours is almost four times that at $65,000.

America's standing has been sliding from historically being about 30 percent of the world's economy. We still take in about 24 percent of the world's income, but we account for only 4.25 percent of the world's population.

There are many more statistics to back trade's worth to Americans, but unfortunately, both Democrats and Republicans have been moving away from the trading system that had so much to do with our enviable financial position and way of life. The trade union base within the Democratic Party always saw it as competition, so the party has been tepid on the issue, but Republicans have historically supported free trade both for ideological and economic reasons. This went out the door in the age of Trump. If Republicans no longer advocate for free trade, who will? We are at a major fork in the road, and I think it's past time for the party to reembrace where it once stood on trade.

A bit of background. Republicans' original belief on the issue was not about economics. It was about that which has always driven conservative thought—personal freedom. For a conservative, there is always the recognition of two choices in a decision that lies ahead: one that allows for more freedom and one that allows the government to make the decision for you. It was never that free trade was a perfect ideal, but it was far better than a government-made decision that crowded out the ability of an individual business to make its own choices.

Think about it this way. In the open marketplace of commerce, you are free to walk into or out of a store of your choice. If you don't like a product you bought from Amazon, you send it back. These are all free choices that are collectively made by billions of people around the world. The thing that connects the world to allow all those choices is what we call free trade. On the other hand, the government certainly has the capacity to obtain for you any of the same goods or services. But providing them takes taxing the citizens to pay for them, and those taxes are compulsory. Don't pay them, and you win a trip to jail. Conservatives' long-held belief was that although certain parts of trade always needed to be controlled by the government to make the playing field as fair as possible, at the end of the day it was worth being biased in the direction of open markets and free trade because individual choices are always better than government edicts.

It needs to be remembered that a tariff is also a tax, and the tariff increases over the last four years have the capacity to wash away all the good Republicans proclaim was done for the economy in tax reduction and regulatory reform.

Conservatives traditionally had some common-sense reasons to be biased toward free trade.

John Donne in 1624 noted that "no man is an island." The concept is a simple one. We all connect—and trade reflects that connectivity.

Isaac Newton's law that every action has an equal and opposite reaction also plays into the issue. At the neighborhood bar, if you get hit, there's a good chance you're going to try to hit back. If you make your markets more open, another country might or might not do the same. But if you raise your barriers with tariffs or blockades, they are most certain to follow suit. We have seen this play out with the trade tariffs that the Trump administration enacted over the last few years. But trade barriers are hardly a formula for growth. If they were, countries like Argentina, Gabon, and Chad would be thriving. They are not, and the operative political question is, how can America avoid a race to the bottom in trade?

David Ricardo in 1817 developed the theory of comparative advantage. It's the main reason we don't all have vegetable gardens in the backyard. A farmer can specialize in growing crops while I specialize in being a great fisherman and while the neighbor down the street specializes in being a banker. By not doing everything and instead focusing on what you can do best, you gain more than you would by diluting your efforts in being so-so at a lot of things. It's the aircraft carrier thing again. Countries and states fit this mold as well. Hawaii is awesome for growing pineapples. Kansas not so much, but it's great for wheat.

If you combine these three concepts, you get an overwhelming reason to keep the bias we've had in the American system toward more in the way of trade rather than less.

But free trade is under assault these days. Over the last four years we have been moving quickly in the wrong direction. Though one event doesn't make that big a difference, trends do, and the trend is toward more in the way of trade tariffs and less in the way of free trade.

It started with tariffs on softwood imports from Canada. It grew to tariffs on washing machines and solar panel imports. Then it expanded to tariffs on steel and aluminum, and here the Trump administration used a section of the law meant for national security concerns. How Canada, one of our longest and staunchest allies, could be viewed as a national security threat was particularly curious, as was the math in that tariff, given that about 50 percent of our own domestically produced steel was being sold to Canada.

The European Union then introduced retaliatory tariffs on 348 American products.

Canada similarly introduced retaliatory tariffs on 135 product categories. This included manufacturers like Zodiac Boats in Summerville, South Carolina, where 25 percent of their sales went to Canada.

Mexico introduced retaliatory tariffs on 145 product categories.

And this was just the blowback from our allies.

With China, things became more heated, but there were limits to what they could do given all they exported to the United States relative to what we exported to them. We announced tariffs of roughly $50 billion on Chinese imports. They retaliated with $3 billion in tariffs based on the steel and aluminum tariffs that we had imposed. By that April, we retaliated to their increase by introducing more tariffs, on 128 products totaling $3 billion. In June, we announced an additional $34 billion in tariffs on China and $14 billion in tariffs without an implementation date. China announced a retaliatory tariff on 659 US products worth $50 billion.

This tit for tat is the way escalating tariffs go. It's like the movie *War Games* from years ago where the closing line was, "The only way to win the war is to stay out of the war." When one party hits, the other hits back.

This was what happened at the onset of the Great Depression as well. Congress passed the Smoot-Hawley Act, increasing tariffs on imports to the highest levels in one hundred years. Not surprising, other countries responded in kind, and over the next four years world trade decreased by 66 percent. By 1934, Congress recognized its inability to manage this process and reversed course, passing legislation granting

President Roosevelt the authority to negotiate lower tariffs with other countries. Since then, every president has been granted authority to negotiate trade agreements specifically aimed at lowering tariffs and opening markets for American products. Congress saw its inability to contain trade frictions, and wisely vested negotiating authority in the presidency. Can you imagine anything worse than having to negotiate with 535 members of Congress for every trade deal? Everyone would want something, and about the time you made your way through the list, random members would want something new or different.

A negotiation dies a death of a thousand cuts when multiple interest groups want to add or subtract from it. As governor, I saw firsthand the importance of vesting negotiating authority in one person. Get your best deal, and then a legislative body or Congress may vote it up or down. That is a reasonable system.

As I see it, there are currently three big threats on the trade front.

The first is increasing rhetoric against trade. The person you can't see is often the person blamed in politics, but Trump took this to a new level as he claimed outsiders of all sorts were the problem. If nationalism now means isolation and turning inward as a country, you don't want it. It's not what marked our Greatest Generation, nor what made this country great. They looked out and with confidence believed that they, and America as a country, could thrive and succeed in competition.

Second, Republicans aren't leading. Republicans once had a very solid tradition in flying the mantle of free trade and engagement. Former president Trump was the first Republican in modern history to come out as definitively as he did against trade and trading agreements when he misused Section 232 to unilaterally impose tariffs. That might make for great politics, but it will make for bad economics. The BMW automobiles manufactured in my home state don't stay in South Carolina any more than the Boeing jets produced in Charleston do.

Finally, while it's one thing to recognize one's own inability to do something and vest in someone else the responsibility for doing it, it's another to just let that someone else simply take something. This is what Congress is now doing in quietly ceding authority to the executive branch. Only Congress can raise taxes, and tariffs are just a fancy word for taxes imposed at a country's border. The Constitution clearly vests Congress with the responsibility to impose tariffs, but what's happened on so many thorny issues over the years is that Congress has punted and let the administration run with the ball. Even before the granting legislation had been enacted, modern history was filled with examples of the executive branch imposing tariffs without Congress's approval or even a congressional debate.

This happened in 1971 when President Nixon imposed a 10 percent tariff, citing the Korean War. The catch was he did it under a 1917 law allowing presidents to restrict trade during times of war. Somehow lost were little details like the fact that the war was never officially declared, and that war effort had ended almost twenty years earlier. President George W. Bush similarly imposed tariffs on steel imports in 2002 under Section 201 of the Trade Act of 1974 and very broadly interpreted the bill's definition of unfair trade practices.

Congress could have made noise on these things, but they didn't. And over the years, no matter whether the White House was occupied by a Democrat or a Republican, the role of Congress in deciding tariffs has been eroded. Too much power and authority have gone from the legislative branch over to the executive branch.

Congress shouldn't have to assert its constitutional authority, but that is now the case. It's time to turn these things around.

SEVEN: REMEMBER THAT EACH BRANCH OF LIBERTY MATTERS. AND YOU CAN'T HAVE REAL LIBERTY WITHOUT CIVIL LIBERTY.

People have become cavalier about this component of freedom. Yet in the same way that a house can't stand without its foundation, liberty can't stand without maintaining civil liberty and the right of citizens to their constitutional privacy. But I still hear all the time, "What do I care? I have nothing to hide. What does it matter if the government snoops on my phone?" I understand that most people are law-abiding citizens. But this is a matter of principle. And of the Constitution. The Founders had strong feelings about this issue, and accordingly they included the Fourth Amendment in our Bill of Rights. It's really clear. "The right of the people to be secure in their persons, houses, papers, and effects, against unreasonable searches and seizures, shall not be violated, and no Warrants shall issue but upon probable cause, supported by oath or affirmation, and particularly describing the place to be searched, and the persons or things to be seized."[48]

The Founders were remarkably deliberate and specific in this amendment meant to limit the reach of government. Without probable cause and a warrant, government couldn't violate your privacy or your personal effects. Government's ability to do so has been made much easier in the digital age, but the Founders believed there were

48 US Constitution. amend. IV

places that government couldn't and shouldn't go without a warrant. This belief was based on their personal experiences in colonial times of British officers coming into a home and searching until they found something to charge the patriots with. The principle of this constitutionally enshrined limit on government should be just as real today as it was then. I believe that civil liberty is a cornerstone to the bundle of rights that go with the liberties our Founders promised.

This is relevant in a fight we had in Congress on the reauthorization of Section 702 of the Foreign Intelligence Surveillance Act (FISA). Led by Justin Amash, a tireless advocate and leader on civil liberties—and a person Trump also pushed from office—a group of us tried to trim its sails. Our amendment would still have allowed the intelligence community to do its job and conduct foreign surveillance, and in no way prohibited the interception of information on non-US citizens. It would not have interrupted the first basket of information-gathering that would have included Americans, and in that regard it represented a compromise. But it prevented intelligence agencies from accessing without a warrant any of the information caught up in their data sweeps if the person was a US citizen.

Currently, FISA allows intelligence agencies to collect the electronic communications of foreign persons. However, not all the electronic communications being collected belong to foreigners. With little oversight, this data on American citizens can be searched without a warrant and used for a wide range of purposes, including domestic criminal prosecutions that are completely unrelated to foreign intelligence.

According to a *Washington Post* report at the time of our debate in Congress, 90 percent of people whose communications were collected were not the intended targets, many of them American. Nearly half of the surveillance files contained names, email addresses, or other details that the NSA marked as belonging to Americans.[49] Even more important was the fact that we had no clue how many Americans were caught up in this surveillance activity. Far worse, the intelligence community routinely refused to provide the American public with this information.

Oversight of a major program with clear civil liberties implications is impossible without some change demanded by all of us, and at a minimum this is what we were asking for with our amendment. We didn't get even this, and again, most members just didn't care.

I won't get further in the weeds here, but George Orwell's book *1984* described the Big Brother power of government, and Big Brother is now here. The revolution that has taken place with tech, artificial intelligence, and data now strengthens the government's hand in oversight at a level that would have been unimaginable to the Founders. The question now is, are we willing to do anything about it? Because though there has always been tension between security and freedom in any open government system, those who have leaned too much toward security have over time lost both security and freedom.

EIGHT: WE MUST MANAGE OUR MONEY.

It is important, even vital, for our government to manage the country's money wisely, because for civilizations to be sustainable, they have to do sustainable things. No surprise there.

---

49 Barton Gellman, Julie Tate, Ashkan Soltani, "In NSA-intercepted data, those not targeted far outnumber the foreigners who are" *The Washington Post*, July 5, 2014.

Printing money is not sustainable. Across the pages of history, it has never worked. It is no road to riches for a country.

Money is one of the pillars of sustaining any institution. Keep it coming, and the institution lives. Kill the money, and it dies. When you discredit or devalue currency, you ultimately discredit or devalue the government that calls it legal tender.

Ranking right up there with adherence to our Constitution, the importance of our institutions, and the rule of law is the question of whether our spending is sustainable. It drives what happens to the value of the money people earn, save, and hold. It matters as much in preserving our country and our way of life as the other building blocks to liberty and self-governance.

Given what our government and central bank have done with money lately, we are headed for uncertain times. If people's savings evaporate, history promises liberty will be threatened. Money doesn't come in red or blue varieties. Whether you are Republican or Democrat won't matter one iota if things go wrong.

Let's look for a moment at money.

Through the ages it has had two primary functions: as a store of value and means of exchange. The workings of a capitalist society rest on people being able to exchange something that represents worth and to know that same worth will be there the next day. If not, the whole system breaks down. The lawyer is stuck growing his own vegetables or finding the one farmer who needs his services on a given day. Bartering each day for goods and services is not only inefficient in terms of time but also often a fruitless effort. The farmer may not ever need the lawyer. There might not even be any farmers where the lawyer lives.

Money has many values beyond facilitating trade and commerce. What if you could only hold your worth in cows? Never mind the difficulty in getting them to and from your points of purchase, what would you do as a city dweller about keeping them? Along with being a store of value, money is also a marking point on the value of all assets. Does it take three cows to buy a hut or four? You used to work two years for a cow, now you have to work three. Money recalibrates everything.

Which brings us to the danger of what the government and the Federal Reserve are now doing. They are playing with our worth and our relative worth. It's wrong. When they deflate the value of money, they deflate the value of your time and even your life. Think about it. Really think about it. If government changes the value of that which we exchange for our work, they change the value of your time on earth. That's a very big deal.

People—and young people in particular—should be embracing this tenet of conservative philosophy rather than math that doesn't add up from people like Andrew Yang. They should be petitioning Washington on a massive scale to defend their futures and their worth, but instead, things are dead quiet. I suspect it will remain so until it is too late. And that won't be long in coming, I fear.

But let's go back to the most disturbing fact—that if you change a person's worth, you change their life. What occurs here makes this a call with moral and spiritual dimensions that go well beyond the capacity or purview of anyone I encountered in my years in politics. It's a decision Janet Yellen, Ben Bernanke, Chuck Schumer, Joe Biden, or Donald Trump were ill equipped even to contemplate making. No one in government should ever be given the power to change our worth, no matter the supposed greater good of making the wheels of an economy run. Our government is run by astoundingly ordinary people who are driven by the same hopes, fears, and ambitions that have always driven mankind. And that should frighten every one of us. It should make us want to be extra judicious in constraining government's powers.

This is the case not only because of government's human construct but also because of its size and its ability to coerce. I love Oreo cookies, but whether I chomp down five or ten isn't going to change my life, and the company I work for can't put me in jail if I splurge and eat eleven. Each day there are millions of conversations from Democrats fearful of Republican intentions and Republicans fearful of Democrats' intentions regarding the way their political actions could be a threat to freedom or our way of life. Talk radio, newspaper headlines, and TV all report on anyone and everyone perceived as a threat. And yet there is total silence on what our government is doing to the value of our worth and work. All that we have saved, and our sweat and toil over the years are at stake, with only crickets chirping politically. It's remarkable, and collectively we are idiots if we don't rise up and do something about what is sure to decimate our lives here.

Sadly, the government's diminishing of our personal worth is not the only problem. Washington's present course also diminishes our relative worth—the haves versus the have-nots. This breeds the very populism that brought Trump to power, and ultimately is even more destabilizing to a political system than the erosion of wealth and savings. Envy is potent in politics. If we are all poor together, it's okay. Look at many countries around the world and you find people surprisingly content in tough situations. But if I get poorer as you get richer, now we have a real problem. It's amazing that people like Bernie Sanders talk as much as they do about income inequality but not about its cause. It is in large measure government-sponsored income inequality. Last year, between the federal government and the Federal Reserve, there was about $7 trillion in stimulus to the economy. The money didn't stay in Washington. It went out and bid up the value of assets. Jeff Bezos and Mark Cuban got much richer. If you had stuff, your stuff became worth more, if you didn't, you effectively fell in worth relative to those who did. Next there will be all sorts of governmental measures designed to combat what the government itself is doing in income inequality, when in fact the government just needs to begin by treating money as money—as a store of value that should be held constant as a reliable means of exchange.

"Leave me the hell alone!" should be our scream at government's appetite for more, but only time will tell whether people wake up to this real threat to our republic, our finances, and our way of life.

I OFFER A FINAL THOUGHT HERE.

In closing out these thoughts on how we might make our nation better, I go back to the Latin phrase *e pluribus unum*—from the many, one. This was indeed the Founders' vision. As Americans, lately we have lost sight of that. We are not in a world war, and in not having to face and confront an outside enemy, we have created enemies in each other. We need to go back to the fundamental principles that brought us together as Americans and the philosophy behind Kennedy's famous "Ask not what your country can do for you; ask what you can do for your country."[50]

One of my favorite stories in this vein occurred in my first stint in Congress as we voted on whether to increase congressional committee funding by 14.5 percent. Several of us believed it represented going back on our word, as we had previously cut committee funding by a full third in living up to our pledge in the Contract with America. On the various whip checks that preceded the vote, a rat pack of eleven junior Republican members, including myself, held consistent in saying not only would we vote against the measure, but we would also vote against "the rule" in attempting to derail it. The so-called rule is a big deal in Washington. It is the mechanism by which the majority party controls the House floor and sets the boundaries for how debate is conducted on the issue at hand. Even if one is planning on voting against a measure that will be debated, for the most part there are complete party-line votes on the rules themselves, with the result that the party in power retains its hold on the House floor.

That afternoon the eleven of us found ourselves in a room just off the House floor that looked down on the Mall. We were being cajoled and lectured to by various House leaders, and different forms of political pressure were applied in attempts to get us back on board. Since there's no physical escape from these sessions, your mind can wander as a way of escape, and I remember thinking about where we sat and the history of every room in the Capitol. I imagined the historic discussions that had preceded us maybe fifty or one hundred years before. I studied the room's stately decor and

---

50 John Fitzgerald Kennedy, "Ask Not What Your Country Can Do for You" (Inauguration Address, Washington D.C, January 20, 1961).

regal moldings. I soaked in the early-evening light and its color in looking out the window and down the Mall to the Washington Monument in the distance. The cajoling went on for hours, but next thing I knew, they called the vote.

As a last plea before we left for the House Chamber, House Majority Leader Dick Armey asked us for our votes. He said, "I've never asked you for one before, but I'm asking for this one." Mark Neumann of Wisconsin was now looking out that same window into the fading light and a darkening sky over the Mall. Mark turned back to Armey and said that of all the members of leadership we might change our vote for, he suspected the group would give our votes to him, but this was a matter of principle, and so he doubted we would. Armey said, "Think about it. We're holding the vote open for another ten minutes," and left. No one said anything, and a few minutes passed. It felt like much longer. Finally, Tom Coburn and a few others rose and headed for the door. Staffers lined our hundred-foot single-file walk to the House floor, and I remember wondering how many people would really vote no once they got inside. I voted no, guaranteeing that the floor would soon be less than hospitable territory, so I turned and left the chamber. Several others did the same, and we walked back to Lindsey Graham's office, where we saw on C-SPAN that, to our surprise, we had defeated the rule.

Moments later our pagers were going off, and we were summoned to a mandatory caucus meeting in room HC-5. Speaker Gingrich was steaming mad, and the first thing the older member sitting next to me said was, "In the eight years I've been here, I've never heard of a mandatory conference meeting based on a vote." I was now thinking this was not going to be good, and I was

quickly proved correct. The Speaker announced that the eleven ge-
niuses who thought they knew more than the rest of the Republican
Conference were going to come up and explain their votes. The guy
beside me now was getting agitated and said, "I've never heard
of anyone having to explain their vote before the membership."
I'm now thinking this is going from bad to worse. Then to com-
pound things, the Speaker said, "Those of you who planned to go
to Congressman John Kasich's wedding on Saturday aren't going.
Those who planned vacations with family aren't going. No one is
going anywhere until we get the votes we need to pass the rule."

In not-so-subtle terms, this meant some of us were expected to
change our vote.

I wasn't thrilled about having to go up to the podium, and
mercifully I didn't have to go first. Oklahoma congressman Steve
Largent, an NFL Hall of Fame wide receiver, walked straight up.
Two hundred and thirty Republican members of Congress were
jammed into the room. None were too happy about the prospect of
delayed trips home.

Steve's first words were addressed to Newt Gingrich, not ten
feet away. His tone was matter of fact, even pleasant.

"Mr. Speaker, I'm not intimidated," he said.

The room went dead silent.

Largent continued. "I've been in rooms much smaller than this
one when I was on the opposite side of teammates during a players'
strike against the NFL owners. The guys in the room weighed 280,
320 pounds and not only wanted to kill me, but if they had gotten
hold of me, they probably could have." With a pause and a smile,
he added, "This isn't the case here tonight," then went on, "More

seriously I'm not intimidated because I feel good about this vote and the principle behind it. The Speaker talked tonight about the eleven of us letting the team down. The more significant question, and the question that never gets asked in Washington DC is, whose team are we on? When I was elected to represent the first district of Oklahoma, I wasn't elected to represent just the Republican or Democratic teams but what I thought was in the best interest of the taxpayers back home. If you stop and think about it, the team we're all on is the American team. And if, as a matter of conscience, I believe a vote is in the best interest of the American taxpayer I represent back home, then I just have to vote that way."

As the drama mounted, Largent continued. "I'd say secondly, in Washington, people forget the significance of a person's word. Many of us were elected in 1994, and before that election we signed a document called the Contract with America. One of its pledges was to cut Washington committee funding by one-third. We kept our word and did just that. Yet this proposal would reverse that cut. We owe it to those same folks to whom we pledged our word to either keep it, or to go back to them and say we're new to the business of running government and we need to make a change.

"It's okay to say we cut too much and we need to change our committee staffing numbers, but whatever we do, we shouldn't do what was proposed today, which typified the Washington way of doing business so many of us came here to change—to take credit for cutting by a third and then below the radar quietly add back the spending."

He went from there to tell the story of how during the NFL player strikes, when his best friends chose to strike, he had gone to them and said, "I understand why you're doing this. I'd like to go with you, but I gave my word to the owners that for X number of dollars, I'd play football." He said to the Speaker, "I couldn't go back on my word then, and I'm not going to now."

Lindsey Graham went next and popped the tension in the room as he began with, "Mr. Speaker, I *can* be intimidated." Laughter filled the room for a moment, and although the rest of us took our turns at the podium, Largent's words had already turned the tide. Instead of piling on the pressure as leadership had intended, our peers identified with our position. A compromise was reached by the early morning hours.

Though I was in Congress for votes on war, votes to impeach the president, votes on a lot of weighty issues, I've always remembered that night as a big one for the way it once again reinforced for me how human Congress is as an institution. Courage, independence, and in Steve's case a willingness to lead, completely changed the course of what had been destined to happen that night.

It's my hope and prayer that our country can find more leadership of this shape and flavor, because without it I have grave concerns about what comes next for America. Each one of us must take on the role of Steve Largent. What we expect and demand from Washington and its leaders will determine what comes from them and Washington.

Change is in *our* hands.

7

THIRTEEN THINGS WE
CAN DO FOR OURSELVES

Throughout this book I've consistently tried to make real the fact that liberty is precious and fragile, and that sustaining it requires effort. Freedom has been fought over and debated through the ages. People across this land are increasingly recognizing that we cannot go on as we are and keep what we have. What comes next will be determined by all our actions. And the beauty of freedom is that we get to pick. We get to make our own movie. But built into that freedom of choice is the important question we must confront at any crossroads: Which path do we take?

We will always have a headwind against us in slowing government because because in reality, in the body politic there is only one party—the party of incumbency. He who holds power wants to hang onto it, and that, unfortunately, always favors spending. It's for this reason Jefferson said that the normal course of things was for liberty to yield and for government to gain ground. When I first became governor of South Carolina, a lobbyist in Columbia referred to a certain group of well-heeled businessmen as the "oligarchs." They were quiet and behind the scenes, but she viewed this group as the people who decided much of what would, or wouldn't, be on the legislative agenda for the House or Senate. Over the years I came to see a fair amount of truth to that. We need to understand there is a headwind to slowing government spending that comes from a powerful combination of human nature, government's very structure, and the allure of power for the party in power.

Just as we have at many times in the history of our republic, we now have some very big choices before us. We must ask ourselves, what are we willing to do about them?

I was there to witness the beginnings of the Tea Party phenomenon and saw the way it was fueled by regular people standing up and saying they didn't like the choices being made in American politics. I joined them in believing we needed to begin a journey down a different path. Things had to change then; they still must change now.

In business, big change is marketed by restructuring. In politics you don't want to wait to the point of big change because the political equivalent of a business restructuring is a revolution. If one waits too long, a lot changes fast. Hyperinflation, deflation, or currency collapse are becoming very real threats, and to avoid these horrors, we must act now.

Our country's way forward must begin within each one of us. In life, everything is created twice—once in our minds and then again with our actions. You must decide there is something you want to change in this country, and then commit to doing your part to bring it about. As I have mentioned more than a few times, I believe one of these actions lies in championing conservative ideals and supporting real conservatives. They are fewer and further between than we might like, but there are great conservative people across this country. They are to be found in all walks of life across this great land, and I'm sure there are many who could rise to the level of service I saw in my dear friend Tom Coburn. Similarly at the state and local levels of government, there are heroes like my friend Tom Davis of Beaufort, and I urge you to actively support and encourage them.

There is a lot that you can do to help direct America toward a bright future. Here are twelve things we can all do as we choose a better road ahead.

ONE: VALUE WORK.

On work, as both a value and an action, we have lost our way of late. It's as real an institution and value to be protected as any other in perpetuating the American way, but we have lost sight of this.

Thomas Jefferson said, "Democracy will cease to exist when you take away from those who are willing to work and give to those who would not."[51] Work is vital, and the term "American work ethic" didn't magically appear from the sky. Hard work was part of our country's religious roots. Puritans believed God had worked to create the heavens and the earth and that we were to follow his good example. A work ethic was part of what defined the Greatest Generation, and it had a lot to do with settling the West, winning both world wars, and much more. But honest work is now under assault as never

---

51 Wilson, R. Blake, Don't Tread on Me: An American Patriot's Book of Quotes. (Boulder: West View Press, 2011).

before. Even prior to the latest efforts that came with stimulus bills and enhanced levels of unemployment compensation, social scientists like Charles Murray were alerting people to the dangers of a growing underclass in America that did not embrace the need to work.

It's something we should again take up as a primary American value, and it's incumbent upon every family to teach the value of work. My father probably overdid lessons here, but they have been important in framing not only my own life but also the lessons I wanted to teach our sons. My father was a successful but relatively simple man who grew up in a little town in North Carolina, and the small-town values that had been embedded in him as a boy, he in turn wanted to pass along to me and my siblings. Consequently, we would find ourselves in the summer heat of August at the family farm frantically baling hay before a gathering afternoon thunderstorm. My dad would be driving the baler, my mom the truck. My sister would be flattening bales so that they could work their way up the pop-up bale loader, and my brothers and I would be catching and stacking hay bales in the back of a C50 Chevrolet flatbed truck. As dark-gray clouds approached in the heat of a late August afternoon, my two brothers and I were convinced that our family's livelihood depended on getting every last bale in the truck before that afternoon thunderstorm came. We didn't know it at the time, but it didn't. Each of my siblings could tell a hundred similar stories all tied to our father's ideas on teaching the value of work. My sons could also give their share of stories about moving rocks and dirt at the farm with the same intended lesson.

In my father's efforts there was a deeper principle that he always tried to get at, which was that work in and of itself was good. Work was part of what people were designed to do, and it was critical to one's sense of self-worth. He believed part of life was defined by what you worked on and toward. He believed the person who was handed things at best gave up the pride that would have come in earning those same things, and at worst would grow not to appreciate the efforts of others on his or her behalf.

All this was one reason that in the depths of the Great Depression, FDR created the Civilian Conservation Corps. It was a vehicle for work rather than simply handing out aid. FDR's words then were, "I propose to create a Civilian Conservation Corps to be used in simple work... More important, however, than the material gains will be the moral and spiritual value of such work."[52]

Dr. Martin Luther King Jr. celebrated work as well when he said,

> "We should set out to do work so well that the living, the dead, or the unborn couldn't do it any better. We must see the dignity of all labor. Even if it falls to your lot to be a street sweeper, go on out and sweep streets like Michelangelo painted pictures; sweep streets like Handel and Beethoven composed music; sweep streets like Shakespeare wrote poetry; sweep streets so well that all the host of Heaven and earth will have to pause and say, 'Here lived a great street sweeper who swept his job well.'"[53]

---

52 Franklin D. Roosevelt, "Message to Congress on Unemployment Relief." March 21, 1933. Online by Gerhard Peters and John T. Woolley, The American Presidency Project. http://www.presidency.ucsb.edu/ws/?pid=14596.

53 Martin Luther King Jr., "Facing the Challenge of a New Age" (Holt Street Baptist Church, Montgomery, Alabama, December 3, 1956).

Whether you take the Bible, history, Dr. King, or FDR as your reference point, it's my belief that reembracing the moral and spiritual elements of work would do us good these days, and go far to continue again making America the most creative, prosperous, and abundant country in the world.

TWO: ACTIVELY LOOK FOR WAYS TO ENGAGE IN OUR POLITICAL PROCESS.

Knowledge really is power, and this is particularly the case in politics. Politicians love to keep things general, and usually want to avoid the specifics because the details are things that have the capacity to offend. You should take it upon yourself to know the details of a bill and its history. Go to town hall meetings and county hearings, and be willing to pleasantly confront elected officials. Being informed is the only ammunition against the platitudes you are likely to hear. As governor I was once at a city hall hearing over a ten-acre park I had proposed on land the state was disposing of in the little town of Port Royal, South Carolina. When I pressed the mayor and city hall members on where they stood, their reply was that they, too, wanted a park. But I couldn't get their plan for the park defined. As much as both the one dissenting council vote and I tried to get a commitment on specifics, they kept giving platitudes.

Generalities are a politician's way of weaseling out of saying no or hiding an agenda. Don't accept it. In the park's case, what they weren't saying was that they wanted every inch of that land not as a park but to develop so the city would get more tax base. They just didn't want to admit it. Knowing the why behind certain actions is vital to smoking out the real course being taken in politics. Be an informed citizen.

Be willing to make your voice heard with bigger microphones as well. Fifty people may hear you at a town council meeting; fifty thousand may hear you through a letter to the editor in your local paper.

Write op-eds.

Put a bumper sticker on your car.

Put a political yard sign up in your yard.

Be willing to financially contribute to a political cause, organization, or candidate.

Invest time, energy, and resources to our political process.

In short, have skin in the deal.

Special interests flourish and have a disproportionate voice because so few everyday citizens contribute financially to the political process. If everyone in this country invested one hundred dollars in politics each year, we would drown out those special interests. It is a way to leverage your voice and time.

Above all else, remember it really is the squeaky wheel that gets the grease in the world, and especially in the world of politics. But one slight squeak doesn't get noticed. The political process responds to sustained pressure over time. Onetime shouts don't really register. I have seen repeatedly the futility of short efforts in politics. People too easily get frustrated and move on to other things. Change takes time. It can't be rushed because the political process by its very nature is designed to move slowly. If something is important to you, you must stick to it.

The beauty of businesspeople is that they are used to getting things done, and the curse of businesspeople in politics is that they are used to getting things done. I remember one friend telling me that he had put a solid two months into an effort to impact an issue, but nothing had happened, so he was going on to more productive things. I asked him if he could imagine any of the Founders coming back and reporting to their colleagues that they had tried talking up the patriot cause for two months, nothing had happened, and therefore they were moving on.

Change takes time. Stay involved for the long run!

THREE: BUILD AN ARMY.

There are a lot of forces out there in the cause of many things It is just a matter of finding the one that fits with your interests and the talents you have to offer. If you like advancing ideas, how about the Cato Institute or the Heritage Foundation? If your view is from the left, then how about Brookings? If you like a direct assault on the mountain of big government, there is an endless number of campaigns and political committees that need your help. Define what you want your army to do and what you want to do in it.

There is absolute strength in numbers when confronting the power of government. No one candidate or one team of new contenders in office will normally make a big difference. Solo doesn't work in politics. For all the vim and vigor of *Mr. Smith Goes to Washington*, too often in real life, Washington changes Mr. Smith more than Mr. Smith changes Washington. I have seen many self-proclaimed agents of change do nothing more than change themselves after coming to Washington. I am not talking about their character or love of country but about their approach as a movement. I saw it with the Tea Party, the Perot deficit phenomenon, the Christian Coalition, and many more. They wither over time. The only antidote to this is new blood and the strength that comes with additions to a cause, what the Bible talks about in the strength of a three-cord rope versus a single strand. Go, do, and bring someone with you!

Limiting government must be sustained from the ground up. As Wendel Phillips once said, "Eternal vigilance is the price of liberty."[54]

Right now it's incredibly important that those of us who want less government get organized about asking for less. Many of the strategies employed by those wanting to have more money or influence from government can also be used in the cause of limited government. I think two organizations that stand out in being organized at a grassroots level are the American Israel Public Relations Committee (AIPAC) and the National Rifle Association (NRA). The NRA has certainly gotten bruised lately based on its own hubris at leadership levels, but its grassroots approach to protecting the Second Amendment has always been strong. AIPAC's purpose is to strengthen and sustain America's commitment to Israel. Whether or not you agree with their objectives, you have to admire the ways in which they have been strategic and organized in their approach. Israel receives over $3 billion a year in foreign aid, in no small measure due to AIPAC's influence. The

---

54 Wendell Phillips, Speeches Before the Massachusetts Anti-Slavery Society: January, 1852. (London: Forgotten Books, 2018).

commitment of both these organizations to their respective causes has been phenomenal. They are in it for the long haul.

The conservative movement needs this same level of organization and commitment. It is consistency of voice over time that makes for political change. Too many organizations make great noise for an election cycle or two and then disappear, and with them go their voices.

Let me give you an example of the level of detail needed if the conservative voice is to be heard in your city hall, state capitol building, or in Washington. In my first race for Congress, a woman by the name of Leah Chase showed up and offered help. From the very start of the campaign, she was there as a volunteer and an occasional campaign contributor. Her help was not overwhelming; she volunteered when she could once every few weeks, and her campaign contributions were modest, fifty or one hundred dollars here or there. But because she had been there from the beginning, whenever she called or needed to set up a visit, I made sure to work it out, because in politics you never forget those who were with you from the start. It wasn't until many years later that I learned several politically interested AIPAC members at the Jewish Community Center had divided up efforts in that congressional race. One person had helped with each race. No matter who had won, someone representing AIPAC would have been a part of that winning campaign from day one. This sort of grassroots involvement is incredibly powerful. To this day if Leah phones, I take the call because I consider her a friend and a supporter who was there at the very beginning of my time in politics.

FOUR: WORK TO TAKE OUT A LONGTIME INCUMBENT.

One of the most glaring examples of how people in government lose perspective over time and become disconnected from the views of most Americans came in my first year in Congress. On Monday nights they hold what are called suspension votes. They're typically viewed as noncontroversial items and usually go through without debate.

I had been standing along the back rail on the House floor on one such Monday night when a colleague who happened to be Republican came up to me and asked, "How are you going to vote on the next one?"

I told him I was voting against it. Dumbfounded, he asked, "Why?"

I said, "Because it costs a bunch of money."

He said, "No it doesn't. It doesn't cost anything."

"Yes it does."

"No it doesn't."

This was our back-and-forth until we finally decided to walk down to the clerk's desk and have a look. When we opened to the bill page and saw that it cost $16 million, my colleague's immediate response was, "See, I told you, it doesn't cost anything."

I was new to Congress at the time and still under the impression that $16 million was a lot of money. I replied, "Can you imagine how many neighborhoods or scattered family farms it takes to send $16 million in taxes to Washington?"

From his perspective—and one that is shared by most politicians in Washington—$16 million is no more than a rounding error when measured against a multitrillion-dollar annual budget.

Perspectives change, and this is part of what goes wrong when well-intentioned people who go off to represent some part of America stay too long.

Humans are remarkably adaptable; it's how we survive. People who are thrown into some horrid prisoner of war camp or other survival situation are amazingly adaptable and often survive in settings that at first glance should kill them. Unfortunately, that same adaptation trait is the fatal flaw that comes with too many years in office. People get used to lots of zeros behind every number they deal with, and the number that would have been shocking when they first got to Washington becomes commonplace and doesn't register as a possible problem. This can be very costly for all us taxpayers over the long run. Human nature doesn't change, and so you can't change this reality of politics. The only cure lies in having those who represent us not stay as long.

At so many levels I have seen firsthand the consequences of endless terms and the attendant need for term limits. I am a fan, but I know in the near term their passage is not going to happen. However, working to dislodge longtime incumbents can have the same affect. When I was in Congress, there was reportedly more turnover in the Russian State Duma than in Washington. Much of this is because of spaghetti-string districts that have little to do with representing people and everything to do with protecting incumbency.

Term limits—or working hard to convince those elected that they should voluntarily limit their length in office—represent probably the greatest tools for disrupting today's poisoned political culture. Actual limits, or the feel of limited time in office, would lead to more pioneering in the political process because as mentioned earlier, limits change the risk of any political decision.

In this vein, I got great advice when I first entered Congress from a Californian by the name of Tom Campbell. We had become friends based on our shared concern over Congress's ceding of war powers to the executive branch and seemingly open-ended "peace-keeping" operations at that time in Bosnia. Tom was cerebral and bright, and prior to coming to Congress had taught constitutional law at Stanford University. He had been in the US House before but had left to run for what had appeared an open shot at the Republican nomination for the US Senate in California. It didn't turn out that way, as a small-town mayor by the name of Sonny Bono had gotten into the race. Tom lost, and at the time thought he was forever out of politics. He had many regrets. He told me that in his first term he had made the usual trade-offs associated with climbing the political ladder. If one made the trade-offs on votes, one could get the right subcommittee assignment, then the right committee assignment, then the chairmanship of the committee or a leadership posting, *and then* one could really do good things.

What he came to realize in his time away from politics was that all those little trade-offs could lead you to vote in a way that was exactly what you had run to change. He promised himself that if he ever got back into politics, he would no longer take votes based on where he calculated they might lead but rather take each vote one vote at a time. He would vote in a way that followed the core convictions that had led him to run, and in ways that he thought represented the majority will of those he represented...and then just let the chips fall where they may. It was great advice, which I adopted. It allowed me to sleep soundly, knowing that I might get votes right or wrong based on the limited information I had at the time I cast it, but I did what I thought was right. I believe term limits move officeholders toward Tom Campbell's clarity by knowing they won't be casting votes forever and that they therefore ought to cast them on behalf of those they represent, rather than their perceived lifelong career in politics.

A challenge is good for the political process in our country and makes people explain their reasoning and their votes. Competition improves the public sector just as it does the private sector. Given the electoral tilting in some districts, though, know what you are getting into. If you are supporting a challenger or even mounting a challenge yourself, define your objective. If the district numbers offer little hope, be coldly analytical in defining your objectives. If you don't, you will shoot not to kill and wind up emboldening the current officeholder.

When I first ran for Congress, I was given little chance because I had never so much as run for dog catcher. So I laid out my objectives. I knew just by running I would hold the microphone that comes with a run for public office and that I could have some degree of educational impact locally on the debt and deficit. So we did things like including the no-ghost sign from *Ghostbusters* over the word *deficit* on our bumper stickers, signs, and stationery because we thought it would cause people to talk about it and in turn think more about the issue. I also knew by entering the race I would to some degree shape it because in any open forum or debate other candidates would have to respond to things I said. Last would be winning and actually doing something about the deficit, and though I considered that a stretch, I was willing to live with winning on two out of my three objectives. Turns out we did win, but it underscores the importance of defining what you hope to win in the contest of politics.

I have a good friend in Charleston, Chad Walldorf, who for the last couple of years has been leading an effort to get folks of all ranks to challenge Republicans who serve that role in name only. For nearly twenty years he was running a handful of ribs and bar-beque restaurants, but has now made this idea of joining armies and challenging the status quo a big part of his life's mission. It's worth following his example.

FIVE: ACTIVELY SUPPORT LEADERS AND LEADING IDEAS.

Dr. Martin Luther King Jr. called it "the drum major instinct,"[55] and he was right. All too many of us want to be the one out front and not the one supporting others. But we can't have all chiefs and no Indians and advance liberty. Not wanting to fall into a sup-porting role is even exacerbated by wealth, as many who have the financial capacity to help often focus on their own ideas rather than the ideas of others. It's a rare bird that says, "Let's leave your name out front," but Warren Buffett certainly did it in pledging his fortune to the Gates Foundation. Probably the most selfless person I ever knew on this front was Foster Friess from Wyoming and his creation of Foster's Outriders and his subsequent investment in each of their causes, but it doesn't happen as often as it needs to

---

55 Martin Luther King Jr., "The Drum Major Instinct" (Ebenezer Baptist Church, Atlanta, Georgia, February 4, 1968).

happen to turn our country around. There is a vital role here, and we all need to find ways to invest in people and causes that push the political frontier.

And to do so, you don't have to be a billionaire. Some of the most extraordinary people just showed up to help in campaigns. Their attitude was "Put me in, Coach," and they worked tirelessly. People like Barbara Boyston, Remington Duncan, Marvin Meeks, Joan Peters, Pat Dansberry, Peggy Bangle, and Barbara Bates are but the first of hundreds that come to mind here. And while on this topic, I can never forget my former wife, Jenny, whose unpaid efforts were extraordinary.

When I was in Congress, I was told I should not pioneer new or controversial issues because it was too risky. After an issue has already been debated and is viewed as safe, politicians are like bees on honey, vying for television and radio time to broadcast their views. But what we need is more initial risk-taking in the political process. We need brave new ideas and people willing to advance them. We desperately need new approaches to offset the many things that are pulling us from the self-reliance and independence that made this country great. With the last economic downturn, people were paid to be out of work for a few years—ninety-nine weeks of federal benefit, twenty-six weeks of state, and thirteen weeks of "extended" benefit. In the Great Depression, they were given a shovel and the opportunity to earn their unemployment benefits. Though we made some modest changes in our state while I was governor— and I was called the Grinch Before Christmas for my efforts—real change in this realm will be driven from the federal level. Whoever is brave enough to lead at any level of government ought to be encouraged and supported because the pioneering process can get lonely in politics.

In his day Paul Ryan was a pioneer. In 2010 he came out with a plan entitled "A Roadmap for America's Future: a Plan to Solve America's Long-Term Economic and Fiscal Crisis." In it he touched all the untouchables of entitlement and tax reform, and rather than getting praise, what he got from other Republicans at the time was distance. They didn't want their fingerprints on it lest they get the proverbial arrow in the back. It's a shame he walked away from much of this when he was elected Speaker, but in his day he was indeed pioneering.

Governor Mitch Daniels did remarkable things in Indiana in privatizing formerly state-owned assets and in offering health savings accounts. Former governor Jeb Bush both in and out of office was an articulate leader in advancing school choice. Governor Rick Perry was willing to take a stand during the original fight on the stimulus. I am sure you could come up with another hundred names at different levels of government, but I mention these because I saw their work firsthand. It is important for each of us to look for ways to seek out and support leaders and leadership ideas.

I know this may sound strange to some, but I also believe an important role to be played in advancing ideas is lifting up in prayer those who advance good ideas. Benjamin Franklin said it best at the time of the Constitutional Convention when he requested prayer to start the day's deliberations.

"I have lived, sir, a long time, and the longer I live, the more convincing proofs I see of this truth—that God governs in the affairs of men. And if a sparrow cannot fall to the ground without His notice, is it probable that an empire can rise without His aid? We have been assured, sir, in the Sacred Writings, that 'except the Lord build the House, they labor in vain that build it.' I firmly believe this; and I also believe that without His concurring aid we shall succeed in this political building no better than the builders of Babel... I therefore beg leave to move that henceforth prayers imploring the assistance of Heaven, and its blessings on our deliberations, be held in this Assembly every morning before we proceed to business."

The tradition holds even to today as Congress begins each session with a prayer.

Similarly, a constant throughout the history of our country is that our presidents have consistently acknowledged that the job required help and guidance from the Almighty. Every prayer helps. For those who don't come from a faith perspective, you can translate this into personal encouragement. None of this means that you should back away from being direct on the ideas that matter. It just means that leaders need encouragement.

Being engaged in the war of ideas on nearly every political level takes its toll. I am not saying this to justify, but merely stating that the obvious byproduct of pushing against the normal course of things in any walk of life will have a personal cost. I remember going to my friend Cubby when I first decided to run for governor and asking him for a contribution to our effort. He refused. He said his first interest was for the health of my family and spirit, and he didn't see how an effort of this scale could be conducive to the good growth of either. I was disappointed and even a little mad at him at the time, but I could never have imagined back then how clairvoyant he would prove to be in his assessment.

I found there was an amazing loneliness that went with pushing against the tide in government. It's easy to get too wound up on the very important but isolating, work at hand. This is particularly true if your efforts represent more than work but rather a burning passion, and for many attracted to politics this calling fits. For me this was absolutely the case, and the higher you climb as a public figure, the more vulnerable you can become as a private figure.

The highs can be deceiving. I remember in the spring of 2009 stepping out onto the Custom House steps in Charleston for what was then the first round of Tax Day Tea Party rallies. As I walked out, the crowd began chanting, "Sanford President, Sanford President." I savored not so much the chant but the energy on the issues of spending and taxes that I had never before seen. After I had pushed for nearly fifteen years, at times in very quiet corners far from where most people were, that moment seemed about as close to political nirvana as I could ever have imagined. That which I considered my life's work and calling in politics was now what the crowd was yelling, and it felt like a glorious vindication for all those lonely votes and actions that had led to that moment.

The lows were real too. More than anything, they came in my trying to do too much and just exhausting myself in the effort. Life during several periods became an insular world of early-morning satellite feeds followed by a day of meetings, visits, and speeches, followed by still more satellite feeds into the late hours of the night. I look back on 2009 and wish I had been wise enough then to slow down. In addition to the busy roles of husband, father, and governor, I was chairman of the Republican Governors Association. I traveled the country to help raise money for their efforts, and was increasingly asked to speak in conservative circles around the country, becoming something of a default national spokesman against the stimulus package—about which I was doing multiple satellite feeds each day. I was also trying to write a book by June, still pulling drill in the Air Force Reserves, and more. I was stupidly busy.

And it's in these clouds of activity that we most need perspective. A spiritual perspective, prayer, and encouragement become lifesaving. People in office need real friends to tamp them down when they are up and to bolster them when they are down. You need friends because of the loneliness that can come in charting a different political path and in managing the additional loads you may take on in the belief that they help the cause that becomes much of your life.

Most of all these friends need to be real. They need to be the friends you had before you got into politics, the ones who will be with you after it's over. After my implosion, a friend said to me that the silver lining was that I didn't have to wait until my funeral to find out who my real friends were. How right he was. The bottom line is that while others may be more disciplined in managing the different pressures that come with political life, it's a handful of relationships that will give you perspective on God's plan in life's busy chapters. I believe thought, word, and prayer can be a great contribution to the larger cause of advancing liberty. For those who don't hold a faith, simple personal encouragement and accountability can help to the same thing.

Just contribute, somehow, someway, to leaders or the ideas they represent. If it's a person of faith, use it. If not, a good word will do!

SIX: REMEMBER THAT POLITICS TRADES ON A DIFFERENT COMMODITY.

I remember long-distance calls being a big deal when I was in college. Lately, I have been amazed at the dropping cost of flat-screen televisions, computers, and more. But we are not so lucky with government. It operates on a different currency. It's much more tied to the exchange of power than profit or efficiency. I remember asking Governor Ed Rendell at a National Governors meeting why the privatization of the New Jersey Turnpike did not go through. It would have brought his state over a billion dollars, relieved them of maintenance costs, and given them a new road. His response was that there were two thousand patronage jobs on the turnpike, split evenly between Republicans and Democrats, and the legislature didn't want to give them up.

When most in politics are presented with the choice between giving something up that will produce real but distant savings, the benefits of which can't directly help them politically, and the ability to "deliver" now, guess which one they pick? In each case the choice is invariably between a job or appointment for a friend or ally and something abstract. Abstract rarely wins in the world of here and now politics, particularly when it is weighed against the future support and power that will come with the job for "Uncle Billy's cousin" or their biggest fundraiser's nephew.

Though the world changes, human nature does not. New technologies and global competition should bring down the cost of government, but that's not government.

The number of legislators who asked me for appointments for sons, daughters, relatives, or loved ones was astounding. They don't do it because they really believe that the person is the most qualified. They do it because they want to "deliver" for someone who supports them. I remember being dumbstruck when I came into office as governor at how real this phenomenon was because it had not been part of what I had seen in Congress.

In my first year as governor, I was summoned for a meeting with the Speaker of the House. The meeting had been described by my legislative team as being very important to our legislative agenda. At the time I naively thought it would entail a discussion on the need for more compromise on some of our budget proposals. I met the Speaker in my office, and immediately after we sat down, he went straight to the point. "I need your help on something that is very important to me." My mind was spinning as he drew out the word *very*. I was trying to anticipate which part of the budget he could be referencing, but as it turned out, I was wrong on all counts. He continued, "You make the appointments to the Workers' Comp Commission, and my brother-in-law is on that commission. It would mean a lot to me if you reappointed him."

I told him I would most certainly consider it and that his opinion on these sorts of things mattered a lot. That was the end of our meeting, and we quickly went our different ways. I debated with the staff on what to do, as I could not imagine appointing my own sister or relative to a board or commission. It didn't feel right. It seemed like that "nepotism thing" I thought we had gotten rid of a long time ago. The legislative team, my policy director, and my chief of staff were all united in asking whether I was out of my mind in even debating what to do. There was not another member of the entire legislature who could more greatly impact our legislative agenda than the Speaker, and if this was important to him, it needed to be done.

Though it never really got reported that way, at the beginning of my time in the governorship, we were earnestly trying to look for compromises and ways to build bridges where we could. As a consequence, I found myself rationalizing and going ahead with this appointment. You say to yourself that these are the inevitable trade-offs that go with politics and that you can't fight every fight, but at a gut level I always regretted whenever I rationalized along these lines. In fairness to the Speaker, he was straightforward in his dealings, which was in real contrast to others in his role, and in this story, he was at least transparent and forthright in his request—a far cry from scores of legislators who hosted familial or financial arrangements with the state that in retrospect made the Speaker's request seem almost benign.

You really can't imagine until you've seen it up close the degree to which politics is enacted at the human rather than the idea level. Though Thomas Friedman talks about a flat world of commerce with rational actors,[56] that's not true in politics. In the governorship I saw this up close as we went through the process of making thousands of appointments over those eight years. Though I had served

---

56 Thomas L. Friedman, *The World is Flat [Updated and Expanded]: A Brief History of the Twenty-First Century* (New York: Macmillan, 2006).

three terms in the US Congress, I frankly didn't really understand politics until I was in Columbia and had countless conversations with legislators about their friends, cousins, brothers, and sisters in filling gubernatorial appointments. I don't remember one instance when these conversations extended over to the larger world of ideas. It was about friendship, support, or allegiance to the individual in question…which makes sense given this is the currency that drives most people's behaviors in politics.

SEVEN: DON'T JUST REMEMBER, *FOCUS* ON HOW POLITICS TRADES ON A DIFFERENT COMMODITY.

The ancient Chinese strategist Sun Tzu argued the key to winning a battle was knowing your enemy, so for those who want to make a difference in politics, let me highlight again the way politics really works.

The commodity of politics too often is power. We need reason. We need ideas. We need constraint. But too often there is simply an unquenchable thirst for more control and power by those who hold it.

I will never forget a meeting early in my governorship with the late Vern Smith. He had been frustrated with my stubborn adherence to limited government, just as I had been frustrated at his adherence to big government. He was a large man, and one afternoon as I paid homage to yet another senior senator, he leaned forward from his desk and said, "We want to make you the best governor South Carolina has ever seen, and if you will just do as we tell you, we will make you the best governor South Carolina has ever seen." I thanked him for the offer but raised the question of what I would do if his requests ran counter to the things I had run on and promised. His reply was, "Don't you sweat those details, son."

I politely told him I unfortunately had to sweat those details and declined his offer. On that day it was about power, as on most days it is, which makes Thomas Sowell's observation that "the most basic question is not what is best, but who shall decide what is best"[57] really important in thinking about politics.

Sometimes the tug-of-war on power becomes extreme—and to the point of kill or be killed—but it's still about power. In this light, a senator by the name of Jake Knotts became my chief critic over my years as governor. If I said the sky was blue, he was sure to counter that it was gray. Though critics come with trying to change anything and are guaranteed in life, his efforts went well beyond this. He was frequently trying through law enforcement circles to find more on my comings and goings, and became the voice for those wanting to register disagreement or displeasure with my administration. In short, it became tremendously personal, as evidenced by his role in the events of June 2009.

The question is, why so personal? After all, other senators (like Phil Leventis or Luke Rankin) and I viscerally disagreed, but it never became personal. What I didn't know then was that Senator Knotts thought he had to make sure that something he believed could kill him politically never got out. He seemed to figure he had to politically kill anyone who might talk, and he figured that was me.

---

57 Thomas Sowell, *Knowledge And Decisions* (New York: Basic Books, 1996), 79.

Early on in my administration a leader in the community had told me to remember that the ones who throw rocks the hardest are the ones who live in glass houses, and that this senator lived in a very glass house. He said the senator had fathered an illegitimate child with a Black streetwalker by the name of Little Bit when he had earlier worked the beat as a police officer. He said the son was now in one of our state's jails and gave me the inmate's name. Given the individual passing me these details was very credible and had no reason to make things up, I wanted to know whether there was any credence to the story. So I pulled the photo for the inmate in question. I found a remarkable visual similarity between the senator and his alleged son. I talked it over with a few key advisers, and we decided to leave it alone. Unfortunately there are no real secrets in politics, and so in the process, one of those advisers must have mentioned it to a friend of theirs, who then took it to the press. The press ultimately raised the question with Knotts. It ended there because when the press sought confirmation, I had told my guys not to comment, so no story ever advanced because no one would go on record.

But there was more than a little bit of irony here. How in the world could a man whose public persona was that of a self-acclaimed redneck—who looked and played every bit the part—hold this little secret? But his knowing that I might know set off a full-scale jihad in my our direction, though actions were never motivated by what they seemed, and personal differences were shrouded and draped as policy differences.

The point here is that power, or the information that creates it, drives an amazing level of activity around politics, and that which may seem petty or small is often driven by hidden fears or hopes on this front.

In other cases, people are just crooked. They want what they want because they want it. Take for instance our airport authority in Charleston. Because state retirement is configured in a way that disproportionately rewards the last three years of service, political folks have long wrangled ways to get themselves a high-paying appointment like the airport authority for a few years to finish their "public service," though in fact it's always about juicing their retirement.

But why wait when you can just do a coup d'état? That's what happened little more than a year ago in Charleston. In this case, Elliot Summey, a board member and coincidentally the son of the mayor where the airport sits, worked with others to appoint himself to the $300,000-a-year job as airport director. Did he have any experience in this? Did he have any experience running a large organization? Did the board conduct any interviews for someone who might? The answer is no to all the above, though it's hardly unreasonable to believe that public boards should operate in the public interest, and that public money should be handled through a public process. But this is just another example of the way politics too often works, and why so many of us become disillusioned by it.

Finally, we need to remember that when it's not about power or self-interest, it's about the power and self-interest that come in delivering for those who help politicians keep power. In other words, it's still about the power.

Consider the Lexington Peach Festival. It comes in the heat of the South Carolina summer, and in the midlands it can be unmercifully hot. I remember how, after just finishing walking the parade,

I was soaked in sweat and heading with others to the gymnasium just trying to cool down. I wasn't alone. The place was packed, and while the crowd was still there, they always held an awards ceremony for the best float, "Ms. Peach," and the like. While our son little Blake was at my feet working on his third bowl of peach ice cream, I was standing onstage with their local delegation listening to members ramble on how though the governor didn't want to help them, the delegation had come through.

At this point they had a chance to show how they could deliver for "their" people. And with the crowd assembled and the local paper there, they held up an automobile-size copy of the $5,000 grant check they had procured for the Peach Festival. It didn't matter that nearly every small town in South Carolina had gotten a similarly wasteful check; what mattered was that they could show a deliverable, and demonstrate they had the power to get it there. So goes the real ways of politics.

EIGHT: GET TO KNOW YOUR CONSTITUTION.

In any modern society there is an endless list of wants and needs, and there are many good ideas advanced to address these in America. But not all are constitutional. Without holding to constitutional limits, there is no end to what government does. The only real and lasting safeguard against this is the educated will of the people.

Read the Constitution, and know it. It is a vital defense against all those great-sounding intentions of so many in politics. The road to hell really is paved with good intentions. Not all of them turn out to be so good. There are limits to what government can do, and grave dangers lie in government doing more than is constitutionally and financially reasonable or possible.

Let me give you a strange example. In the fall after I was elected governor, the state comptroller general discovered an illegal and unconstitutional $155 million deficit. Our state, like many, has a balanced budget requirement that would make a deficit impossible, but nonetheless one had been swept under the rug in the closing chapter of the previous administration. It was something we had to deal with, so I met with House and Senate leadership. As a result, we drafted the Fiscal Discipline Act. It committed us, even if we were to have South Carolina's worst three budget years going forward, to allocating $50 million each year to extinguish this unconstitutional deficit. I had conversations with the credit agencies in New York that were involved, laying out a payment plan and how the legislative body was willing to commit it to law.

Our legislative session is held between January and June, and in April of that year our state saw something of a spring thaw regarding the economy and money coming into the state government. We now had the capacity to completely pay off the deficit that same year. But after going through weeks of back-and-forth in the budget process, we finally found ourselves just $16 million short of completely extinguishing the deficit. We had reached an impasse. Legislative leadership made the point that politics was about compromise, and that our administration had gotten almost all of what we wanted in paying back this debt. They argued that we should declare victory and move on. My point to them was that though I understood political reality, there were certain absolutes dictated by the state constitution. We couldn't just get "close" on the balanced budget requirement. I had placed my left hand on the Bible, raised my right hand, and sworn to uphold the constitution, and in this case it was crystal clear about not getting close and declaring victory. It said the South Carolina government was to balance its budget each year.

As the legislative session was wrapping up, we would have one final bite at the apple with my budget vetoes. Using vetoes to close the gap would work and would even be expected, given I was known to be a penny-pincher. In addition to my belief in the substance of the vetoes, they would also offer legislators a political way out that would allow them to save face. They could place any blame for pork projects not coming back to their districts on me. Accordingly, on May 4, we offered about double the budget vetoes they needed to close the deficit. They could choose à la carte the ones that were the least politically sensitive and look like heroes for saving half of my much longer list of vetoes. Our team thought it was a pretty good approach. We offered a way forward, compromise, and a way for legislators to save face. I would get my constitutionally required balanced budget, and the legislators would get political cover to blame me for unpopular spending cuts.

It didn't work out that way.

In South Carolina, the governor has five days to sign or veto a bill after the conference report between House and Senate passes both bodies. In this case, while creating our list of vetoes, the staff worked through all five nights to produce a well-justified list. Unfortunately, on the day the House was to take up our vetoes and their accompanying messages, I learned that the House was not even going to debate them. They would instead vote them all down together as a block. I went upstairs to meet with the Speaker and leadership team, and their response was, "We got to do what we got to do." My reply was, "If you don't even take the time to debate the merits of the vetoes we have offered, then I'll be forced to look for some more colorful way of raising what I think is a critical financial and constitutional issue."

We had tried the deliberative approach, and it had gotten us nowhere. Was there something else that would cause them to look at this issue differently?

Our team held a brainstorming session on how to make this constitutional issue real to the public so we could make their voice heard to the legislative body. One of the team members came up with the idea of pigs. "What they are really doing is putting pork for their district ahead of that which they are constitutionally required to do." Within an hour there was a highway patrol vehicle picking up pigs in Lexington County, and the next thing I know, I'm walking upstairs to the entrance of the chamber of the House of Representatives with a squealing pig under each arm—one named Pork, the other named Barrel.

Needless to say, all hell broke loose. The Speaker accused me of a terrible breach of decorum, and I have to admit that squealing pigs doing some of the things pigs do was probably a low point of the episode. But the people got it. Talk radio was massively on our side, and legislators heard the voice of their constituents loud and clear. A few days later, the $16 million was quietly found over on the Senate side, and the unconstitutional deficit was just as quietly extinguished.

I didn't like using political instruments quite that blunt, but when push came to shove, there was no other way to garner the attention of the public, who in turn could demand change in the legislative body.

In instances like these, I think it is important to use any and all tools available. I've always wondered why it took that much effort to derail just $16 million in pork bound for the districts of House members, especially when faced with a deficit that was unconstitutional. But in the end, it is just a reflection of the way the system works. What is close and personal for a politician's district pretty much always trumps distant and abstract, or even constitutional, which makes it vital we all know what the constitution has to say about the issue at hand.

NINE: STUDY THOSE WHO HAVE LOST FREEDOM— OR THOSE FOR WHOM IT IS FRAGILE.

I was invited to Nicaragua to be an election observer when I was in Congress, and as we flew in on the morning of the elections, I looked out the window of the descending airplane and saw something I will never forget—lines and lines of people that went on for blocks. There was a light drizzle, and yet people at different neighborhood polling places were standing patiently in lines that ran down the street and stretched block after block. Voting was a fundamental right they had been denied for years, and now that they had the chance, they were exercising it. With few exceptions, everyone in that country was voting—far from the 30 percent turnouts America has come to expect in our non-presidential national elections.

I remember the words of Paul Kagame, the current president of Rwanda, when he started out in that office. "The progress we made in democracy is because somebody was whipping us with a stick. We believe in freedoms…we believe in democracy, not because anybody tells us to do so."[58] At that time he had directly seen and felt the reasons freedom mattered. Highlighted in movies like *Hotel Rwanda*, his country was torn apart as eight hundred thousand men, women, and children were brutally murdered in just over one hundred days as Hutus targeted minority Tutsis for genocide. Kagame led the guerilla effort to take back the country and end the bloodshed, and in those early days in office, he said, "For so long I've lived injustice, and have had to struggle and fight for my freedom... I think you tend to have more passion for freedom and for rights to exist, for you and for everyone... With that kind of life, you don't take things for granted, you want to earn every step of your life. You want to work hard, you want to achieve, you want to reach where you have not been before."

Those words fit with the remarkable experience Kagame and his countrymen had experienced in Rwanda, and I remember being struck by his story and his presence as a young member of the International Relations Committee in Congress. And yet the democratic process has gone from dust back to dust in his country. Kagame is now regrettably one more example of an officeholder gone bad, and of the need for term limits and short stays in office. He's yet another political criminal, and his $500 million net worth stands as a testament to this.

The transformation from pain to hope and back into pain in Rwanda is a vivid and poignant reminder of how watchful we need to be in safeguarding the institutions and traditions of freedom, in watching its ebb and flow and vigilantly protecting it here at home.

---

58 Anne Jolis, "A Supply-Sider in East Africa" Wall Street Journal, April 24, 2010.

TEN: STAY FOCUSED ON SPENDING.

In the 1992 presidential race, political strategist James Carville coined the phrase "It's the economy, stupid." Those words hung in the Clinton campaign war room, and it became Carville's job, no matter the debate or issue being discussed, to always keep the campaign focused on those four words. Given the state of things today, we would be wise to do the same on spending. However, I won't further beat the dead horse of my oft-mentioned beliefs here. Much.

It's the spending, stupid.

ELEVEN: DON'T LET CIVIL LIBERTIES GET BRUSHED ASIDE.

The aim of our Founders was to maximize personal liberty. Spending and economic freedom are certainly a huge part of this, but let me circle back again to civil liberty. In today's never-ending War on Terror, many components of our personal liberty are being pushed to the back seat. The idea that anyone can be held in a jail for a long period of time without formal charges being brought against them is scary, and I firmly believe it is unconstitutional. Some level of risk will always come with a free and open society, and if we ever get to the point where there is no risk, we will no longer be living in a free and open society. For this reason, over my time in politics I wound up in a variety of fights about civil liberties, but let me tell you of yet another to underscore the importance of this issue.

Do you remember the tragic story in March of 2020 about Breonna Taylor? She was sitting in her apartment in Louisville, Kentucky, with her boyfriend when people broke the door down and entered. Her boyfriend does what every red-blooded White South Carolinian would do and fires a warning shot, trying to fend off these would-be intruders. It turns out the intruders were plainclothes police officers in search of Breonna's old boyfriend, and they returned fire. Firing thirty-two shots, they hit and killed Breonna.[59]

Civil liberty is real. This is not an abstract. The police argued they did not need a warrant because Breonna's old boyfriend was out on parole, and therefore the normal requirements for a warrant were not needed. The problem is that's not what the Fourth Amendment says. It doesn't have carve outs. It's for this reason that ten years before Breonna's case made national news I vetoed a bill passed by the House and Senate that would have allowed exactly what happened to her.

The bill in South Carolina had been pushed hard by the chief of police in North Charleston, and accordingly had all the backing of law enforcement. It would have allowed officers to search people released on probation or parole without a warrant. At the time I showed how there was no evidence that giving law enforcement the additional authority would decrease crime or reduce recidivism, and I highlighted how the protection from warrantless home searches was an essential safeguard of liberty. Our fights then and Breonna's tragedy are but another reminder of how important it is we stay focused on preserving civil liberty.

---

59 Richard A. Oppel Jr., Derrick Bryson Taylor, Nicholas Bogel-Burroughs, "What to Know About Breonna Taylor's Death" *The New York Times*, April 26, 2021.

TWELVE: SUPPORT GROWTH IDEAS.

In reality, government is never really cut. The best any legislature can do is slow its advance. A budget cut is seldom what you and I would see as a budget cut. It's usually just a cut from the level government would have grown to in the next year. In budget language, this is known as the baseline. But who really cares…it all means government keeps on growing. The only other avenue to shrink the government relative to the size of our economy is to grow the economy. I'd ask you to brainstorm with friends on ideas that you think might work, or borrow ideas that have worked in other places. Estonia has a transparent and flat tax system. Why can't we? Some places solve traffic issues with variable pricing and tolls so they can harness the private sector in building more roads sooner. Why can't we? In places like Belgium, the Netherlands, and Ireland, school choice is a constitutional right. Why is it so hard here? Singapore is much more robust in its use of medical savings accounts. Why are reforms not more abundant here? You could come up with your own list, I'm sure, but the point is we need to think of and apply more growth- and freedom-focused ideas if we are going to keep government confined to its once-limited role.

THIRTEEN: RECOGNIZE THAT THE SEEDS OF POLITICAL REVIVAL AND CHANGE ARE ALREADY IN PLACE.

Renewal, rebirth, and redirection are cornerstones in the Christian faith, our human journey, and America's political history. In 1992, Democrats swept through to control the White House, Senate, and House, and at that time who would have thought that in twenty-four months Republicans would take back the House and Senate? From the Republican high-water mark of 1994 when there were literally front-page stories asking whether the president was relevant, who would have imagined the loss of both House and Senate again in just a handful of years? With Obama, the White House, House, and Senate all went to the Democrats in 2008. Since then, things have swung back to Republicans and then Democrats again.

Government is always changing, and the seeds of hope, growth, and redemption in our lives and in the body politic always seem to come in the wake of our biggest losses.

Sir Winston Churchill observed years ago that "America will always do the right thing…after having exhausted all other possibilities."[60]

I have seen the spontaneous combustion of political revival. During my battle as governor against the stimulus in 2009, teachers from across the state held a political rally on the State House steps to encourage me to change my position on education stimulus funding. It was organized by different interests that, not surprisingly, wanted the money. Amazingly, Tea Party participants from across the state began arriving to form a counterrally to support my stand against the stimulus funding. This spontaneous counterrally grew organically in proportion to the rally calling for the stimulus. My office didn't call a single person. It just happened. And those sorts of things don't happen in politics unless the seeds of change are already in place.

Whether we liked them or not, it was that same energy behind Obama's election and Trump's. People are always looking for hope and change.

---

60 Winston Churchill, Richard M. Langworth, Churchill by Himself: The Life, Times and Opinions of Winston Churchill in His Own Words. (London: Ebury Press, 2008).

The big question of the conservative movement lies in whether we are willing to accept the fact that our work is never done. There will always be a tension between security and freedom and between the authority of government and the free will of man. In calibrating this and in getting it right, we should remember Jefferson's words. "Every government degenerates when trusted to the rulers of the people alone. The people themselves are its only safe depositories."[61] Similarly, FDR observed, "In the truest sense freedom can't be bestowed, it must be achieved."[62]

Indeed, these things are so, and so I close this chapter with Ronald Reagan's words to each one of us as conservatives on the importance of our duty to keep alive our birthright of freedom. Reagan presented "A Time for Choosing" on behalf of Republican candidate Barry Goldwater during the 1964 US presidential election campaign, and in it he said simply, "You and I have a rendezvous with destiny. We will preserve for our children this, the last best hope of man on earth, or we will sentence them to take the first step into a thousand years of darkness. If we fail, at least let our children and our children's children say of us we justified our brief moment here. We did all that could be done."[63]

---

61 Thomas Jefferson, Notes on the State of Virginia. (New York: Penguin, 1999).

62 Franklin D. Roosevelt, Public Papers of the Presidents of the United States: Franklin D. Roosevelt. (Best Books, 1938).

63 Ronald Reagan, *A Time for Choosing: The Speeches of Ronald Reagan, 1961-1982* (Gateway Books, 1983).

PARTING THOUGHTS

I n conclusion, I'd like to tell you a story.

It all came together for me in May 2021. I had gone to Washington to be with our youngest son over his graduation weekend from Georgetown. I was staying on Capitol Hill, and that Saturday, in making the trip back across town, I decided to go into the Capitol. I hadn't been there since I left Congress, and was curious to see how it looked after the events of January 6. It was eerie, even surreal, to see the grounds encased by a steel fence. Over the years, I had come and gone from this place so freely. It had always been so alive, and I particularly remembered meeting school groups and seeing throngs of visitors this time of year when Washington for a short season escaped the heat of summer and the cold of winter. This was no more. As I approached the guard gate, two officers stepped forward to stop me, then recognized me and waved me in. At the second post, I got into a conversation on how different things were, and by the time I got to the third line of defense, I asked one of the officers to show me a little more of what had happened in

January. He showed me cracked glass and other windows covered by plywood, and talked of how violent the day had been. Of bear spray to the face, metal framing and guardrails being reconfigured to break glass and be used as weapons. It sounded so distant from what I knew of the Capitol during my twelve years working there. I went on to walk into, and through, the Capitol alone. It was like a morgue. A place I had known to be of never-ending activity and always filled with the echoing sounds of tour groups was still and quiet.

When I got to the rotunda, I decided to just sit, soaking in the Capitol's stillness. In this magnificent cathedral built to celebrate our nation's birth and origin, you could have heard a pin drop. George Washington looks down from the heavens in Brumidi's *Apotheosis of Washington* centered and visible through the oculus far above. Silent watchmen surround you in the stern busts of Grant, Eisenhower, Reagan, King, Jackson, Lincoln, Jefferson, and more. At the edge of the rotunda hang eight paintings, four that depict scenes from our Revolution and four on the exploration and colonization of America. They are grand and life-size renderings. The *Surrender of Lord Cornwallis*, the *Declaration of Independence*, the *Discovery of the Mississippi*, and the *Embarkation of the Pilgrims*—all these events are made so real in these paintings.

In those moments I soaked up our country's grand journey and thought about my place in it. Had my decades of effort been worthwhile? How had we gotten to where we were now? Would we find a way forward? In my quiet isolation, I didn't have answers, but pondered how much this place and its institutions had come to mean to me. In a single sitting it's hard to digest twenty-five years, but in that moment I felt the weight of all the time, experience, and perceptions that I had drawn over my time in politics.

Four things particularly hit me.

One: How elegant and thoughtful but fragile was the design of our republic and the freedoms for which it stands. The Capitol is its physical representation, but as surely as I had just seen plywood-covered windows and broken glass and heard the officer's tales of assault, so, too, was our system currently undergoing assault. I had seen this over the airwaves for months and years, but it crystallized in my guide's tales, and in seeing the high steel fence at the building's edge. Fragile things require care, and we are not giving our democracy the care it needs to sustain itself.

Two: It struck me how much this place had come to mean to me. A major part of my life had been invested here, and over time we grow to love our major life investments. Our work, our children, our faith…these points of focus indeed represent the great loves of one's life. But to love an established thing, or way of doing things, does not make you part of the establishment. It's instead just recognizing the established wisdom of the past. It's part of being conservative. It's part of paying homage to the wisdom of those who came before you. I had fought with everything in me against the normal course of doing things at many points along the way in my career, but that didn't mean I wanted to blow the system up and start all over. Even if major refinement and overhaul were necessary, I had never given up my belief in our traditions and the system of governance that was represented there in the rotunda of the US Capitol. But somehow, the political climate in our country had gotten to a point where many believed that anything short of upheaval was an embrace of the status quo. This was wrong, I thought. But how had we gotten to this unexpected place?

Three: I was struck by how humbling it was to work on something so much bigger than I was. This had been my work in Washington and South Carolina. Given its size, scale, and grandeur, the rotunda itself is humbling, but when one adds in the history of its hallowed ground and the memories of this history that surround you there, it's overwhelming. It certainly was for me at that moment, as I asked myself how voters—and why God—had put me in that chapter of my life. I thought about what I had learned from it all, how I had contributed, and what I might do with everything I had learned going forward.

Fourth: I had to ask myself whether I honestly believed my boys would continue to know what I had known and experienced of freedom. Was it a standing capacity of the American experiment? Would it last? To sit alone in the rotunda is a spiritual exercise because in the same way that the grand cathedrals of Europe were designed to inspire one's thinking toward God, our rotunda represents the American cathedral of freedom. And although the freedoms we enjoy today have been protected by the brave souls memorialized by the white gravestones that dot the hills of Arlington, who will guard it tomorrow and over the months and years ahead? What would happen to this great institution during my boys' lives?

To each of the questions that ran through my head that afternoon, the answer was the same. Though I might have a unique vantage point, I had been but one soldier in what General McArthur described in his final address to the cadets at West Point as the long gray line. In our country's march to sustain freedom, it has required from its defenders a chapter, chapters, or even the last full measure of life itself. In short, freedom has never been free.

And so the questions I pondered were ultimately never questions reserved only for me in what I had seen and observed over my time in politics. Rather, they were questions for all Americans, for we should all contemplate what each one of us might do to make our union more perfect and complete. What the Founding Fathers wrote in the Preamble to our Constitution began with the words "We the people." So it has been, so it is, and, I believe, so it always will be.

What comes next in the blessing of freedom and this unique land we call America is in the hands of "we the people." May we act in good judgment.

Godspeed in the journey.

EPILOGUE
EPISTLES

A book is not a letter, and a letter is not a book. Yet as I wrote the closing chapter of this one, I was struck by the fact that I needed to try one last time to convey this book's themes in a more concise and direct way. This is the nature of a letter. It is generally sent to one person and by its very nature requires conciseness. My hope is that the letters that follow will serve as nothing more than examples of what we all should do in contacting neighbors, friends, and representatives—with the hope that they in turn will do the same. Our country's time is running short, and it's important for each one of us to look for ways to elevate ideas in a political world that seems to have lost its way regarding ideas that do matter.

TO DEMOCRATS

Dear Democrats,

We find ourselves in a contest to determine whether we sustain the heart and soul of what it means to be an American. We are living in fateful times, and what we last saw with Trump's crass ways and shredding of long-established political institutions and norms could indeed hasten our demise as a republic. He is frightening, and that's why I stood against him. It was never an academic call but a visceral belief that he was so bad that I had little choice but to make a stand that cost me my job in Congress.

I share your concerns.

But I think it's important to see that he is in many ways a symptom rather than a cause. Fredrick Hayek's book *The Road to Serfdom* chronicles Hitler's rise to power in post–World War II Germany,[64] and from it I have always taken two lessons. One, desperate people

---

64 Friedrich Hayek and Bruce Caldwell, *The Road to Serfdom: Text and documents: The definitive edition*. (Routledge, 2014).

do desperate things. Germany at that time had a well-educated population and stood as a well-developed industrial power. But when you can't feed your family or care for those you love, political ideology goes out the window. And two, the bigger the government gets, the more inefficient and bureaucratic it often becomes. Combine this with a downward economic spiral, and you have an environment ripe for a political strongman. Hitler's basic promise was that he could fix things, and people were so desperate for things to be fixed that they would turn to most anyone who professed to have the answers…and indeed they did.

For four years we also had a political strongman, and he appalled those of us who believe in democratic rule, checks and balances, and an open political system. But he was not a skillful political operator, and he made it a point to needlessly offend the very people who could keep him in power, so he may simply have been setting the stage for someone else who will take America's now-diminished political norms and run with the divisiveness they have created.

Before that happens, it's time to look inward and ask what each one of us contributed to the screenplay that brought Trump to Washington. The Bible says, "He who is without sin among you, let him cast the first stone."[65] And it says, "Why do you see the splinter in your brother's eye, but not notice the log in your own?"[66]

The following are just two of many things I see in Washington that my Democratic friends should think about as we contemplate where we go from here.

One: extreme political hubris and double standards. President Trump was a reaction to the belief that no one would stand up and

---

65 John 8:7.
66 Luke 6:41.

fight against Obama or Clinton. Trump has taken hubris and double standards to new levels, but the wrecking of political norms and the sustained growth of an imperial presidency continued from President Obama. It was Obama who ignored and refused to enforce the law. It would have required the deportation of eight hundred thousand young illegal immigrants, dubbed Dreamers. Instead he chose to selectively enforce the law—which in layman's terms means he refused to enforce the law. And if partial adherence to the law is okay, why don't we all try paying half our taxes? Either law stands supreme, or it does not.

His Environmental Protection Agency drastically intensified regulations, thereby bypassing Congress in the process of what used to be debate on things that impact people and their lives. The same holds true on his use of executive orders, or in his Justice Department, where without any real public debate, they abruptly interpreted Title IX to cover transgender high school students and create yet another round of federal mandates for school districts across the country. In each instance the issues were not the actual issue; instead, people felt that their way of life and things they held dear were changing without an adequate debate on the public square. They wanted someone to fight for them. You need to recognize how President Obama and many of his supporters set the stage for Trump to take on the role of fighter, to step forward and present himself.

Two: Bernie Sanders and our government's continued growth also created Trump. Granted, in recent years Republicans have been pathetic at even pretending to still want to limit government's growth, but Democrats have been even worse. You haven't worked to limit the reach and scope of government, except perhaps in the battle over civil liberties. This doesn't resonate in America's heartland. Bernie's plan was to expand the cost of government by $60 trillion. Not to be outdone, Alexandria Ocasio-Cortez came up with a Green New Deal whose cost would run somewhere between $52 and $93 trillion. With numbers like these, how can anyone be surprised a figure like Trump comes along, particularly when he was promising to eliminate the debt over the eight years he might be in office?

And it wasn't just crazy financial numbers or perceived threats to cultural norms that frightened people and helped them to rally around a fighter, it was the way too many leaders on the left looked the other way when members of their political base abused freedom. An injustice received or perceived does not give one license to bring injustice to another. Whether on immigration, trade, or race relations, we do have laws and a system that regular working people believed should be used before looters were given a pass on taking to the street and burning a downtown. The fact that actions in Portland, Kenosha, or Minneapolis weren't condemned by Democratic leaders gave Trump additional lift.

Over my last few years in Congress, the polarization has made the place dysfunctional. Both sides spend too much time delegitimizing each other rather than advancing ideas they believe in. George Washington warned about this in his farewell address. He spoke of factions, what we would now consider parties, when he said,

> "The alternate domination of one faction over another, sharpened by the spirit of revenge natural to party dissension, which in different ages and countries has perpetrated the most horrid enormities, is itself a frightful despotism. But this leads at length to a more

formal and permanent despotism. The disorders and miseries which result, gradually incline the minds of men to seek security and repose in the absolute power of an individual; and sooner or later the chief of some prevailing faction, more able or more fortunate than his competitors, turns this disposition to the purposes of his own elevation, on the ruins of public liberty."

Abraham Lincoln in a different way said the same thing. He warned in 1858 that a house divided would not stand. He had pulled it from Matthew and Mark in the Bible, where Jesus warns that "every kingdom divided against itself is brought to desolation; and every city or house divided against itself shall not stand."[67]

To Democrats and Republicans alike, I'm suggesting that we need to walk softly. We all need to have humility in attempting to understand the things that brought Trump to power and recognize our own role in it. Not doing so could unleash something even more venomous in our political waters. Social justice and charity toward all don't begin in Tibet; they start in a place much tougher—right here at home with the obnoxious neighbor down the street who had the big Trump sign in his yard. Blaming the other side will not be the answer. If we are going to fix what's before us, a touch of charity, grace, and understanding will be vital to begin the journey of bringing our country back from the edges—to the center that has long made it great.

Sincerely,
Mark Sanford

---

67 Matthew 12:25

TO THE TRUMP VOTERS

Dear Trump voters,

I understand your frustration and appreciate your pain.

Through no fault of your own, you, those you love, your way of life, and even our country are being torn and splintered in ways few of us would have imagined, having been born to and aspiring to the American Dream.

It used to be that you could graduate from high school and, just by being industrious and persistent, build a life for a family. The jobs that made this possible have vanished with globalization, and with them a way of life across America.

Even if you have a job these days, it feels like you are getting nowhere as the rich and elite get richer. Income has gone flat. After adjusting for inflation, today's average hourly wage is about where it was fifty years ago, which is to say anyone earning it is a lot poorer than they were fifty years ago. Wages in fact slid backward in the 1980s and early 1990s. How could you not be frustrated? What happened over these fifty years is a generation's worth of financial stagnation.

Same with life spans. America is the only wealthy country in the world where the life expectancy needle is moving backward. Between 1959 and 2014, American life spans were on the rise. Since then, and now for three consecutive years in a row, they have been declining. I could cite the *Journal of the American Medical Association*, but you are living it and don't need a study to tell you what you see.

During all this, you have elites from both coasts who would not survive a week without your toil and effort telling you what to do. These elites think differently than you. That somehow law and order do not matter. That it's fine for people to just walk across the border and take your job. That boys can call themselves girls and help themselves to your thirteen-year-old's bathroom at school.

It's all too crazy, and you know it must end. You feel it in simply trying to make it through each day, and I could cite a lot of statistics here, but they all point to the same thing—something had to change.

To make matters worse, in each election cycle a new crop of Republican politicians comes through and sells you the same garbage on wanting to change things…and then they don't. They offer you yet more excuses. Too many don't appreciate your struggle, and even more are hypocrites. Ted Cruz heads for Cancún as people are left without water in Texas.

The definition of insanity is doing the same thing over and over and expecting a different result. So along comes Trump. And he is different. He is unorthodox. He calls it like he sees it, in simple terms. He's a refreshing change from the picture-perfect political figure who has failed to improve your life.

You gave it a go, and I understand that.

But here is where we part paths. The pain was real; Trump's prescription was not. His approach was not a new one. Machiavelli's work in the 1500s could be summed up in one phrase: "Tell people what they want to hear." And that's exactly what Trump did.

He offered you something he could never deliver on. But you desperately wanted to believe it could be so.

His approach was fundamentally autocratic, and unless we dissolve our American democratic traditions, it could never work.

Nonetheless, the promises sounded sweet. And you doubled down on your beliefs, just as some do in a bad marriage, thinking that simply believing and hoping could somehow solve the problems at hand.

And so we end up with a strange reality. The golden Trump statue wheeled out at the CPAC conference in Florida symbolized all that traditional conservatism, and even the American Founding Fathers' political ideas and the Constitution were designed to guard against—faith and allegiance to one person. A golden image of one man at the premier gathering of alleged "conservatives" is neither what conservatism is about nor representative of any one-man-one-vote system. Any one person strong enough to give you things will be strong enough to take them away. The Founders had seen up close the capricious nature of man and the need to guard against the prerogatives of one person with power in government. That's why we have the Constitution and Bill of Rights.

The Republican Party needs to remember how the golden calf story ends. Moses destroyed the image of their worship. No false gods before the one true God, was his thinking, and it ought to be ours when we consider where we should place our trust in political matters. As real as the Bible is in laying out the path to a good life, our Constitution—with its faith in institutions and limitation of the powers of any one man—should be our country's path to a good life.

Much has been sacrificed to build what was once a conservative movement and Grand Old Party, and given what's become of it, many of you want to tear it down. But the stands I see taken don't represent construction. Throwing away principles like free trade and limited government is not a win. Evangelicals sacrificing what has been a historic commitment to godliness in public servants is not a win. Conservatism itself, once seen as a thoughtful intellectual tradition, devolving to a base level and degrading even further during Trump's watch is not a win.

You sacrificed a lot in this political experiment of trying something different. The promises are still out there; the results are not. At the end of the day, it was the same thing you have seen so many times before—empty promises from yet another politician.

And the question now lies in where we turn going forward. Like the Israelites so many years before us, hopefully we turn back to a true God—in our case a governing philosophy in America that, while certainly not perfect, has brought more freedom and more opportunity than any other system devised by man. Or will you turn to continued trust in one man? A man who says nothing is his fault, it's always someone else. The Chinese, the Mexicans, the deep state…always someone else out there. That is not the America I believe in. Let's find things wrong and deal with them, but not trust in one man as the answer to getting these things done. Let's trust in the Constitution, truth, humility, and law and order.

That, to me, is the American way.

Sincerely,
Mark Sanford

TO THE MAGA FOLKS

Dear MAGA folks,

I hear you. The rich keep getting richer, the federal government has become a feeding system for those in and around power in Washington, and elites on both coasts have seemingly no compassion, appreciation, or even concern for your lives. It's maddening. The feeling that the American Dream is dissolving before our eyes is real. That dream and our way of life have been predicated on the American way offering high levels of opportunity and being fair, and I know for many working people these days, both appear to be mirages.

What's occurring was best captured a few months ago on US Highway 17, just north of the Point South exit outside of Beaufort, South Carolina. There in front of a beekeeper's home sat a tombstone, and beside it a toilet with a green Statue of Liberty model sitting inside the toilet bowl. The tombstone simply read "RIP, My America, 1776 to 2020," and at its bottom were the words "Made in China." The Statue of Liberty in the toilet needed no explanation.

People are frustrated, but the question now is, how are we going to fix things? For nearly every problem that confronts society, there are two answers—one with more government as the answer and the other with less. Neither is perfect, and in many cases we pick a blend. But the starting point in getting things right for you and those you love is to figure out whether the road you are on will get you there.

On thisquestion, it's worth studying history. If you don't want to do that, how about studying folks in your neighborhood, at work, and in church? Does it really work out well for the bully down the street? Not in one unpleasant exchange but over the long haul? How about the person in the church meeting who just won't shut up? How about the person running the business that always tilts the table in their direction and leaves no room for give-and-take?

I respect the fact that President Trump identified feelings that were real for you. I just think his approach was harmful over the short run and horrendous to our system of government over the long run. To be fair, some things he worked on were good and long overdue. The Chinese made a mockery of many of our free trade agreements, and it wasn't right that there was a blind eye offered as immigration laws were ignored and cheap labor walked across our southern border.

But in recognizing those problems, has he created still bigger problems that will haunt us? I'd argue yes.

He has given us easy answers to hard problems. There is no free lunch, but he has promised many. Remember when the Mexicans were going to pay for the wall? Through the pages of time, charlatans, promoters, and con men have promised people a free lunch.

They have always claimed someone else was the problem—and the solution to be used in paying for the problem. The fact is, we are all part of any solution.

By telling people what they want to hear and making it sound like a wand could be waved to solve much of what confronts us, Trump has allowed us to sleepwalk our way into the world of easy answers. Life is hard. I can't find easy answers for my own family… and they are even harder to find for our American family of over 350 million people.

Trump has also said *he* is the answer, and that's not the American way. Although he may not exploit this notion, someone in the future surely will. Trump is stretching the limits of what we will accept as Americans on democratic versus autocratic behaviors. His push against long-established American norms of behavior and political traditions made what would have been unacceptable a few years ago the new normal. Making these negative changes acceptable in the eyes of far too many is broadening a landing strip in the jungle of American politics for someone in the future to use them in all the wrong ways.

If we really want to move to a fairer playing field for all and break the imperial structure and power of Washington, why not have the humility to honor the playbook of the *original* team that wanted to make America great? These men, our American Founding Fathers, were making it up as they went along. They went up against the greatest power on earth at that time, and pushed all the cards onto the table. They knew if their effort for liberty failed, they would lose a lot more than honor or possessions. It would be to the gallows they go.

With an appreciation of history and a clear understanding of the importance of not putting their faith in one man or woman, they constructed institutions and traditions that would divide and separate power. Our Founders were terrified of too much power residing in any one place and skeptical of those who held power. The idea that "I can fix it all" ran counter to their belief in the fallibility of man.

The American way came with no master and no king. In our country you would be judged by your merits, not your connection to political power. Think about this concept in local terms. Would you trust your neighbor down the street with your future, or would you want to try and shape it on your own? While I agree that elites, the media, and Washington have been determining far too much for you, we should not replace them with a new form of centralized power.

One of the greatest definitions of a free society is that you don't ever have to think about who governs you. That's not Trump.

The Preamble to our Constitution reads, "We the People of the United States, in Order to form a more perfect Union, establish Justice, insure domestic Tranquility, provide for the common defense, promote the general Welfare, and secure the Blessings of Liberty to ourselves and our Posterity, do ordain and establish this Constitution for the United States of America."[68]

From this starting point, the Constitution lays out the building blocks of a limited but effective government designed to protect life, maximize liberty, and give each one of us discretion in our pursuit

---

68 U.S Constitution. pmbl.

of happiness. You were rightfully upset by power and its rewards having disproportionately calcified around those with connection to Washington. But in fixing this, we mustn't weaken the system of limited government and checks and balances, or dissolve the political norms, traditions, and institutions that were designed as guardrails to protect the outer limits of what a republic can endure and still survive.

Finally, the national debt exploded under President Trump's watch. It's growing even faster under Biden. Our finances are spinning out of control. The things you want in maintaining American freedom don't fit with a huge national debt. Unsustainable growth in a national debt kills civilizations in the same way that stacking up enough credit card debt can kill a family's finances. In business, Trump has proclaimed himself the king of debt, and he has stiffed plenty of creditors over the years. But this doesn't work for a country.

So be mad and stay mad. Our country needs your voice. But it also needs reason and a few conservative remedies as part of your formula to make America great again.

Sincerely,
Mark Sanford

TO EVANGELICAL
CHRISTIANS

Dear friends,

I have long believed in the good to be found in the church and people of faith, but I was disappointed in the way you excused things with Trump. Some of you seemed blind to what really matters to a person of faith. Others were spellbound in hearing what you wanted to hear. In this you aren't doing what the church is supposed to do. Dr. Martin Luther King Jr. once said, "The church must be reminded that it is not the master or the servant of the state, but rather the conscience of the state. It must be the guide and the critic of the state, and never its tool."[69]

I get it that each one of us wants to be relevant. We want our views to be accepted and, better yet, to prevail. No one wants to sit in the corner being ignored by friends. We want to be heard, and there is a universal need to be perceived as winning rather than

---

69 Martin Luther King Jr., "The Conscience and the State" (Memphis, April 3, 1968).

losing. If we can't win ourselves, then many identify and put great hopes in the sports team or athlete who does. Trump has always understood this, and consequently he promised everyone a win. As a developer he promised those who bought his properties would be "winners" as residents there. His words in politics to every audience were the same. "Come with me, and you will get tired of winning."

Faith is a commitment to the things we can't see, touch, or feel. People of all faiths across time have shared this belief, and accordingly the winning in our day-to-day here on earth shouldn't take center stage for people of faith. The Bible tells us that as Christians, and therefore evangelicals, we are to be in the world but not of it. There is but one true question for evangelicals, and it's not based on worldly outcomes. It's based on whether what's before us brings us closer to God.

We are certainly to "render unto Caesar that which is Caesar's, and unto God that which is God's."[70] But expectations as laid out in the Bible are very clear—seek first his kingdom and his righteousness, and all these other things will be added. It's not just that the ends justify the means; the right court appointments or abortion language in a bill should not make us look past the Bible's clear dictates on what comes first and what matters.

Behavior is made clear in the Bible. Our behaviors are to be driven by what it calls the fruit of the spirit—love, joy, patience, kindness, goodness, and more. None of these fit with Trump's approach.

Conservative Christian leaders strongly helped to elect President Trump, and according to Pew Research, 81 percent of White evangelicals voted for him in 2016. This is amazing to me given the lectures I

---

70 Matthew 22:21

have gotten from evangelical friends on the importance of morals and walking the straight line. That view is right, and I got crushed on this front after 2009. Yet some of those who were most condemning of me then proved a few years later to be Trump's staunchest cheerleaders.

It's been perplexing as I watched friends switch gears and make excuses for behaviors they had only months earlier condemned. It made me scratch my head wondering how heartfelt these beliefs really were, because true principles and ideals don't change with officeholders. This phenomenon has become even more startling in the wake of the storming of the Capitol in January. At a time when I heard many friends say, "What happened at the Capitol was the last straw," this sentiment has not resonated with Republicans at large or friends in the faith community. Remarkably, polling suggests 75 percent of Republicans want Trump to "play a prominent role" in the GOP going forward. It's for this reason Mitt Romney said in a February interview, "He has by far the largest voice and a big impact in my party. I don't know if he's planning to run in 2024 or not, but if he does, I'm pretty sure he would win the nomination."[71]

Christ's admonition to Christians in Matthew 5.13 is so right. "You are the salt of the earth. But if salt loses its flavor, how can it be made salty again? It is no longer good for anything except to be thrown out and trampled on by people."

People bend to power, and the federal government has never before been as mighty. Whether one is a churchgoer or an evangelical is immaterial in why what's happened with the church and Trump should matter to all of us. He is an example of the mighty power that

---

71 "DealBook DC Policy Project: Mitt Romney on the Search for Common Ground" *The New York Times*, February 23, 2021.

comes with government and why its power should always be limited. How could it be anything but an illustration of the need to limit its size when even those who profess not to be driven by the earthly cares and concerns of the world so quickly fall under the sway of its power? In and outside of church circles, many who had expressed reservation and caution about him as a candidate became full-throated supporters once he took office. Certainly, we all have our share of hypocrisy in us, but for me alarm bells went off in watching what happened and what continues to happen with friends in churches where they say they a know better way.

These friends say they are being pragmatic. Trump's views were more closely aligned with theirs than Clinton or Biden's. I get and respect that, but faith, ideals, and values are not pragmatic and conditional. Holding a view centered in faith would suggest agreeing where one agreed and disagreeing and speaking out where one disagreed. Looking the other way doesn't fit with my definition of real beliefs and faith.

In all this I go back to Dr. Martin Luther King Jr.'s wise admonition. "The church must be reminded that it is not the master nor the servant of the state, but rather the conscience of the state. It must be the guide and the critic of the state, and never its tool."[72] Indeed these are words to live by as we all try to find true north in these tumultuous times.

Sincerely,
Mark Sanford

---

72 Martin Luther King Jr., "The Conscience and the State" (Memphis, April 3, 1968).

TO THE COMMENTERS ON MY FACEBOOK PAGE

Dear Facebook friends,

This morning I had the misfortune of reading through comments that came in response to a few of my recent posts on Facebook. At one level I'd say to get a life…and at another I should say thank you, as we all have things we need to be reminded of. Having the major failure of your life retumbled in comment after comment as if in a giant dryer takes me back to a place I've tried to learn from but move past.

I have been warned many times over by folks much wiser than I am that living while wallowing in old regrets isn't living, and doing so keeps you from finding new joys. They have said to me that although Satan is said to be the great tempter, once we have fallen in some form or fashion, his greatest strength is as the great reminder. He, through others, reminds us that we are not worthy of speaking up and saying what's in our heart or contributing because we did something that now makes us inferior to others. But going back in our hole and staying clear of others is hardly a recipe for using whatever limited talents we have toward useful ends and helping other people. That's what I know in my head, but when one reads enough of "Go back to Argentina" and more, I simply want to let it all go and retreat to our family farm because it's safe. Each of us after failure finds our own place of refuge, but a refuge is not living a life, it is a refuge from living it.

Many comments are nothing more than from trolls paid to launch their venom on me as a public figure, and I really don't care about them. The attempted slings and arrows are just what come with public life. But to the well-meaning folks from home, I'd just say I'll always keep trying to listen as best I can. June of 2009 and its aftermath certainly humbled me, and it made me more real and empathetic. I hope to use those attributes going forward with you and others to make a difference in things that matter.

At a policy level, I am struck by four recurring themes that come up in your comments: you wanted change, you had given up on the GOP, you were angry, and you believed Donald Trump was fighting for you.

Let's examine these themes.

One: You wanted change. The status quo wasn't working for you and those you loved. You wanted it gone. It's understandable. You were right to want something different. Between 2000 and 2016, middle- and lower-income families in America saw their incomes and wealth fall. After more than four decades as the nation's economic majority, the American middle class was now matched by those in the economic tiers above and below it. That's a disturbing first, because part of our strength as a county has always rested in having a robust and strong middle class. Because Trump came to represent a change from the status quo, I understand how those wanting change would see anyone who challenged him as a part of the status quo.

In my case, I just wish those people had done a little home-work. If they had, or did today, they would find a guy who ironi-cally spent his entire time in politics trying to challenge the status quo. It's hard to go from being a Tea Party favorite and endorsed by the Tea Party patriots in my last election to a defender of the status quo. But in the age of Trump, perceptions quickly became political realities, and anything less than a wholehearted embrace of President Trump somehow meant status quo.

Two: You had given up on the GOP because you believed you had been abandoned by the GOP. There were many comments call-ing me "No better than a Democrat," "RINO," etc. And they all point to the utter breach of trust that had taken place between many conservative voters and the GOP. As a party, Republicans said we were about a lot of things and then just didn't work on those things. It was brand destruction in its purest form.

It's usually not just one thing that breaks trust—it's a thou-sand little cuts. I remember coming into Congress in 1994 as part of the so-called Republican revolution that was in part fueled by the "Contract with America." The contract promised that if you elected us and Republicans took back the Congress, we would work to deliver on ten things. One was term limits. Yet as soon as we were elected, the majority leader, Dick Armey, began to backtrack on term limits. He said now that Republicans had taken control, term limits were no longer necessary! Similarly, Republicans kept talking about shrinking government. And yet the government kept getting bigger. So again, I understand your skeptical look at anything viewed as being close to the traditional GOP.

Three: You were and are angry. The anonymous nature of the internet and social media seems to harness negative energy. People will say the craziest of things to you in a post, things they would never say to your face. My friend Cubby up in Columbia used to say, "When emotion is high, discernment is low." Indeed, this seems to be the case with much of the destructive babble on social media. But for one moment let's look past the negative and look to its positive. It means you care. Hope and anger are first cousins. In a relationship, if someone is yelling, there is still a chance to fix things because they are still engaged. But if they quietly go off to the other room and no longer engage, now we have real problems.

Respectfully, some of the anger may be misdirected, and people may not have done any homework to see what political actors have "done" other than noting whether they were for or against Trump. But the bright side to all this is that you still care, and for America's sake caring is an important first step to fixing things.

In fairness, you have reason to be angry. You have been disappointed by Republican politicians for a long time. Trump was just a symptom, a reaction, to what had long been festering. You have seen your way of life, finances, and the culture around you challenged and deflated as never before in our country's history.

Four: You believed Trump was fighting for you. Though I have agreed with where you were coming from on the other three sentiments, on this one I have to disagree with you on two levels.

First, at times Trump just liked to fight. It energized those who supported him and thereby energized him. Over my sixty-one years, I have never seen a president so insecure and in need of affirmation as Trump, and this became something of a vicious cycle in his presidency. Tell the crowd what they want to hear, and get some praise. The problem is this is not real leadership. Lincoln hardly told people what they wanted to hear at the time of the Civil War. Conflict without a policy objective is just war for the sake of war, a fight for the sake of a fight.

Which brings me to my second point. Despite what you might believe, outside of the good federal court appointments—which he had in fact offloaded to the Federalist Society—there really weren't a lot of wins for the people Trump professed to want to protect.

Claiming to be draining the swamp all while putting family members and the likes of Bannon or Manafort in high offices... growing the debt to levels never before seen in American history while promising to eliminate it...were these wins for you? The list goes on. For all his boasting, there have not been a lot of true political wins for those most enthusiastic about President Trump.

Which brings me to my final point. Commenters on my social media are understandably mad and upset. But just being mad and upset and wanting to burn the whole thing down won't make our lives better. As Americans we have got to find a way to look beyond our own hurt feelings and past wrongs, and humbly but forcefully begin to build things again in the political arena. We have gotten too good at vilifying the other side and pointing fingers, but this is not where solutions come from in politics. Walt Kelly years ago paraphrased the words of Oliver Hazard Perry, an American naval officer in 1813. "We have met the enemy and he is us."[73] Indeed

---

73 Walt Kelly, Pogo: We Have Met the Enemy and He is Us. (New York: Simon & Schuster, 1987).

there is truth to this. As much as one is free to suggest otherwise from the obscurity and comfort found in social media, this idea is right on target. It's not all someone else's fault. And the fact is, we can all learn from others if we are so bold as to listen.

Sincerely,
Mark Sanford

TO CONGRESSMAN JIM JORDAN

Dear Jim,

Based on a shared ideology, you invited me to be a part of the Freedom Caucus, which at its start was filled with conservative firebrands like you, Meadows, Mulvaney, and more. There is strength in numbers, and accordingly, it matters to me that you would invite me to be a part of a group that would consistently point the Republican caucus to what we believed was "true north" in conservative stands. That's what I believed at our start. Now I don't know what to believe, given the way the so-called Freedom Caucus devolved into nothing more than Trump's biggest defender on the Hill.

Indeed over the six years that I was last in Congress, I thought I got to know people like you and Meadows or Mulvaney. But after the way ideals were abandoned over the last few years so that the group could stay relevant—and you or Mark could make mention of regular calls from President Trump—I feel I didn't know you at all.

I have always admired your energy and what I thought was your philosophical tenacity, but based on my uncertainty now on the second point, let me just say a few things. I realize this may fall on deaf ears, given what's become apparent in your focus on the here and now of politics…but do you really want to be a coconspirator in planting the seeds that will lead to the destruction of our republic?

We are spinning apart as a democracy, and sadly, you are helping to create the centrifugal force that pulls us apart. When President Trump doesn't even feign concern for democratic norms, when he lies with abandon, when he says that our system is rigged and that election fraud is rampant, and you say nothing, you are breaking new ground for what's acceptable in the Founders' deliberate but delicate design of political balance. Without balance, our system fails, and we start the march toward oblivion that so many civilizations before us have taken—sometimes at a run, other times at a walk. Liberty is fragile and has been consistently lost as tyranny claims its hold on power and exercises its seemingly unquenchable thirst for dominion over our lives.

Unfortunately, in many such instances over the past four years, you haven't kept quiet—which would have been destructive and bad enough—but you have gone the extra mile and actually supported his crazy claims.

Sir Isaac Newton said that for every action, there is an equal and opposite reaction. In politics, the act of escalating crazy to acceptable inevitably leads to the reaction coming back as destruction. The former president was dangerous in the way he disregarded political norms and traditions, but it's much worse than that. In politics, we both know words matter, and in every way, words are acts. A president's misguided words can create a false perception, and in politics, that perception can quickly become a reality that far too many believe is true. For a president to say the democratic process is corrupt makes it so in the minds of many citizens.

Most political figures at some point in their career have convinced themselves of some truth as they saw it. But this is a long way from daily shattering any idea that truth matters, as this president has done. The norms of truth and political civility represent the glue that holds our differing political institutions together. These things can be stretched only so far. All relationships have limits, and what the president did was test and enlarge what once were long-established political speed bumps and limits.

Break enough of them in any functioning democracy, and it's lethal. The Roman Republic didn't fall in a day. Julius Caesar didn't just stroll in randomly and change the show. His ability to grab the reins of power and move Rome from a functioning republic to his autocratic rule was made possible by the leaders who had preceded him, along with the slow unraveling of political and cultural norms that had held the Roman democratic system together.

Your complicity threatens my four boys' odds of living in a free political system. You are aiding and abetting in our country the very things that caused the Roman Republic to die. It was this breaking of political norms and traditions, what the Romans called *mos maiorum*—the way of the elders—that really paved the way for Rome to lose its standing as a democracy and fall to the whims of Caesar and the sixty-nine emperors who followed. We are at just such a gut-check moment today, and all this puts you at a crossroads.

As members of Congress, you and I have had the unique honor of raising our right hands and swearing to defend the Constitution. Not many people have stood in the Capitol and pledged, "I do solemnly swear that I will support and defend the Constitution of the United States against all enemies, foreign and domestic; that I will bear true faith and allegiance to the same; that I take this obligation freely, without any mental reservation or purpose of evasion; and that I will well and faithfully discharge the duties of the office on which I am about to enter. So help me God." I have always done my best to uphold that sacred oath.

Few people set out intending to do bad, but little choices over time can get you there. Trust me, I know about this. But Trump's commitment has not been to the Constitution or to the institutions, norms, and traditions that have kept our republic alive.

So my question is, will you change course and make a stand for the Constitution? Our republic has been kept strong thanks to a lot of little choices made by those who preceded us. Now it's our turn. What will your choice be?

In life every one of us at some point must decide what we stand for, and for many it's just the chance to stay relevant. I was struck by this in you at the time Trump came after me a few years ago. A friend sent me a clip of Trump droning on about me and the Appalachian Trail before a rally. He then calls your name, and I remember being taken back by the way you ran up to him onstage for a hug in the same way a small boy runs to his father for attention.

A connection to the president and his conspiracies certainly keeps one relevant. But my question to you is, what is the cost to your soul and to the freedoms of our children? I leave this for you to ponder.

Sincerely,
Mark Sanford

TO SENATOR TED CRUZ

Dear Ted,

Ambition is disorienting. What we know to be true can be rationalized away under the pretext of working our way up the ladder so we might do even greater good. But that kind of ambition is toxic. Its blinding effects are cancerous, and I would respectfully suggest that you have the disease.

Life is short, people see more than you think, and what a person stands for really does matter.

I think most people would say they perceive you as one who would say almost anything to stay in office. They couldn't tell you all the stands you have taken, it would come instead as a gut reaction. There is not a particular rhyme or reason in the way perceptions are formed, but perceptions are all too real in politics. In watching those of us in its arena, people get the big picture much more than we realize. Twisting one's views to fit the moment is by no means unique to you, but what is unique is that you absolutely know better. Your law professor at Harvard described you as

244

"off-the-charts brilliant." You graduated cum laude from Princeton and magna cum laude from Harvard Law School.

Knowing better puts you in a curious spot, given what the Bible says. "To whom much is given, much will be required."[74] Too often through the ages, the people who could have made a difference stayed silent or simply looked the other way when their country or civilization was at a difficult fork in the path. We are there and living in a political moment that can't afford the luxury of those who have the power to change things instead looking away. Given all you have been blessed with, I would suggest even more is required of you.

If nothing else, given the brevity of life, aren't there things that matter far more than reelection? Is that really what we will look back on in the eleventh hour of life and be proud of?

Aren't there ideas and ideals worth living and sacrificing for? That our Founders would risk all they did for ideas they believed in says it all, and what they did is pretty much the opposite of contorting one's views to fit the moment.

Which brings me to three very real beefs I would ask you to think about.

One: You and I share a strong belief in our Constitution, and in fact you know far more about it than I do. You wrote a 115-page senior thesis at Princeton on the separation of powers in the Constitution. Yet somehow you have now been able to bring yourself to vigorously defend President Trump and his assault on those same separated powers. Then, doubling-down on harm, you went

---

74 Luke 12:48

full bore on attempting to nullify the 2020 presidential election, even hours after the assault on the Capitol on January 6. These things represent playing not with fire but with nitroglycerin in any open political system—and you of all people know this.

Two: Quit being a hypocrite. Many of us applauded your push back against Obama on his executive orders on immigration reform and more. You were right. What you did goes to the heart of the separated powers that you wrote so eloquently about at Princeton. But then when Trump began taking even simpler toxic actions by executive order, you said not a word.

We undermine whatever authority we have, especially as conservatives, when we apply principles only to the opposing side but not to ourselves. You, unlike many of your colleagues, have the mental bandwidth to recognize these inconsistencies and the impact they'll have with the very voters who watch not what we say but what we do.

Three: Be a man. Part of what people hate about politicians is their gratuitous insincerity. You take this to new levels. Trump called you Lying Ted. He said your dad was part of killing John F. Kennedy. He was more than tough on your wife. He said things like, "This guy Ted Cruz is the single biggest liar I have ever dealt with in my life. I mean it… He will lie about anything. I've met much tougher people than Ted Cruz. He's like a baby… He's like a little baby. Soft, weak, little baby by comparison. But for lying, he's the best I've ever seen… A guy like Ted Cruz, he has no clue. He never employed anybody. He's a nasty, nasty guy."

Wow.

And this insulting vitriol does not matter? You chose not only to support him but to vigorously defend him?

Again, wow.

I wish I could say that I don't understand, but unfortunately I do. I have seen ambition's ability to cloud a good man's vision.

I ask you to take the time to reappraise. Begin with the end in mind and what you think will really matter to you and your children at your deathbed. My suspicion is you would choose a different path.

I'll be watching with anticipation to see your take on what should come next.

Many thanks, and take good care.

Mark Sanford

TO SENATOR JOSH HAWLEY

Dear Senator Hawley,

I think your stands are inhibiting our party and our country's ability to have a second chance, and accordingly I thought it was worth writing to you. As busy as you are, I hope you will find the time to read this because—though in a different light—I have walked in your shoes. In doing so, and in this greater journey we call life, I have been struck by many things, but two stand out as I have watched you in the news.

One: Our strengths are always also our weaknesses. You're obviously bright, Stanford followed by Yale Law School is not the curriculum of the ordinary mind. Nor is it the background or educational pedigree one typically finds in the people whose views you now profess to represent. Too many of them struggled just to get their hand onto the first rung of the economic ladder, while you became accustomed to being at the front of the class. This is not an indictment of you, but a recognition of a walk that I have seen before. Those with genuine talent rightly want to make something of it. But if one is not careful, one can fall into the savior trap.

Discussing this would lead to a much longer conversation on faith and the spiritual plane, but in some form we all want to be a savior. We want to have significance and have it matter that we lived, whether in providing for those we love, in being a good Little League coach, or in serving the country in Congress. Universities across this country are filled with the names of people who had the financial means to express this. Donating in exchange for their name on a building is some people's way of exercising this need. You are bright, talented, and hardworking enough to climb to a place of recognition and for people to see you as an answer. But here's the danger: we can come to believe it's true. Not that one is perfect, or indeed a savior, but thinking that we could really make a difference has its own corrupting influences. We rationalize many things as we begin to believe it's incumbent upon us to stay in the mix to indeed make a difference.

Two: Ambition combined with politics is deadly fuel, and represents my second point. You had to be ambitious to get into Stanford. It's in your DNA. But the toxic formula of politics lies in the adulation that comes with doing the right things and the people seeing you as a leader. It's heady stuff. People begin to credit you with all sorts of things, and you think if you just stay on the train that is fueling your rise, you could do even greater things. You could make an even greater difference. Who knows, you might even become president.

Truly wise kings of the past had someone in their court to remind them of the ways they were not. These days we don't have a king's court, but I have known some wise men over the years. One was Tom Campbell. We met when I was a freshman in Congress, and ironically, he used to teach constitutional law at Stanford. I got some really great advice as we served in the House together. It was his second time there. In his first trip, he had been filled with the ambition that captures most anyone with drive. So he made the trade-offs that ambitious people do. But it all came crashing down. He had left the House for what he thought was a good chance to get to the Senate. Instead he was left with no political platform—and only regret over some of the political trade-offs he had rationalized. He vowed that if he ever had another shot at politics, he would cast votes according to what he really believed in and had promised voters when running for office rather than where he thought they might take him. That happened, and I had the privilege to serve with a man I considered one of the most principled people I have ever met in my life.

I'd ask you to examine your soul and ask yourself whether you have recently been making stands and casting votes based on your beliefs or took the road of expediency too often traveled in politics. It's important because, as the Bible says, there is nothing new under the sun.[75] This is true of ambitious young rising stars, just as it is true of political strongmen and charlatans simply telling people what they wanted to hear. The question is not our role in all this, but whether we study and learn from those who have gone before us. Your actions represented work that undermined the delicate balance of what our Founders built.

---

75 Ecclesiastes 1:9

As Republicans we have always claimed that we believe in checks and balances in power, and in federalism, which dictates that whenever possible decisions should be made by those who hold power at a local or state level, rather than in Washington. Our electoral process is one that is from the bottom up. Good people in our hometowns drive it at the precinct and county level. Another branch of government, represented by our court system, has come in and overwhelmingly said that the election was not a fraud.

And yet you joined a president who promulgated every conspiracy theory under the sun because the people's verdict in the election did not favor him. I don't understand it.

Or maybe I do. It's that if you can just climb one rung higher, you can do some really great and worthy things.

But if you didn't do any of those great things, would it really be worth the trade-offs in the future opinion of your two young kids about the kind of America they will one day inherit?

That's my thought for the day. I wish you well in your contemplations.

With respect and sincerity,
Mark Sanford

TO MATT GAETZ AND MARJORIE TAYLOR GREENE

Dear Matt and Marjorie,

Have you completely lost your minds? Or, given the actions I have seen of late, maybe they were never there to be found. Maybe it's just wild ambition. Maybe lust for the adulation of the crowd. Maybe it's the stupidity that can come with thinking more of oneself than one should.

Whatever it may be, it needs to stop, because with great power should come great responsibility. People who have been given the authority that comes as a member of the US Congress don't have license to go out and say and endorse crazy. This is not professional wrestling. It's not entertainment. What happens next on the national stage will impact people's lives and the composition and duration of our republic. That's reality, even while you now attempt to host America First rallies around the country. To spike the ball in Wyoming with an anti-Cheney rally at the state capitol says all too much about your desire to mimic former president Trump's bullying ways, but I'd just ask you to remember that what goes around comes around in life. What's happening here is wrong and won't end well. It's time to wake up, smell the salts, and regain some measure of consciousness lest your crazy be mimicked by others.

With due respect,
Mark Sanford

TO NANCY PELOSI

Dear Nancy,

I believe in what the Bible talks about in first taking the log from your own eye before worrying about the splinter in someone else's. For that reason, this book has been aimed at conservatives and Republicans. I am a conservative and believe we need to clean our own house first before we worry about the perceived wrongs of another political philosophy or party.

But because you are now the third-highest officeholder in the land, among the most powerful Democrats in the country, and the Speaker of the House, I think it's worth writing a few thoughts to you on your party's direction, given how much your role will help shape and determine the national debate before us.

I think our country is at a tipping point, and since I know you love our country, respectfully, I feel it's time for you to put our country before your party or your role as Speaker.

I fear for your grandchildren and for my boys alike.

Although we held strongly opposing political views when I was in Congress with you, in no way do I doubt your patriotism or your sincere wish to do what you think is best for our country. Similarly, I have always admired your work ethic. Your knowledge of your caucus's districts and their consequent political needs is second to none.

But your direction, I strongly believe, is wrong.

There is no example in history that suggests good things will come from further expanding government when we have no capacity to pay for the expansions already promised. We have already reached peacetime highs on both what our federal government spends and the accumulated debt that comes with that spending. And yet the Democratic Party enthusiastically proposes even more debt and spending.

This is the big lie that no one talks about—how to pay for it. I fully understand the electoral advantages to offering more and more, but I cannot see any rational way to hold this position when it's clear there is no way to pay for it all. It is a lie as big as any Trump has told.

We all have blind spots. It's difficult to see and feel things that are not part of our own life experience. Not seeing something doesn't make us bad, it just makes us blind in that particular area. You have become insulated from financial reality. Life as a member of Congress insulates one from some of the world's rough edges, and this is put on steroids when one is a part of leadership. A security team transports you from point A to point B, and never again do you think about the logistics of getting somewhere or filling the gas tank to get there. As Speaker, you are also afforded the luxury of an Air Force jet in getting around.

You grew up in a political family with a father who was both in Congress and mayor of Baltimore, and these experiences led to a very different perspective on money than if your father had worked at the local lumber or steel mill. Similarly, your husband, Paul, has been a great success, and you have homes in both San Francisco and Washington, coupled with a vineyard in Napa and a family net worth of a few hundred million dollars.

That is not the experience of most people.

It's not wrong to be in the top one-tenth of 1 percent as you are, but it is wrong to institute policies that would hinder our children from getting to the same place.

I offer three bits of perspective.

First, money can't be spent by the government until it is made somewhere, then taxed and sent to Washington, DC. I have always been astounded by how casually people can spend other people's money, and how particularly true this is in Washington. I have seen too many times how little appreciation is shown for the people who earned the money sent to Washington, and how readily people in office respond in sending money to most anyone who asks. I understand it's a political system, not an economic one, but even so, I have always been aghast at how much money was squandered on Capitol Hill. The numbers become really significant as we now regularly talk of trillion-dollar spending bills in Washington.

It's past time someone got real. You are in a unique position to lead on this front.

Second, please help us meet in the middle and get back to the center. Neither party is doing this now, and therefore, the center that has defined our political system for two hundred years is disappearing. Left gets more left and right gets more right.

You have the opportunity to be part of fixing this.

If not, centrifugal force is sure to tear our political system apart, because tribalism is not a political system. The year I joined your Congress, the economist Laurence Iannaccone wrote a paper entitled "Why Strict Churches Are Strong." In it, he highlighted a great paradox in American faith. Religiosity was declining overall, but denominations with strict rules and restrictions, such as Mormonism and Orthodox Judaism, which asked their congregations for the most sacrifice, were growing. He argued that niche beats general, and fervent devotion beats moderation in religion.[76] I would say the same of politics.

Think about your time in politics. Not so many years ago strong parties preferred moderate candidates. But the days of backrooms and party bosses are gone, and now with weak parties, orthodox candidates often build the most devout followings. This is true of politicians like Bernie Sanders and Alexandria Ocasio-Cortez on the left, just as it was true with Trump and Ron Paul on the right. But this doesn't make it a good thing, and you have the capacity to push your party back from the edge.

Finally, leaving money aside, the concept of government giving something away for free works against a market-based

---

76 Laurence R. Iannaccone, "Why Strict Churches Are Strong." (*American Journal of Sociology* 99, no. 5, 1994), 1180-211.

economic system, and it's the market-based system that has protected many of the freedoms we enjoy as Democrats, Independents, and Republicans. The "free" education, health care, and more that the Democratic Party proposes have a corrosive effect well beyond what happens economically.

I tried to get an Uber the other night, and twenty-seven minutes later when one finally appeared, the driver told me they were tough to get because drivers had gotten stimulus money and consequently were not working.

If the road to riches were as easy as just printing and distributing money, then places like Zimbabwe would be lined with gold. But they are not, and what's being attempted and advanced by your party will have disastrous consequences for our economic system and the behaviors key to its survival.

In any case, when our paths next cross, I will be sure to give you an earful. But for now, I wish you and your family well.

Sincerely,
Mark Sanford

TO FORMER PRESIDENT DONALD TRUMP

Dear Donald,

Either you are wrong and I am right, or you are right and everything I thought I knew about life and the ways in which we should conduct it are wrong. It's one or the other, but not both.

That is not to say that we don't have our days. I have certainly had mine, and consequently I throw no stones from my glass house. But being imperfect does not absolve any of us from calling things as we see them. Standing for truth as we see it is a job for both saint and sinner here on earth.

What I see in you is profound bluster to make up for profound insecurity. Why this is so I don't know, but what I do know is that one's imperfection is worth embracing...or at least accepting. This may make me a loser, but if so, I gladly embrace that because failure has a way of making us real. When one person tries to be perfect while another is also trying to be perfect, we have nothing more than two peacocks preening. People don't open up when they think another person is perfect while they are not But the fact is we all have days we wish we could do over. It's life. Our shared humanity is not found in our triumphs. I would argue it's in our weakness and blunders.

Which brings me back to you.

Either you are right or you are not. If you are, then I don't know why the beatitudes were written in the Bible. Or maybe the Bible is just a losers manual. But to me and millions around the world, its words matter.

"Blessed are the poor in spirit, for theirs is the Kingdom of Heaven. Blessed are those who mourn, for they will be comforted. Blessed are the meek, for they will inherit the Earth. Blessed are those who hunger and thirst for righteousness, for they will be satisfied. Blessed are the merciful, for they will be shown mercy. Blessed are the pure in heart, for they will see God. Blessed are the peacemakers, for they will be called children of God."[77]

Or for that matter, why would Micah 6:8 be as emphatic as it is? "He has shown you, O mortal, what is good. And what does the Lord require of you? To act justly, to love mercy, and to walk humbly."

I could give lots of other biblical references, and people of different faiths could give the same lessons from their own faith traditions, because through the ages all religions have embraced a few simple truths, and among them are the importance of qualities like humility, mercy, and empathy.

---

77 Matthew 5:3-9

Either this stuff really does matter, or this "new way" that you have exalted throughout your life is the way to go. But it can't be both. I think everyone has a duty based on our own faith to stand up and say that your "new way" is wrong. I believe that to the core of my being.

I believe history points to the wrong found in your approach. Our very political design was set up by the Founders to guard against an authoritarian. You have spoken highly of the strength found in Vladimir Putin's approach. But in speaking to the British parliament in 1982, President Reagan predicted the opposite. He believed that the march of freedom and democracy would "leave Marxism-Leninism on the ash heap of history, as it has left other tyrannies which stifle the freedom and muzzle the self-expression of the people."[78]

Either one believes in the institutions and traditions of democratic rule, as cumbersome as they are at times, or one does not. I spent twenty-five years of my life each day becoming more in awe of the wisdom found in what the Founders created. But history shows how fragile that system can be. Your approach fueled people's skepticism of processes and institutions vital to sustaining what we have here. Though I have had my personal share of inaccurate stories, the press is never an enemy of democratic tradition.

Two other thoughts regarding the crossroads before us.

Either truth matters or it does not. I believe it does. You have had a very casual relationship with the truth for the whole of your life. The accounts of you pretending to be a publicist for yourself— "John Miller" or "John Barron"—should neither be celebrated nor

---

78 Ronald Reagan, "20 Years Later: Reagan's Westminster Speech" (*The Heritage Foundation*, June 4, 2002).

emulated. It's a tragic commentary on American society that you have been given a pass for a lifetime of exploiting the extreme version of self-promotion you call "truthful hyperbole" to get what you want. More plainly, you lie to get what you want.

From one who told a perceived small white lie, I can say with authority that there is no such thing as a little white lie. Truth is the cornerstone of all human relations. Truth matters, and your approach to the presidency represented an assault on this simple but essential principle. The question now is whether "we the people" will let this approach stand.

Finally, do all those lessons we teach our children matter, or do they not? I believe they do matter. I tell my children not to bully others. This has not been your approach, and some of your bullying I have experienced firsthand. I say treat others with respect. You say to Billy Bush, "When you're a star, they let you do it, you can do anything...grab them by the pussy."[79] I say it's not winning or losing that counts but how you play the game. You say it's all about winning, no matter how you get there.

I could go on, but my point is that there can only be one right choice in each of these situations before us. Your approach is one way. The approach tested through the ages in all faiths, history, and even the school of hard knocks in our own lives is the other. Your presidency gave each of us a chance to take stock of what we believe and how firmly we believe it. My choice cost me a job in Congress that I felt called to, but I take solace in the wisdom of Matthew 16:26, which says, "For what will it profit a man if he

---

79 Jane C. Timm, "Trump on Hot Mic: 'When You're a Star ... You Can Do Anything' to Women" (*NBC News*, October 7, 2017).

gains the whole world and forfeits his soul? Or what shall a man give in return for his soul?"

It's food for thought, and though contemplation doesn't exactly fit your appetite, it's worth your consideration.

Sincerely,
Mark Sanford

TO PRESIDENT JOE BIDEN

Dear President Biden,

There are always two roads ahead of each one of us in the choices we make, and before us as a country there is a crossroads with two very different paths. Which one we take will in part be determined by your leadership.

Which path will you take? It matters. My son's lives and the trajectory of our country's future will be affected by your choices over the next four years.

I am writing to ask that you help move our country back to its vital center. Your language has been good here. Your actions have not. Just as Obama pulled health care forward on single-party Democratic votes, so, too, was the recent stimulus bill passed in the Senate. It has only been Democratic Senator Joe Manchin from West Virginia insisting that Republican considerations must also be included on future votes. It should be you speaking up here.

I understand that moving to the center won't be easy.

I talked with my friend and former congressional colleague Mike Flanagan, and his prognosis was sobering. He believes that we are at a point where our country's political problems might not be fixable. We could go the way of the Roman Republic. That legislatively, anything other than lots of "more" for all the warring tribes isn't happening, and that nuanced legislation has become impossible. He believes we have come to a point through the Obama and Trump presidencies where, rather than rolling up sleeves and looking for a bipartisan way forward, executive orders drive the day. They stand for four or eight years only to be undone by the next presidential change of power.

In that process, the certainty needed for long-term investments evaporates, and the legislative branch renders itself impotent in solving the problems that need changing in an evolving society. People who are frustrated by politics become more so in this environment. They don't feel heard, because their sentiments don't make their way forward legislatively.

In announcing his decision not to run for reelection to the Senate, my former House colleague Roy Blunt put it more candidly.

> "I think the country in the last decade or so has sort of fallen off the edge, with too many politicians saying, "If you vote for me, I'll never compromise on anything," and the failure to do that—that's a philosophy that particularly does not work in a democracy. We've seen too much of it in our politics today at all levels, and rather than spending a lot of time saying what I'd never do, I'd spend more time saying what I'd try to do and be willing to move as far

in the direction of that goal as you possibly could rather than saying, "I'll never do this."

Former president Trump was sending out a statement at the same time.

"No more money for 'Republicans in Name Only.' They do nothing but hurt the Republican Party and our great voting base. They will never lead us to greatness. Send your donation to Save America PAC at DonaldJTrump.com. We will bring it all back stronger than ever before."[80]

Blunt's statement represents a political swim upstream, and Trump's was just more of the madness. The same dynamics are at play in your party with Alexandria Ocasio-Cortez attempting to purge the Democratic Party of centrists and move it left.

But our situation is dire, and if you as president don't begin to move us back to some semblance of a center, our country can't withstand too many more years of wild oscillation between left and right in Washington.

As I see it, there are but three civic choices before us.

We can separate, we can subjugate, or we can reconcile.

We have already separated. Republicans demonize Democrats, and Democrats demonize Republicans. Politicians rationalize these actions by saying, "It's just red meat for the base," "They are just

---

80 Domenico Montanaro, "No More Money For RINOs': How Trump's Fight With The GOP Is All About Control" (*npr.org*, March 9, 2021).

words," or, "It's necessary for fundraising." Trump took crazy to new levels in his willingness to say anything, and there will be lasting damage and reaction to his words. How your words and actions can help heal a nation politically separated should be your first order of business.

We can subjugate. We have tried this too. It just happened in the Senate when Democrats used a party-line vote to move the stimulus bill. Before that, Republicans used straight party-line dominance against Democrats, just as before Obama lectured on how "elections had consequences." So goes the ping-pong match. But just as the Bible says that while all things are lawful, not all things are wise,[81] in this case the ability to politically subjugate the minority party in Washington is not wise. It invites revenge. And so the question for you now that Democrats hold the House, the Senate, and White House is, what will you do?

Which brings me to the last choice, indeed the road less traveled in politics today. Will you try and reconcile our two parties? Will you help the country find our center and a sustainable way forward? It's one of those things that has enormous long-term benefits but is so hard to do in the here and now of life. No political force within your own party will push you in this direction. It's not comfortable, given the leftward push within the base of the Democratic Party. It's not comfortable for those who would want to exact revenge for slights endured during Trump's time in office. It could make you look weak, and no one wants to look weak in the theater of politics.

But it's the right thing to do.

---

81 1 Corinthians 10:23

I know this from my own life. The benefits of looking beyond the past, reconciling, and finding a way forward can last through the generations.

If my former wife Jenny and I had been able to find a way back to the center and reconcile, it would have impacted not only our lives and the story of our four sons going forward, but the story of their children and that of those who follow them.

The Bible that we both look to for guidance is replete with stories on the importance of turning the cheek and finding a way forward. Can you imagine the power that would come in laying down the gloves and saying to Republicans across the heartland of this great country that you want to find a way forward with them? And not just with words—and you have at times been eloquent on this front—but with actions. Saying to leaders in the House and Senate that we won't pass legislation on a single party vote would represent a path not often walked in Washington. But it's one that history, life experience, and the wisdom of the ages found in faith would say is worth the risk.

We can't keep doing what we have been doing. We need a change. Godspeed in your deliberations.

Sincerely,
Mark Sanford

TO MY SONS

Marshall, Landon, Bolton, and Blake,

Life is but a blink. I'm struck by this here on the eve of yet another birthday, and by the respective deaths over the last year of four great men who really meant a lot to me. I will be joining them all too soon, and in my passing you will be left with only the memories of our times together, and a few of the many life lessons I tried to convey to each of you.

In this writing, I'll mercifully spare you from my tendency to preach with a life lesson, and simply leave you with three thank-yous.

Thank you for your very considerable investment in politics. As a percentage of life, yours has been gargantuan. It's what you grew up with, and there aren't many who grow up thinking it's normal to get in the back of a Chevy Suburban on a Saturday morning and head off to yet another parade or festival. It wasn't normal. And for the heat, cold, and crowds endured at tender ages, I thank you. Above all, your presence gave meaning to events I would have otherwise had to have attended alone, and for our odd but most special times here together, again, thank you.

Thank you as well for your moral clarity. Life's worth is defined by the things we stand and fight for, but in the heat of battle, it's easy to lose sight of what's important. You never have. Each one of you has been crystal clear in reminding me of what matters, and for this I'm most grateful.

Finally, thank you for being an inspiration. You represent the most important work of my life and the audience that matters most to me. I am very proud of each of you. You have risen to the occasion in making me and Mom most proud of the young men you have become. I am thankful God made me your dad and you my sons. I most look forward to watching what comes next in each of your lives.

With all my love,
Dad

ACKNOWLEDGMENTS

I happen to believe strongly that no one gets anywhere on their own in life. At critical moments along the way we get a hand from a loved one, friend or acquaintance and these things, great or small, as Frost suggests - make all the difference. Accordingly I am profoundly grateful for the many who have made my life's journey possible - and all the richer for their presence in it.

I begin with the spiritual side of life. I certainly have been on and off the path over the years, but to a God that knows if a sparrow falls to the ground and indeed the number of hairs on my head, I am most thankful for his guidance, blessings, corrections and love over my 61 years. Also in this light I am thankful he made me the son of Marshall and Peggy, they were wonderfully loving parents who inspired me to try to make the most of each day in this amazingly short journey we call life.

In acknowledgement here on earth, I begin with our four sons: Marshall, Landon, Bolton and Blake. Special thanks to each one of you. You are superheroes in my book. You've not only made the journey lighter and more fun, but you have given it meaning and purpose that would not be there without each of you in it. Special thanks for the sacrifices you made along the way. I'll never forget Landon at a tender age turning back to me at the start of a parade's walk and saying he was afraid. It led to an important conversation on the fears that came to all of us, and for his bravery in walking that parade and life since, he has my admiration. Each of the four boys could tell of similar stories and experiences and of all the endless parades, festivals and events that marked our life in politics together - and for your sacrifices in them, again, thank you. You guys light up my life. I love you and am most proud of each one of you.

In campaigns and politics, you also end up with a second family composed of the people who bring an office and campaigns to life. This team grew to mean the world to me. Given I was notoriously frugal with government money as well as my own, they put up with less than robust compensation for a workaholic's hours and time demands. They did it with grace, patience and an ease that looked past the many demands that were placed on them each day. So to my staff who did so much to guide, help, and facilitate my years in office, thank you. Marie Dupree, Tom Davis, Martha Morris, Chad Waldorf, April Paris Derr, Carl Blackstone, Catherine Kellahan, Scott English, Jay Fields, Mary Neil Stroud, Jeff Schilz, Ben Fox, Olivia Edwards, Cameron Morabito, John Mckinney, Merredeth Myers, Brent Gibadalo, Kathy Worthington, Jon Kohan, Jessica Gonzales, Elizabeth Cruise, Cris Steel, Jerrod Martin, Andrew Ochoa, Henry White, Swati Patel, Chris Allen, Laurie King, David John, Herbert Aimes, Clare Morris, Leigh LeMoine, Lindsey Heiser, Justin Ouimette, Sarah Kimball, Grant

Gillespie, Bryan McLelland, James Braid, Kim Brown, Matthew Taylor, Austin Smith, Walt Roberts, Lisa Kindwall, Laurie Turner, Joe Taylor, Jon Ozmint, Bob Faith, Michael Paul Thomas, Joey Peoples, Justin Evans, Douglas Mazyck, Sidney Rainwater, Brian Benfield, Jordan Pace, Sunny Philips, Paige Herrin Stowell, Kristie Lumley, Rita Allison, Judy Nance and Lawson Manzell represent but the start of a list - but I am most thankful for all you did for me and our efforts to advance the conservative cause and limit government spending.

Finally, when I think of those who helped lighten the load or inspire in life's journey, I want to add a few additional names. My former wife, Jenny, for not only being a remarkable mom but for her many herculean efforts in campaign, after campaign, after campaign. Thank you. To four great men who were in their own ways each inspirational to me in politics, and who died over the last year: Foster Friess, John Rainey, Paul Barringer and Hayne Hipp, I miss you. To the many who offered wisdom with geographies and personalities as disparate as Jim Wheeler, Tom Bell, Kevin Luzak, Ethan Penner or Tony Page, thank you. And to a list too long to score of those who offered financial help or time that kept each campaign alive and afloat, I profoundly and indeed thank each one of you.

In short, it was quite an effort over these last twenty five years, and I couldn't have done it without you. For your presence in my life, I am most thankful.